LEGO® STAR WARS: THE FORCE AWAKENS™

Official Guide

Written by Ken Schmidt & Michael Knight

GAME BASICS

The First Order has risen from the ashes of the Galactic Empire and seeks a position of dominance over the galaxy. Standing in its way is the Resistance, the New Republic, and you. To learn more about the adventure that awaits you, read on! May the Force be with you.

How the Game Flows

STORY MODE

Your first trip through an area takes place in Story Mode. The characters available for use are limited. You may use any of the preselected characters and switch (or "tag") freely between them. Holding the Change Character button brings up the character wheel, which displays all characters currently available for use.

These preselected characters possess the skills needed to meet the objectives of the level, but they may lack the abilities required to uncover every collectible. Collecting everything is reserved for Free Play.

NEW STAR WARS ADVENTURES

These bonus chapters provide insight into the events that took place previous to the main adventure. There are two steps to unlocking these chapters. First, complete a specific chapter to unlock a New Star Wars Adventures level. Second, acquire a number of Gold Bricks by any means (completing levels, hitting True Jedi targets, and so on).

For example, you discover the first New Star Wars Adventures chapter (Poe to the Rescue) when Poe Dameron speaks with C-3PO on D'Qar before departing for Jakku. However, you need to collect 10 Gold Bricks to unlock the chapter and play through it.

FREE PLAY

Once you clear a chapter in Story Mode, it becomes available in Free Play. When you visit a level in Free Play, you may choose to play as any character you've unlocked, and then put their skills to use in gathering every collectible in each level. You're also able to start at any of the checkpoints in a chapter, allowing you to skip areas where you've already uncovered every collectible.

HUBS

You get sneak peeks of the game's five hubs between Story Mode chapters. Your ability to explore is limited until you complete the main adventure. You eventually gain the ability to switch characters freely, which allows you to gather collectibles, undertake quests, and much more. To move through hubs quicker, summon a speeder bike, landspeeder, or any microfighter.

Fighting for the Fate of the Galaxy

The adventure spans multiple planets, and sometimes in the space around those planets. Expect to run, climb, fight, and encounter a variety of puzzles while you strive to keep the galaxy safe. Before you hop into your Corellian YT-1300 Light Freighter, take some time to familiarize yourself with the basics of the newest LEGO *Star Wars* game.

CHARACTER PORTRAIT

The character portrait provides an at-a-glance overview of the status of the character you're currently controlling. When you're piloting a vehicle, the information remains the same, except that vehicles do not use the combat bar.

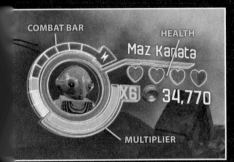

Health is measured by the four hearts (red for characters, gray for vehicles). Taking damage once causes a heart to become half empty. Taking damage a second time empties that heart, which vanishes. Picking up a heart dropped by a defeated enemy returns a heart half full, or refills a partially empty heart. When a character's health is depleted, they drop a pile of studs before reappearing in the same spot. Quickly recollect these studs to minimize any losses.

Multiplier increases the value of studs collected. For more information about the multiplier, look under "Studs and the Multiplier" later in this section.

Combat Bar is an important aspect of winning battles. To learn more, skip ahead to the "Combat" section.

ABILITIES

Abilities are the one piece of information you can't learn about characters from the character portrait. Abilities are special powers and gadgets possessed by characters. Examples include jetpacks that allow bounty hunters to extend the distance of their jumps, protocol droids speaking multiple languages, and using the Force to control objects and people.

Some characters have a special ability tied to the Use button. Other abilities are passive traits that grant resistances to hazards, such as toxic gas and extreme cold. These abilities are the keys to finding all the collectibles and hitting 100% completion. There's a complete breakdown of abilities, including the abilities each character possesses, in the Characters section of this guide.

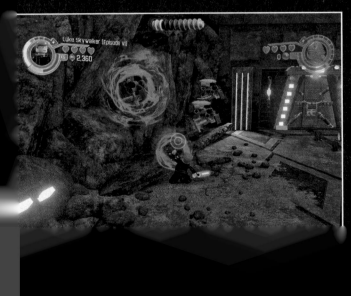

OVERCOMING OBSTACLES

Some hallways are blocked by more than enemy troops. You can't leap over every gap, even with jetpack-boosted jumps. Sometimes you must push heavy objects or turn valve wheels to make it possible to continue your exploration.

Common Obstacles

Many obstacles can be overcome by any character; all you need to do is press the correct button or move the control stick in the indicated direction. You may need to hunt down a yellow valve wheel and attach it to a machine before it works, but any character is capable of turning the wheel once it's in place. The grip handles attached to a vertical face of a cliff or cave wall are available for anyone to use, but be ready to quickly tap a second button if your character's grip slips!

While most terminals require a character to be part of a group (being a protocol droid or a member of the Resistance for example) to use it, a scanner opens for anyone wearing the proper hat. You must obtain this hat from a nearby hat dispenser.

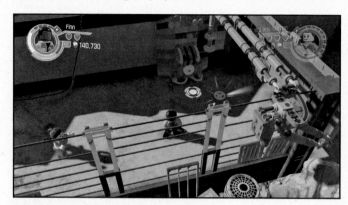 

Obstacles that Require Abilities

When characters encounter something unknown to them, whether it's a terminal they can't access or an object they can't clear, they'll helpfully shrug their shoulders and hint at someone who could help. If you run into something you haven't encountered before, refer to the following list for assistance in moving past it.

CRACKED LEGO OBJECTS

Cracked bricks come in many shapes and sizes, but characters must have the Cracked ability to break them down. Some mountable creatures, such as luggabeasts, allow anyone to break through these bricks.

GOLD LEGO OBJECTS

Rapid fire attacks, such as Captain Phasma's blaster rifle, steadily heat up gold bricks until they explode.

ICE LEGO OBJECTS

Without help from a conveniently placed X-wing thruster, only fire-based attacks like the Flametrooper's flamethrower can melt frozen bricks.

LEGO BRICKS—SILVER

Silver bricks sparkle and shine to stand out from the metal used to construct buildings and spaceships. When you need to get it out of the way, target them with an explosive attack like Chewbacca's thermal detonators.

FORCE LEGO

Force-sensitive characters, such as Luke Skywalker, must be called in to handle sparkling LEGO bricks. Jedi repair broken components, or gently move blocks from their path. Sith violently destroy whatever they can reach with the Force. Sith characters use dark side Force powers against dark bricks highlighted by red sparkles. Green sparkles indicate only a Jedi can move the object.

ACCESS HATCH

Access hatches link two areas. But only characters of small stature, like Maz Kanata, are able to pass through them.

WALL RUN

These arrows are typically white or orange and your character runs across the wall at the arrows.

ASTROMECH ACCESS

Astromech droids and BB-8 are able to interact with these ports, which require you matching up layers of shapes by spinning the pieces before they lock in place.

CLIMB WALL

These walls with thin LEGO handholds can be scaled by agile characters like Rey.

LIGHTSABER CUT

Glowing lines on a wall or door must be cut open with a lightsaber.

DIVE POOLS

Aquatic characters, like Admiral Ackbar, jump into these small bodies of water and emerge a short distance away.

FIRST ORDER ACCESS TERMINAL

These stormtrooper-colored terminals require membership in the First Order to operate. You must cycle through the top, center, and bottom sections until each displays the white figure segments.

FREEZING AREAS

There are two types of freezing areas. The first type is so cold that it instantly freezes any character. The second type gives enough of a warning that characters back away automatically when they move too close. Only characters with Immunity (Cold), like Snowtroopers, can handle the temperature.

GRAPPLE HANDLE

Orange grapple handles work a few ways, but only characters with grapple guns, such as Poe Dameron, can use them. Grapple handles allow characters to open containers and doors, and swing over a gap or up to a higher level. There are two different command inputs for grapple handles: the first is tapping a button, the other is holding a direction on your control stick.

MULTIPLE GRAPPLE HANDLES
Encountering two grapple handles together means you need two characters with grapple guns working together. Four grapple handles clustered together means you need to look up the Command ability in the Characters section!

GRIP WALL

Jumping up these walls requires either an agile character like Rey, or a character carrying a lightsaber.

LAUNCH PAD

This orange and white device is designed specifically for BB-8. The launch pad sends the versatile droid to higher spots.

ELECTRICITY CHARGE

When BB-8 or GNK-143 interface with these nodes, you must keep the arrow balanced in the green area of the meter long enough to restore power.

PROTOCOL ACCESS TERMINAL

These gold terminals require the language skills of a protocol droid. Note the order of the colors and simple images shown in the main window, then select the three smaller images in the same order.

RESISTANCE ACCESS TERMINAL

Green terminals are reserved for members of the Resistance. When the changing symbol matches the symbol above it, tap the button underneath that column to lock it in place. Match all three columns to activate the terminal.

ROTARY CONTROL

This orange and white interface is designed specifically for BB-8. Rotary controls work with a number of different machines. The lights on the interface turn green when BB-8 moves in the correct direction.

SCAN SPOTS

Watch for columns of white symbols floating in mid-air. These symbols indicate something is hidden from regular view. Only characters with quadnoculars can uncover these hidden objects. Move your goggle view until the two indicators move close together and a button prompt appears.

STAFF SPINNERS

When you encounter a spinner switch, you need to supply a staff to make it work. Switch to staff-wielding characters, such as Lor San Tekka, who employ their staff as a lever to turn the switch. Push the control stick in the indicated direction to open gates, or move large objects.

STRENGTH HANDLES

As the name implies, you need to tag in a strong character like Chewbacca to move strength handles. Strength handles work three different ways: push the control stick in a direction, tap a button repeatedly, or time your button push when the arrow is in the center of a meter.

SHARPSHOOT TARGET

To hit a target, all you need is a ranged attack. Characters, like Finn, that carry a blaster or hurl a melee weapon, like Darth Vader, are able to take out targets.

TOXIC GAS

Rooms, corridors, and even open spaces become impassable when filled with green gas. Regardless of where it's encountered, only gas masks or lack of breathing allow characters to pass through safely.

TWIRL POLES

Twirl poles are another way to cross wide gaps safely. Most characters simply hang from twirl poles, but agile characters like Rey spin around the poles and can leap between them with a single button press.

> **EMPTY SOCKET**
> Some rows of twirl poles include an empty socket. A staff thrown into these sockets acts like a twirl pole. You must keep that character on-screen or their staff vanishes.

COMBAT

Every character can mix it up with enemies in close quarters. Many characters carry a weapon that allows them to strike from long range. When characters have a ranged attack, the attack they use depends on how close a target is when you press the Attack button.

Melee Attacks

The majority of characters attack with punches and kicks, but a few carry weapons such as a staff or lightsaber.

Ranged Attacks

For characters with a ranged attack, tap the Attack button to shoot in the direction they are facing.

SHARPSHOOTER

When characters possess the Sharpshooter ability, you can hold the Attack button to bring up a reticle on the screen. Move the reticle around to acquire targets (you can target more than one item/enemy) and release the button to attack each marked target. Sharpshooter works with any weapon, including staff, lightsaber, and blaster.

Combat Bar & Special Attacks

The segmented ring around a character's portrait that ends with a lightning bolt is the combat bar. Segments of the combat bar are filled each time your multiplier (there's more on the multiplier later in this section) increases. The combat bar stays with the player, so switching characters will not change it, but characters losing all their health will empty it.

One full segment is required to perform a special attack (button prompt flashes blue or yellow). A fully charged combat bar, indicated by a flashing lightning bolt segment, unleashes a more powerful attack that damages multiple enemies, provided they are within range of the attack. Your character must be in melee combat range to perform any special attack.

MORE SPECIAL THAN OTHERS

While many characters with similar weapons use nearly identical special attacks, prominent characters (such as Poe Dameron) have unique full-charged special attacks. Take the time to try out each character's fully-charged special attack to find your favorite.

Blaster Battles

Blaster Battles are a new form of combat that uses cover (from barricades to broken columns) to avoid incoming blaster fire. Forward movement is restricted, but moving from side to side is allowed as long as cover is available. Characters recover health while protected by cover. Any time their health gets low, stay down and wait for a few hearts to return.

To shoot back, press the indicated button to pop out from behind cover and press the Attack button to shoot. Your control stick moves the aiming reticle that appears on-screen. Watch for yellow prompts over the heads of enemies. The prompt indicates when someone is acquiring a target and is ready to fire.

Listen for the sound and watch for the flashing button prompt that indicates your combat bar is full. Activating the combat bar in a Blaster Battle slows down the action and supercharges weapons, causing them to shoot faster and deal more damage.

BLASTER BATTLE MEDALS

The medal that appears next to your character's portrait indicates how well you're doing in a Blaster Battle. Each player (not character) begins with a gold medal. If a character loses all of their health, your medal (but not the other player's) flips and turns silver. If it happens again, the medal turns bronze. A third loss of health results in the medal fading away. At the conclusion of the Blaster Battle, your gold, silver, or bronze medal spins in the center of the screen and increases your stud count.

Aerial Combat

Portions of many chapters take place inside a starfighter's cockpit. Directional controls can be inverted if that's your preferred method of flying. You can activate thrusters to increase your speed, but weapons aren't available while thrusters are active. You also have a button for quick turning and flips when sudden changes of direction are required.

Starfighters are equipped with blasters that you're free to fire with the Attack button. If you keep an enemy in your aiming reticle, your targeting computer will help aim your shots. The Use button is linked to a secondary attack that tracks targets once you've acquired a lock on to them. Fill your combat bar to activate your secondary attack.

Attacking the Environment

Wars fought to stave off intergalactic domination won't win themselves. Sometimes things need to get messy, so don't worry about destroying every container and machine in your quest for studs and building bricks.

Most objects and studs fade away shortly after they appear but some bricks remain no matter how long you wait. In fact, they'll wiggle and bounce to get your attention. These are the bricks you use for building.

BUILDING

With the exception of certain droids, all characters will assemble bouncing bricks when you press and hold the Use button. Objects built in this way are necessary for completing a task. If you're stuck and unsure of what step to take next, attack every nearby object and see if there's something you can build.

MULTI-BUILD BRICKS

This brand-new type of building brick works a bit differently than what you've used in previous games. First, when you stand near these glowing bricks, you are shown a preview of the different spots they can be used.

Sometimes, the bricks can be used once. Most of the time you can build something, then knock it down and rebuild it (or one of the other options) as often as you like.

Rewards

Beyond the sense of satisfaction you get from keeping the galaxy safe from the First Order, there are additional rewards you can earn at the same time.

STUDS AND THE MULTIPLIER

Studs act as money in LEGO games. You need them to purchase the characters, vehicles, and cheats unlocked while playing through the game. Studs are found everywhere. Even when you don't see any studs, attack any object in the area and it will most likely turn into studs. The color of a stud indicates its base value.

Silver studs increase your stud count by 10

Blue studs increase your stud count by 1,000

Gold studs increase your stud count by 100

Purple studs increase your stud count by 10,000

To increase the total value of the studs you collect, boost your multiplier. The multiplier appears beside your active character's portrait. Build your multiplier by defeating enemies quickly. The multiplier decreases by one each time the thin line above the combat bar empties.

The multiplier begins with a x2 value and can grow up to x10. The number in the multiplier is how much the value of the studs increases. For example, picking up a blue stud (base value 1,000) with a x5 multiplier results in your stud count going up by 5,000.

> ### TRUE JEDI
> Each chapter of Story Mode (the main adventure, and New Star Wars Adventures missions) and Dejarik Battle on the Millennium Falcon have a True Jedi stud count target. When you reach that target stud count, the game rewards you with a Gold Brick. To make this an easier task, build your multiplier before picking up the studs in an area.

MINIKITS

Minikits are glowing, canister-like objects with blinking lights. Every Story Mode chapter has 10 Minikits, meaning there are 180 for you to find. When you collect all the Minikits on a level, you earn a Gold Brick and unlock a new vehicle.

RED BRICKS

Red Bricks unlock cheats that you must then purchase and activate. Visit D'Qar, or use the Character Wheel, to purchase the cheats after collecting the Red Brick associated with it.

Red Brick	Where Obtained	Cost	Description
Stud Magnet	Prologue: The Battle of Endor	100,000	Lets you build objects from bricks very quickly
Infinite Torpedoes	Poe to the Rescue	500,000	Ships are always stocked with the maximum number of torpedoes during flight levels
x10 Stud Multiplier	Lor San Tekka's Return	200,000	Allows for blue guide studs to be collected
Fast Force	Rathtar Hunting	200,000	Instantly complete astromech access, protocol droid terminals, First Order terminals, and Resistance terminals
Imperial Inaccuracy	Crimson Corsair	1,000,000	Enemy blaster accuracy reduced to 0% and will always miss the player
Combat Bar Rengen	Trouble Over Taul	1,000,000	Combat bar constantly recharges when emptied
Studs x2	Chapter I: Assault on Jakku	1,000,000	Multiplies the value of studs you collect
Quick Access	Chapter II: Escape from the Finalizer	200,000	Replace Torpedoes with comedy items (Banana, Carrot, Rubber Duck)
Studs x8	Chapter III: Niima Outpost	4,000,000	Multiplies the value of studs you collect
Studs x2	Chapter IV: The Eravana	200,000	Draws in nearby studs for easier collecting
Studs x6	Chapter V: Takodana Castle	3,000,000	Multiplies the value of studs you collect
Destroy on Contact	Chapter VI: Attack on Takodana	200,000	Destroys all damageable LEGO objects on contact
Super Slap	Chapter VII: The Resistance	500,000	One-hit KO from melee attacks (doesn't work on all enemies)
Studs x4	Chapter VIII: The Shield is Down	2,000,000	Multiplies the value of studs you collect
Regenerate Hearts	Chapter IX: Destroy Starkiller Base	500,000	Lost hearts are slowly restored over time
Collect Ghost Studs	Chapter X: The Finale	5,000,000	Multiplies the value of studs you collect
The Funk Awakens	Epilogue: Luke's Island	1,000,000	Characters start to dance to music / Player idle actions are replaced with dancing
Explosive Bolts	Ottegan Assault	200,000	Every blaster bolt fired is a different color; cycle through the rainbow of colors with each shot fired

OTHER GAME MODIFIERS (AVAILABLE IMMEDIATELY)

Description	Cost	Description
Super Detonators	200,000	Thermal detonators cause a larger explosion
Super Silly Sabers	200,000	Sabers appear as silly LEGO pieces rather than the standard beam (tennis racket, golf club, etc.)
Disco Sabers	100,000	Lightsabers cycle through various colors when used

Description	Cost	Description
Squeaky Voices	100,000	All character voices are pitched higher
Collectable Detector	1,000,000	Helps you track down collectibles during missions
Fast Force	200,000	Building and repairing objects with the Force completes faster
		Destruction with dark side Force powers occurs instantly
Super Strength	100,000	All characters can use strength handles and smash cracked LEGO bricks

GOLD BRICKS

Gold Bricks are important collectibles that can be obtained in many ways. There are 250 Gold Bricks to acquire in the game. You earn Gold Bricks by:

- Completing a chapter in Story Mode
- Achieving the True Jedi target in a chapter
- Collecting all Minikits in a chapter
- Discovery in Hubs (Carbonite and Gold Bricks)
- Complete Quests in Hubs

Getting 100% Completion

The game keeps track of your progress, showing the percentage of the game that you have completed. To get to 100%, you must do the following:

- Obtain every collectible in Story Mode levels and Hubs (Carbonite, Gold Bricks, Minikits, and Red Bricks)
- Hit the True Jedi target for all levels
- Unlock and purchase every character
- Unlock every vehicle

CHARACTERS

Unlocking Characters

Characters can be unlocked in several ways. Most characters used in Story Mode are yours to use, free of charge. After completing Story Mode chapters, you unlock additional characters that can be purchased. To purchase a character, speak with them in a hub or buy them from the Character Wheel during Free Play.

The final group of characters are unlocked with the discovery of carbonite in the hubs. The Decarbonizer inside the medical building on D'Qar provides a list of the characters that are unlocked with this method.

However, Carbonite Bricks shown in the Decarbonizer do not specify what character will be unlocked for each Carbonite Brick. Even when you collect the Carbonite Brick in the Hubs, it does not tell you what character is frozen in it. You only discover who is in a brick when you thaw it in the Decarbonizer.

CODES TO UNLOCK CHARACTERS

While these characters are unlocked during the Story Mode, you can use the following codes to get access to them immediately. To input the following codes, choose the Enter Code option in the Pause Menu, then enter the codes.

Character	Code	Character	Code	Character	Code	Character	Code
Caluan Ematt	26F2CF	Quinar	A4EHFJ	Mi'no Teest	GBE8ZC	Major Brance	Q8KRC6
Chief Petty Officer Unamo	2DZXDM	Monn Tatth	A5JR9V	Officer Sumistu	GVNBWB	B-U4D	QLLJXD
GTAW-74 "Geetaw"	2YU4NX	R-3PO	BEMT2T	Snap Wexley	HTN3RD	Goss Toowers	QZTZX9
FN-2187 (Helmetless)	3RRVAV	Dasha Promenti	BJZA6F	Wollivan	J3GMHE	Jessika Pava	SBUSCW
FN-2112	4T3UNK	Crokind Shand	BQPKPA	Oskus Stooratt	K6JXJT	Hoogenz	V3H6RU
Special Forces TIE Pilot	59J67X	Guavian Security Soldier	C73CNV	Flametrooper	LRYUBB	R2-Q5	VVVSEA
Trentus Savay	638FNX	Teedo	CP6ETU	Korr Sella	NGSEKH	Lieutenant Bastian	XQZ7C6
Kaydel Ko Connix	9FJKF4	Hobin Carsamba	E889GQ	Nien Nunb	P8KXSA	Unkar Thug	YABPYU

Character Abilities

The following table provides details about the abilities your characters possess.

Ability	Description
Agile	Agile is a blanket term that covers a few abilities. Agile characters can swing between twirl poles, double-jump to reach more distant locations, ascend climb walls covered in thin LEGO bricks, and cling to grip walls. Most Agile characters can also wall-run from platforms marked by white or orange arrows.
Aquatic	A rare trait that opens up dive pools for use.
Charge Up	Only BB-8 and GNK-143 can connect to power jacks and restore power to devices or machines.
Command	Issue orders to groups of troops, but the troops must be of the same affiliation (Resistance, First Order, etc.).
Cracked LEGO	Demolish Cracked LEGO bricks to reveal what's on the other side.
Dark Side Force Powers	Enables dark side Force characters to manipulate all objects that sparkle with energy, except green glowing objects.
Force Choke	A dark side Force attack that holds its target in place, and that target can be thrown at another enemy or into an object.
Force Freeze	A dark side Force attack that holds its target in place.
Force Lightning	A dark side Force attack that incapacitates its targets, and allows you to move them around.
Force Powers	Enables light side Force characters to manipulate all objects that sparkle with energy, except for red glowing objects.
Gold LEGO	Rapid-fire weapons overheat otherwise indestructible gold LEGO bricks, causing them to explode.
Grapple Gun	A grapple gun allows characters to target and pull grapple handles for a variety of benefits.

Ability	Description
Immunity (Cold)	Cold-resistant characters can enter locations that drive away (or freeze) anyone else.
Immunity (Toxic)	Gas masks (or lacking the need to breathe) make it possible to enter areas covered in green gas.
Jedi Mind Trick	An ability that dazes its targets, causing them to attack your enemies.
Jetpack	Allows characters to hover an additional distance after jumping. The distance can be longer or higher, depending on the direction you hold the control stick.
Lightsaber	An elegant weapon for a more civilzed age that also cuts through glowing lines on doors and walls.
Quadnoculars	By employing quadnoculars, characters can reveal the location of otherwise hidden objects and bricks.
Sharpshooter	Sharpshooter allows characters to aim at a target that is otherwise out of range. Some characters can aim blasters, while others throw melee weapons, such as a staff or lightsaber.
Silver LEGO	Explosive attacks that can destroy objects built from silver LEGO bricks.
Small Access	Characters of small stature can crawl through access hatches to reach hidden areas.
Staff	This melee weapon doubles as both a lever for spinner switches, and a twirl pole in empty sockets.
Strong	Call on Strong characters to deal with strength handles, which are used to open new paths or position objects.
Thaw LEGO	Flamethrowers are difficult to use in battle, but are the only way to melt frozen bricks and bricks frozen in ice.

Character Class

Some characters have an additional trait that allows them to use restricted terminals, or accept specific quests in hubs.

ASTROMECH DROID

Astromech droids can use an astromech access, which perform various functions. Unfortunately, they are incapable of jumping or building with bricks.

> **BB-8**
> BB-8 is a special astromech droid (the only one that can jump) who is the only character capable of using rotary controls and launch pads.

BOUNTY HUNTER

Bounty Hunters can accept bounty hunter quests. A few bounty hunters are equipped with jetpacks, which allow them to reach places other characters can't. Athgar Heece and Boba Fett are examples of bounty hunters.

FIRST ORDER

The most numerous class, First Order characters can access First Order terminals and accept First Order quests.

RESISTANCE

Resistance characters can access Resistance terminals and accept Resistance quests.

PROTOCOL DROID

These polite droids can activate protocol access terminals by decoding mysterious patterns. They also speak multiple languages, a necessary skill to begin a few quests. They also can't jump, so they need help reaching higher spots.

SCAVENGER

Scavengers are not an organized group. The only thing they have in common is they'll accept quests that others will not. Scavenger examples are Rey (Scavenger) and Teedo.

Character List

icon	Got It?	Character	Cost	Level Unlocked	Abilities
				CHARACTERS	
		A-Wing Pilot	Carbonite	D'Qar (Hub)	Sharpshooter, Grapple Gun
		Adan Mose	150,000	Rathtar Hunting	Sharpshooter, Silver LEGO, Immunity (Toxic)
		Admiral Ackbar (Classic)	Carbonite	D'Qar (Hub)	Sharpshooter, Aquatic, Command, Staff
		Admiral Ackbar (Resistance)	N/A	Poe to the Rescue	Sharpshooter, Aquatic, Command, Staff, Resistance
		Admiral Statura	150,000	Chapter VII: The Resistance	Sharpshooter, Quadnoculars, Resistance
		Anakin Skywalker	Carbonite	Starkiller Base (Hub)	Sharpshooter, Force Powers, Jedi Mind Trick, Lightsaber
		Anakin Skywalker (Podracer)	Carbonite	Jakku (Hub)	Quadnoculars, Small Access
		AT-ST Pilot	N/A	Prologue: The Battle of Endor	Sharpshooter, Quadnoculars
		Athgar Heece	N/A	Lor San Tekka's Return	Agile, Sharpshooter, Jet Pack, Silver LEGO, Immunity (Toxic), Scavenger, Bounty Hunter
		Bala-Tik	250,000	Chapter IV: The Eravana	Sharpshooter, Grapple Gun, Silver LEGO
		Bazine Netal	350,000	Chapter V: Maz's Castle	Agile, Sharpshooter, Silver LEGO, First Order
		Bith	Carbonite	Jakku (Hub)	
		Blass Tyran	50,000	Crimson Corsair	Sharpshooter, Quadnoculars, Silver LEGO, Bounty Hunter
		Boba Fett	Carbonite	Jakku (Hub)	Sharpshooter, Grapple Gun, Quadnoculars, Jet Pack, Silver LEGO, Immunity (Toxic), Bounty Hunter
		Bobbajo	50,000	Lor San Tekka's Return	
		Bollie Prindel	200,000	Trouble Over Taul	Sharpshooter, Aquatic, Strong, Resistance
		Caluan Ematt	150,000	Chapter VII: The Resistance	Sharpshooter, Quadnoculars, Resistance
		Captain Phasma	N/A	Trouble Over Taul	Sharpshooter, Grapple Gun, Quadnoculars, Command, Gold LEGO, First Order
		Chancellor Palpatine	Carbonite	Takodana (Hub)	Small, Command
		Chewbacca	N/A	Prologue: The Battle of Endor	Sharpshooter, Strong, Silver LEGO, Resistance
		Chewbacca (Twon Ketee)	N/A	Rathtar Hunting	Sharpshooter, Strong, Silver LEGO, Immunity (Toxic), Resistance
		Chewbacca (Wounded)	N/A	Chapter IV: The Eravana	Sharpshooter, Strong, Silver LEGO, Resistance
		Chief Petty Officer Unamo	100,000	Escape from the Finalizer	Sharpshooter, Quadnoculars, First Order
		Constable Zuvio	200,000	Lor San Tekka's Return	Sharpshooter, Staff
		Count Dooku	Carbonite	Starkiller Base (Hub)	Dark Side Force Powers, Force Lightning, Lightsaber
		Cratinus	50,000	Chapter V: Maz's Castle	Small Access

CHARACTERS

icon	Got It?	Character	Cost	Level Unlocked	Abilities
		Crokind Shand	75,000	Chapter IV: The Eravana	Agile, Sharpshooter, Silver LEGO, Bounty Hunter
		Croll Jenkins	75,000	Rathtar Hunting	Sharpshooter, Grapple Gun, Immunity (Toxic)
		"Crusher" Roodown	200,000	Lor San Tekka's Return	Strong, Cracked LEGO, Scavenger
		Darth Maul	Carbonite	Starkiller Base (Hub)	Agile, Sharpshooter, Dark Side Force Powers, Force Choke, Lightsaber
		Darth Vader	N/A	Prologue: The Battle of Endor	Sharpshooter, Dark Side Force Powers, Force Choke, Lightsaber
		Dasha Promenti	75,000	Chapter I: Assault on Jakku	Agile, Sharpshooter, Quadnoculars, Scavenger
		Davan Marak	75,000	Lor San Tekka's Return	Sharpshooter, Strong, Silver LEGO, Staff
		Death Star Trooper	Carbonite	Starkiller Base (Hub)	Sharpshooter, Quadnoculars
		Ello Asty	125,000	Chapter X: The Finale	Strong, Grapple Gun, Resistance
		Emperor Palpatine	Carbonite	Jakku (Hub)	Dark Side Force Powers, Force Lightning, Lightsaber
		Finn	N/A	Chapter III: Niima Outpost	Sharpshooter, Grapple Gun, Immunity (Toxic), First Order
		Finn (Junction Box)	N/A	Chapter IX: Destroy Starkiller Base	Sharpshooter, Grapple Gun, Immunity (Toxic), Lightsaber, First Order
		Finn (Starkiller Base)	N/A	Chapter X: The Finale	Sharpshooter, Grapple Gun, Immunity (Toxic), Lightsaber, First Order
		Finn (Takodana)	N/A	Chapter VI: Battle of Takodana	Sharpshooter, Grapple Gun, Immunity (Toxic), Lightsaber, First Order
		First Order Fleet Engineer	50,000	Escape from the Finalizer	Sharpshooter, Quadnoculars, First Order
		Flametrooper	125,000	Chapter I: Assault on Jakku	Gold LEGO, Thaw LEGO, First Order
		FN-2187	N/A	Chapter I: Assault on Jakku	Sharpshooter, Grapple Gun, First Order
		FN-2187 (Helmetless)	N/A	Escape from the Finalizer	Sharpshooter, Grapple Gun, First Order
		FN-2199	N/A	Trouble Over Taul	Sharpshooter, Cracked LEGO, First Order
		Gaff Kaylek	75,000	Rathtar Hunting	Sharpshooter, Grapple Gun, Immunity (Toxic)
		General Hux	75,000	Chapter IX: Destroy Starkiller Base	Sharpshooter, Command, First Order
		General Hux (Aerobics)	125,000	Poe to the Rescue	Agile, Grapple Gun, First Order
		General Leia	N/A	Chapter VII: The Resistance	Sharpshooter, Grapple Gun, Command, Resistance
		General Leia (Formal)	75,000	Chapter X: The Finale	Sharpshooter, Grapple Gun, Command, Resistance
		Goss Toowers	50,000	Chapter VII: The Resistance	Sharpshooter, Resistance
		Gray Squadron Pilot	Carbonite	D'Qar (Hub)	Sharpshooter, Grapple Gun, Resistance
		Greedo	Carbonite	Jakku (Hub)	Sharpshooter, Grapple Gun, Bounty Hunter

CHARACTERS

icon	Got It?	Character	Cost	Level Unlocked	Abilities
		Grummgar	200,000	Chapter V: Maz's Castle	Strong, Cracked LEGO, Bounty Hunter
		Guavian Gunner	100,000	Chapter IV: The Eravana	Gold LEGO
		Guavian Security Soldier	75,000	Chapter IV: The Eravana	Sharpshooter, Grapple Gun, Silver LEGO
		Han Solo	N/A	Chapter IV: The Eravana	Sharpshooter, Grapple Gun, Quadnoculars, Resistance
		Han Solo (Classic)	Carbonite	Millennium Falcon (Hub)	Sharpshooter, Grapple Gun, Quadnoculars, Resistance
		Han Solo (Endor)	N/A	Prologue: The Battle of Endor	Sharpshooter, Grapple Gun, Quadnoculars, Resistance
		Han Solo (Starkiller Base)	N/A	Chapter VIII: Starkiller Sabotage	Sharpshooter, Grapple Gun, Quadnoculars, Resistance
		Han Solo (Stormtrooper)	Carbonite	Starkiller Base (Hub)	Sharpshooter, Grapple Gun
		Han Solo (Twon Ketee)	N/A	Rathtar Hunting	Sharpshooter, Grapple Gun, Quadnoculars, Resistance
		Hobin Carsamba	75,000	Chapter III: Niima Outpost	Quadnoculars, Immunity (Toxic), Scavenger
		Hoogenz	50,000	Chapter III: Niima Outpost	Sharpshooter, Immunity (Toxic), Scavenger
		Ilco Munica	50,000	Chapter I: Assault on Jakku	Sharpshooter, Strong, Scavenger
		Imperial Royal Guard	Carbonite	Starkiller Base (Hub)	Staff
		Infrablue Zebeddy Coggins	50,000	Chapter V: Maz's Castle	Sharpshooter, Small Access
		Jawa	Carbonite	Jakku (Hub)	Sharpshooter, Small Access, Scavenger
		Jessika Pava	75,000	Chapter IX: Destroy Starkiller Base	Agile, Sharpshooter, Grapple Gun, Resistance
		Kanjiklub Gang Member	50,000	Chapter IV: The Eravana	Agile, Sharpshooter
		Kanjiklub (Sniper)	75,000	Chapter IV: The Eravana	Sharpshooter, Quadnoculars
		Kaydel Ko Connix	75,000	Ottegan Assault	Sharpshooter, Quadnoculars, Resistance
		Kinn Zih	50,000	Chapter I: Assault on Jakku	Sharpshooter
		Korr Sella	50,000	Chapter VI: Battle of Takodana	Sharpshooter, Resistance
		Kylo Ren	N/A	Ottegan Assault	Dark Side Force Powers, Force Bubble, Force Freeze, Lightsaber, First Order
		Kylo Ren (Hooded)	250,000	Chapter IX: Destroy Starkiller Base	Dark Side Force Powers, Force Bubble, Force Freeze, Lightsaber, First Order
		Kylo Ren (Unmasked)	250,000	Chapter X: The Finale	Dark Side Force Powers, Force Bubble, Force Freeze, Lightsaber, First Order
		Lando Calrissian	N/A	Prologue: The Battle of Endor	Sharpshooter, Grapple Gun, Command
		Lieutenant Bastian	75,000	Chapter X: The Finale	Sharpshooter, Grapple Gun, Immunity (Toxic), Resistance
		Lieutenant Mitaka	50,000	Chapter IX: Destroy Starkiller Base	Sharpshooter, Quadnoculars, First Order

CHARACTERS

icon	Got It?	Character	Cost	Level Unlocked	Abilities
		Logray	N/A	Prologue: The Battle of Endor	Small Access, Command
		Lor San Tekka	N/A	Lor San Tekka's Return	Grapple Gun, Quadnoculars, Staff, Scavenger
		Luke Skywalker (Stormtrooper)	Carbonite	Starkiller Base (Hub)	Sharpshooter, Grapple Gun
		Luke Skywalker (Episode IV)	Carbonite	Jakku (Hub)	Sharpshooter, Grapple Gun, Lightsaber
		Luke Skywalker (Episode VI)	N/A	Prologue: The Battle of Endor	Agile, Sharpshooter, Force Powers, Jedi Mind Trick, Lightsaber
		Major Brance	50,000	Trouble Over Taul	Sharpshooter, Quadnoculars, Command, Resistance
		Major Kalonia	50,000	Chapter VII: The Resistance	Sharpshooter, Quadnoculars, Resistance
		Maz Kanata	N/A	Chapter VI: Battle of Takodana	Sharpshooter, Quadnoculars, Small Access
		Mi'no Teest	50,000	Chapter VI: Battle of Takodana	Sharpshooter, Grapple Gun
		Monn Tatth	50,000	Chapter III: Niima Outpost	Grapple Gun, Quadnoculars, Scavenger
		Nien Nunb	75,000	Chapter IX: Destroy Starkiller Base	Sharpshooter, Resistance
		Nien Nunb (Classic)	75,000	Chapter VII: The Resistance	Sharpshooter, Resistance
		Obi Wan Kenobi (Episode III)	Carbonite	Takodana (Hub)	Sharpshooter, Force Powers, Jedi Mind Trick, Lightsaber
		Obi Wan Kenobi (Classic)	Carbonite	Jakku (Hub)	Sharpshooter, Force Powers, Jedi Mind Trick, Lightsaber
		Officer Sumitsu	50,000	Escape from the Finalizer	Sharpshooter, Quadnoculars, First Order
		Oni Jass	75,000	Rathtar Hunting	Sharpshooter, Silver LEGO, Immunity (Toxic)
		Ophi Egra	50,000	Chapter I: Assault on Jakku	Sharpshooter, Scavenger
		Oskus Stooratt	50,000	Crimson Corsair	Sharpshooter, Silver LEGO
		Ottegan Acolyte	75,000	Ottegan Assault	Sharpshooter, Grapple Gun
		Ottegan Warrior	75,000	Ottegan Assault	Sharpshooter, Staff
		Ozeer Tenzer	50,000	Rathtar Hunting	Sharpshooter, Grapple Gun, Immunity (Toxic)
		Padmé Amidala	Carbonite	Jakku (Hub)	Agile, Grapple Gun
		Pamich Nerro Goode	75,000	Ottegan Assault	Sharpshooter, Quadnoculars, Resistance
		Petty Officer Thanisson	75,000	Escape from the Finalizer	Sharpshooter, Quadnoculars, First Order
		Poe Dameron	N/A	Chapter I: Assault on Jakku	Sharpshooter, Grapple Gun, Quadnoculars, Resistance
		Poe Dameron (D'Qar)	N/A	Chapter X: The Finale	Sharpshooter, Grapple Gun, Quadnoculars, Resistance
		Poe Dameron (Flight Suit)	N/A	Chapter VI: Battle of Takodana	Sharpshooter, Grapple Gun, Quadnoculars, Resistance

icon	Got It?	Character	Cost	Level Unlocked	Abilities
		Poe Dameron (Helmetless)	N/A	Poe to the Rescue	Sharpshooter, Grapple Gun, Quadnoculars, Resistance
		Poe Dameron (Prisoner)	N/A	Escape from the Finalizer	Sharpshooter, Grapple Gun, Quadnoculars, Resistance
		Prashee	50,000	Chapter V: Maz's Castle	Small Access
		Praster Barrun	75,000	Ottegan Assault	Sharpshooter, Command
		Praster Ommlen	75,000	Ottegan Assault	
		Princess Leia (Classic)	Carbonite	D'Qar (Hub)	Sharpshooter, Grapple Gun, Command, Resistance
		Princess Leia (Endor)	N/A	Prologue: The Battle of Endor	Sharpshooter, Grapple Gun, Command, Resistance
		Princess Leia (Ewok Village)	Carbonite	Takodana (Hub)	Sharpshooter, Grapple Gun, Command, Resistance
		Pru Sweevant	N/A	Crimson Corsair	Sharpshooter, Small, Silver LEGO, Bounty Hunter
		Queen Amidala	Carbonite	Takodana (Hub)	Agile, Sharpshooter
		Qui Gon Jin	Carbonite	Takodana (Hub)	Sharpshooter, Force Powers, Jedi Mind Trick, Lightsaber
		Quiggold	N/A	Crimson Corsair	Strong, Gold LEGO, Bounty Hunter
		Quinar	50,000	Chapter III: Niima Outpost	Sharpshooter, Strong, Immunity (Cold), Scavenger
		Rancor	500,000	Poe to the Rescue	Cracked LEGO
		Razoo Qin-Fee	250,000	Chapter IV: The Eravana	Sharpshooter, Silver LEGO
		Rebel Commando	Carbonite	Takodana (Hub)	Sharpshooter, Grapple Gun
		Rebel Fleet Trooper	Carbonite	D'Qar (Hub)	Sharpshooter, Quadnoculars
		Resistance General	75,000	Chapter VII: The Resistance	Sharpshooter, Quadnoculars, Command, Resistance
		Resistance X-Wing Pilot	75,000	Chapter VI: Battle of Takodana	Sharpshooter, Grapple Gun, Resistance
		Rey	N/A	Chapter III: Niima Outpost	Agile, Sharpshooter, Quadnoculars, Staff
		Rey (Junction Box)	N/A	Chapter IX: Destroy Starkiller Base	Agile, Sharpshooter, Quadnoculars, Staff
		Rey (Resistance)	N/A	Epilogue: Luke's Island	Agile, Sharpshooter, Quadnoculars, Staff, Lightsaber, Resistance
		Rey (Scavenger)	N/A	Escape from the Finalizer	Agile, Sharpshooter, Quadnoculars, Staff
		Rey (Starkiller Base)	N/A	Chapter X: The Finale	Agile, Sharpshooter, Quadnoculars, Staff
		Rey (Takodana)	N/A	Chapter V: Maz's Castle	Agile, Sharpshooter, Quadnoculars, Staff
		Rey (Young)	75,000	Chapter V: Maz's Castle	Small Access
		Sache Skareet	50,000	Trouble Over Taul	Sharpshooter, Grapple Gun, Resistance

CHARACTERS

icon	Got It?	Character	Cost	Level Unlocked	Abilities
		Sarco Plank	250,000	Chapter III: Niima Outpost	Sharpshooter, Silver LEGO, Immunity (Toxic), Staff, Bounty Hunter
		Scout Trooper	Carbonite	Starkiller Base (Hub)	Sharpshooter, Quadnoculars
		Sidon Ithano	N/A	Crimson Corsair	Agile, Sharpshooter, Grapple Gun, Quadnoculars, Immunity (Toxic)
		Snap Wexley	N/A	Chapter VI: Battle of Takodana	Sharpshooter, Grapple Gun, Resistance
		Snowtrooper	75,000	Chapter VIII: Starkiller Sabotage	Sharpshooter, Grapple Gun, Immunity (Cold), First Order
		Snowtrooper Officer	125,000	Chapter X: The Finale	Sharpshooter, Command, Silver LEGO, Immunity (Cold), First Order
		Snowtrooper (Classic)	Carbonite	Starkiller Base (Hub)	Sharpshooter, Immunity (Cold)
		Special Forces TIE Pilot	75,000	Chapter VIII: Starkiller Sabotage	Sharpshooter, Grapple Gun, First Order
		Stormtrooper	50,000	Chapter I: Assault on Jakku	Sharpshooter, Grapple Gun, First Order
		Stormtrooper (Aerobics)	125,000	Poe to the Rescue	Agile, Sharpshooter, Grapple Gun, First Order
		Stormtrooper (Heavy)	125,000	Poe to the Rescue	Gold LEGO, First Order
		Stormtrooper Captain	100,000	Chapter IX: Destroy Starkiller Base	Sharpshooter, Grapple Gun, Command, First Order
		Stormtrooper (Classic)	Carbonite	Takodana (Hub)	Sharpshooter, Grapple Gun
		Stormtrooper Combat Engineer	75,000	Chapter IX: Destroy Starkiller Base	Sharpshooter, Grapple Gun, First Order
		FN-2112	75,000	Chapter VIII: Starkiller Sabotage	Sharpshooter, First Order
		Stormtrooper (Hot Tub)	75,000	Chapter VIII: Starkiller Sabotage	Sharpshooter, First Order
		Stormtrooper Sergeant	100,000	Crimson Corsair	Sharpshooter, Command, Silver LEGO, First Order
		Sudswater Dillifay Glon	50,000	Chapter V: Maz's Castle	Sharpshooter, Small Access
		Taryish Juhden	50,000	Chapter III: Niima Outpost	Sharpshooter, Quadnoculars, Staff
		Tasu Leech	250,000	Chapter IV: The Eravana	Agile, Sharpshooter, Grapple Gun
		Taybin Ralorsa	50,000	Chapter V: Maz's Castle	Sharpshooter, Quadnoculars, Resistance
		Technician Mandetat	50,000	Escape from the Finalizer	Sharpshooter, Quadnoculars, First Order
		Teedo	75,000	Lor San Tekka's Return	Sharpshooter, Small Access, Staff
		TIE Interceptor Pilot	Carbonite	Starkiller Base	Sharpshooter, Grapple Gun, Quadnoculars
		TIE Pilot	50,000	Escape from the Finalizer	Sharpshooter, Grapple Gun, First Order
		Trentus Savay	75,000	Ottegan Assault	Sharpshooter, Grapple Gun, Resistance
		Trinto Duaba	50,000	Chapter VI: Battle of Takodana	Sharpshooter, Staff

icon	Got It?	Character	Cost	Level Unlocked	Abilities
		Tusken Raider	Carbonite	Jakku (Hub)	Staff
		Ubert "Sticks" Quaril	50,000	Chapter V: Maz's Castle	
		Unkar Goon	75,000	Chapter III: Niima Outpost	Sharpshooter, Strong
		Unkar Plutt	150,000	Chapter III: Niima Outpost	Sharpshooter, Strong, Quadnoculars
		Unkar Thug	75,000	Chapter III: Niima Outpost	Sharpshooter, Strong
		Varmik	100,000	Chapter V: Maz's Castle	Agile, Sharpshooter, Strong, Silver LEGO
		Varond Jelik	N/A	Rathtar Hunting	Agile, Sharpshooter, Immunity (Toxic), Staff
		Volzang Li-Thrull	125,000	Chapter IV: The Eravana	Gold LEGO, Thaw LEGO
		Wampa	250,000	Poe to the Rescue	Strong, Cracked LEGO, Immunity (Cold)
		Wedge Antilles	N/A	Prologue: The Battle of Endor	Sharpshooter, Grapple Gun, Quadnoculars
		Wi'ba Tuyill	57,000	Crimson Corsair	Sharpshooter, Grapple Gun
		Wicket	N/A	Prologue: The Battle of Endor	Sharpshooter, Small Access, Command
		Wollivan	100,000	Chapter VI: Battle of Takodana	Sharpshooter, Small Access
		Yoda	Carbonite	Takodana (Hub)	Sharpshooter, Small Access, Force Powers, Jedi Mind Trick, Lightsaber
		Zev Senesca	Carbonite	Takodana (Hub)	Sharpshooter, Grapple Gun
		Zylas	100,000	Rathtar Hunting	Agile, Sharpshooter, Immunity (Toxic)
		B-U4D	100,000	Chapter VII: The Resistance	Immunity (Cold), Immunity (Toxic), Resistance
		BB-8	N/A	Chapter I: Assault on Jakku	BB-8, Charge Up, Small Access, Immunity (Cold), Immunity (Toxic), Astromech Droid
		C-3PO	N/A	Chapter VII: The Resistance	Protocol Droid, Immunity (Cold), Immunity (Toxic)
		C-3PO (Classic)	N/A	Prologue: The Battle of Endor	Protocol Droid, Immunity (Cold), Immunity (Toxic)
		EGL-21 "Amps"	75,000	Lor San Tekka's Return	Immunity (Cold), Immunity (Toxic)
		GA-97	75,000	Chapter VI: Battle of Takodana	Immunity (Cold), Immunity (Toxic), Protocol Droid
		GTAW-74 "Geetaw"	50,000	Lor San Tekka's Return	Immunity (Cold), Immunity (Toxic)
		GNK-143	150,000	Trouble Over Taul	Charge Up, Immunity (Cold), Immunity (Toxic)
		HURID-327	400,000	Chapter V: Maz's Castle	Strong, Cracked LEGO, Immunity (Cold), Immunity (Toxic)
		K-3PO	125,000	Poe to the Rescue	Immunity (Cold), Immunity (Toxic), Protocol Droid
		M9-G8	75,000	Lor San Tekka's Return	Immunity (Cold), Immunity (Toxic), Astromech Droid

CHARACTERS

icon	Got It?	Character	Cost	Level Unlocked	Abilities
		MSE-E	75,000	Trouble Over Taul	Small Access, Immunity (Cold), Immunity (Toxic)
		0-MR1	N/A	Trouble Over Taul	Immunity (Cold), Immunity (Toxic), Protocol Droid, First Order
		PZ-4CO	125,000	Chapter VII: The Resistance	Immunity (Cold), Immunity (Toxic), Protocol Droid
		R-3PO	125,000	Escape from the Finalizer	Immunity (Cold), Immunity (Toxic), Protocol Droid
		R2-D2	N/A	Epilogue: Luke's Island	Immunity (Cold), Immunity (Toxic), Astromech Droid
		R2-Q5	75,000	Trouble Over Taul	Immunity (Cold), Immunity (Toxic), Astromech Droid
		R2-KT	75,000	Chapter VII: The Resistance	Immunity (Cold), Immunity (Toxic), Astromech Droid
		R3-A2	N/A	Chapter VIII: Starkiller Sabotage	Immunity (Cold), Immunity (Toxic), Astromech Droid
		R5-D8	75,000	Chapter V: Maz's Castle	Immunity (Cold), Immunity (Toxic), Astromech Droid
		R5-J2	75,000	Poe to the Rescue	Immunity (Cold), Immunity (Toxic), Astromech Droid
		SN-1F4	75,000	Lor San Tekka's Return	Immunity (Cold), Immunity (Toxic)
		Kintan Strider	N/A	Millennium Falcon (Dejarik Battle)	Strong, Cracked LEGO
		Mantellian Savrip	N/A	Millennium Falcon (Dejarik Battle)	Strong, Cracked LEGO
		Molator	N/A	Millennium Falcon (Dejarik Battle)	Strong, Cracked LEGO
		M'onnok	N/A	Millennium Falcon (Dejarik Battle)	
		JJ Abrams	N/A	Epilogue: Luke's Island	Sharpshooter, Grapple Gun, Quadnoculars, Command, Resistance, First Order
		Kathleen Kennedy	N/A	Epilogue: Luke's Island	Sharpshooter, Grapple Gun, Command, Silver LEGO, Gold LEGO, Resistance, First Order

PROLOGUE:
BATTLE OF ENDOR

TRUE JEDI REQUIREMENT
80,000

VEHICLES UNLOCKED (FREE)

 Millennium Falcon (Classic) (and Microfighter)

 Rebel Alliance X-wing (and Microfighter)

 Endor Speeder Bike

COMPLETED MINIKIT VEHICLE

 Imperial AT-ST (Microfighter)

STORY MODE CHARACTERS UNLOCKED (FREE)

 AT-ST Pilot

 Chewbacca

 Darth Vader

 Han Solo (Endor)

 Lando Calrissian

 Logray

 Luke Skywalker (Episode VI)

 Princess Leia (Endor)

 Wedge Antilles

 Wicket

 C-3PO (Classic)

 R2-D2

Endor Shield Generator

CHEWBACCA, HAN SOLO (ENDOR), PRINCESS LEIA (ENDOR), R2-D2, WICKET

ELIMINATE 12 IMPERIALS

You begin in the middle of an intense firefight. Imperial stormtroopers and scout troopers drop into the small basin where your forces begin the fight.

After the twelfth trooper falls, an AT-ST moves into position to block the path ahead. It blasts an Ewok glider from the sky, scattering Multi-Build bricks near your characters.

MINIKIT:
MULTI-BUILD TRAMPOLINE

Use the Multi-Build bricks to assemble a trampoline against the ledge on the right. Bounce up to the ledge to reach the Minikit.

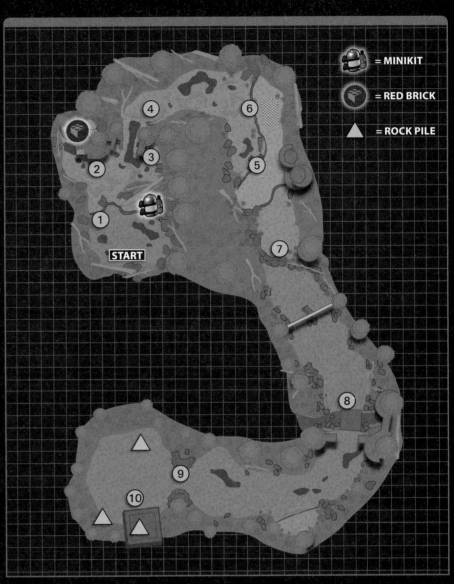

= MINIKIT

= RED BRICK

= ROCK PILE

START

FREE WICKET AND CRUSH THE AT-ST

Assemble a trampoline under the ledge on the left ① and bounce to the ledge. There's a small access hatch at the base of the tree that's too small for your starting characters to use. Fortunately, there's a recruit available who's just hanging out.

Tag to Han Solo or Princess Leia and target the grapple handle attached to the net hanging from the tree's boughs above ②. Tap the indicated button to free Wicket, who joins your group.

Send Wicket through the access hatch, which deposits him on a platform built in the branches above. The strength handles are too much for him, but he can push the weapon rack over the side.

STUD MAGNET

Use the Multi-Build bricks to craft hanging bars against the ledge beyond the tree. Hop between the bars to reach the top ledge and the Red Brick.

Construct a ladder that leads from the ground up to the platform. Tag to Chewbacca, ascend the ladder, then pull the strength handles to position the first log.

Stick with Chewbacca and move to the other side of the AT-ST. Imperial forces remain in the area, so be ready to fight. Pull the strength handles ③ on the base of the tree to position the second log. An Ewok swings an axe to take care of the rest.

BLASTER BATTLE

Tap the indicated button to take cover ④ from the incoming weapons fire. You must take out five stormtroopers and four scout troopers standing in front of the barricades and lining the ridge above.

When they're out of the way, your characters automatically advance toward the AT-ST. It's immune to blaster fire, so aim for the target on the red canisters at the feet of the AT-ST.

RESCUE R2-D2

Continue ahead until you encounter a trio of Ewoks pinned down by another AT-ST. R2-D2 is above them ⑤, trapped under a giant log. Tag to Wicket and recruit the Ewoks by speaking with them.

Backtrack slightly to an access hatch ⑥ in the hillside. Crawl through, then push the rack of large logs over the side. Wicket can't do it himself, but the three Ewoks following him provide the extra muscle needed to take out the AT-ST.

From the Multi-Build bricks left behind, construct the closest object, a turret. A few well-placed blasts destroy the log and free R2-D2. Build a ramp from the bricks left behind to create a path to join Wicket.

— MINIKIT: —
IN A TREE

The Multi-Build bricks become a lift and control node when directed under a nearby tree. Set one character on the platform, then a second on the control node. Jump to the platform built around the tree.

TAKE AN AT-ST ON A TEST DRIVE

Use the Multi-Build bricks under the ledge on the right. Tag to R2-D2 and connect with the interface port. Complete the shape-matching puzzle to power the platform. Ride the platform to the higher ledge.

Smash the storage containers ⑦ until there are enough bricks to build a banner and grapple handle. Target the grapple handle with either Han Solo or Princess Leia. After landing atop an AT-ST, pull open the hatch and throw out the pilot with a well-timed button press. Tap the indicated button when the indicator is in the green.

REACH THE SHIELD GENERATOR BUNKER

Don't bother with the Imperial forces in this area. They can't damage an AT-ST and you can't earn a multiplier while driving. Target the wooden palisades with the AT-ST's blasters. Move forward until a raised bridge (8) blocks your progress. Blast the two rock-filled nets hanging on either side of the bridge to lower it.

The AT-STs on the ridge beyond the bridge are your primary targets. Take them out from long range, then clear out the barricades set up by Imperial forces. There's an additional AT-ST to eliminate before you reach the bunker clearing.

Advance into the clearing (9) and take one final AT-ST. Blast the red canisters atop the bunker, which also destroys a turret. A large log drops into place, sealing off possible Imperial reinforcements.

Don't exit your AT-ST until after you blast three piles of rocks scattered around the clearing. One pile is on the bunker's roof. A second pile is on the ground next to the bunker. The final pile is on the opposite side of the clearing.

After dropping the giant tree trunk in place and leaving the AT-ST cockpit, tag to Princess Leia and speak to the trio of Rebel soldiers near a downed AT-ST. Rip off the walker's hatch to expose a Minikit.

After the log drops, Chewbacca, R2-D2, and Wicket rejoin the group. Han Solo and Princess Leia can exit their AT-ST as well. Look for a pile of Multi-Build bricks in front of the bunker (10).

You have two possible build options here, and either choice completes this portion of the mission. Choose left to construct a giant movie screen. Choose right to assemble a hat dispenser. Select an Imperial pilot's hat from the dispenser and interact with the scanner outside the blast doors.

Death Star Interior

LUKE SKYWALKER (EPISODE VI), DARTH VADER

DEFEAT THE EMPEROR

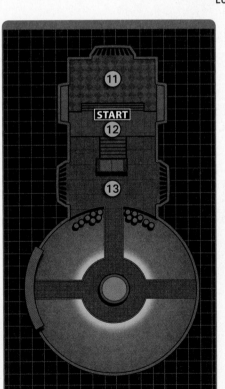

Eliminate the Imperial Guard, then use the Force on the two large structures hanging above the Emperor (11). Each can be used once before the Emperor rips them out and sends them across the room, where they become Multi-Build bricks (12).

Choose right to make an X-wing, which Luke Skywalker can guide with the Force. Choose left to build a TIE fighter, which Darth Vader can hurl at the Emperor with the power of the Dark Side. Each attack can be used once. The Emperor destroys rebuilt mini-starfighters with Force Lightning.

The Emperor moves the fight down a flight of stairs (13). He shields himself in Force Lightning, summons additional Imperial Guardsmen, and hurls assembled debris at the Skywalkers.

There are two ways to damage the Emperor here. The first is to throw a lightsaber at the targets high above the Emperor, which spills a pile of junk on him.

The second way is to use the Force to pull objects from the walls on either side of the staircase. Hold the cylinders with the Force until they slam into the Emperor.

The final stage pits Darth Vader against the Emperor. Tap the button that appears to advance Darth Vader, and end the fight with a mighty heave.

Death Star Escape

MILLENNIUM FALCON (CLASSIC), REBEL ALLIANCE X-WING

REACH THE CORE

The Millennium Falcon and Wedge Antilles's X-wing zoom over the surface of the Death Star, and then through its partially-constructed interior on the way to the core. You can't get lost here, so focus on flying through the rings of studs or blasting TIE fighters.

MINIKIT:
TOWER TURRETS

Watch for turbolaser turrets while flying on the surface and down to the core. Blast five total to earn a Minikit.

DESTROY THE DEATH STAR

The Death Star's power core is sheathed in metal, which breaks down under concentrated fire from the Millennium Falcon and the X-wing. Target the glowing blue discs to destroy the barrier. Advanced TIE fighters appear next, and they carry exactly what you need to finish the battle.

Destroy the Advanced TIE fighters for the proton torpedoes they carry (your battle computer marks them red) or pick up torpedoes from the dispensers along the exterior wall. There are three targets in the center of the core. Each must be hit with a proton torpedo. You can either gather multiple proton torpedoes at once, or make a run each time you collect a single proton torpedo.

MINIKIT:
POWER PYLONS

Destroy the three blue pylons above the Death Star's power core.

FREE PLAY:
THE BATTLE OF ENDOR

Endor Shield Generator

Death Star Interior

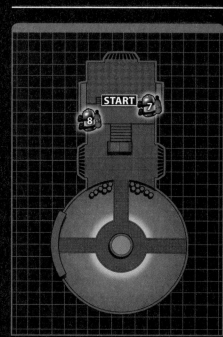

 = MINIKIT   = RED BRICK

 = ROCK PILE

 = MINIKIT

Minikit 3
The Multi-Build bricks become a raising platform and control node when directed under a nearby tree. Set one character on the platform, then a second on the control node. Jump to the platform built around the tree.

Minikit 4
Select an aquatic character and jump into the dive pool on the wooden platform. Assemble an explosive bundle from the bricks tossed out from the water. The now-open door leads to a large wooden platform and three Ewoks. Break down the rack and other primitive items. Rebuild each item as a musical instrument. The Ewoks begin playing the instruments and the bricks for a Minikit appear between them.

Minikit 5
Don't exit your AT-ST until after you blast three piles of rocks scattered around the clearing. One pile is on the bunker's roof. A second pile is on the ground next to the bunker. The final pile is on the opposite side of the clearing.

Minikit 6
After dropping the giant tree trunk in place and leaving the AT-ST cockpit, tag in Princess Leia to speak to the trio of Rebel soldiers near a downed AT-ST. Rip off the walker's hatch to expose a Minikit.

Minikit 1
Use the Multi-Build bricks to assemble a trampoline against the ledge on the right. Bounce up to the ledge and claim the Minikit.

Minikit 2
Select a character with Force Powers, like Luke Skywalker, to pull down the insect hive above the AT-ST's location at the end of the Blaster Battle.

STUD MAGNET
Use the Multi-Build bricks to craft hanging bars against the ledge beyond the tree. Hop between the bars to reach the top ledge and the Red Brick.

Minikit 7
During the first stage of the battle against the Emperor, build a rotary control next to the screen on the room's right side. Guide the ship through the course and avoid the obstacles.

Minikit 8
After the fight moves down stairs, use dark side Force powers to pull away a panel on the left, which exposes an access hatch. There's a Minikit on a walkway on the other end of the hatch.

Death Star Escape

Minikit 9
While flying outside the Death Star and through it (but before reaching the core), watch for turbolaser towers. Blast five to earn a Minikit.

Minikit 10
While attacking the Death Star power core, aim for the three pylons above it.

HUB:
D'QAR

CHARACTERS NOW AVAILABLE FOR PURCHASE	NEW LEVEL UNLOCKED
None	None

Resistance Base
POE DAMERON, BB-8

GET A GOLD BRICK

When you assume control of Poe Dameron and BB-8, exit the command center and stop to speak with C-3PO ① before continuing to an X-wing ② being prepped for its trip to Jakku. The stairs leading up to the X-wing are destroyed.

Move Poe Dameron near the pile of bricks (BB-8 is unable to build) and note the two locations of orange outlines. Two outlines means these Multi-Build bricks can be used in one of two ways, depending on which way you push the control stick while you hold the Build button.

Build to the right to add a motor to the lift ③, which lowers the lift's platform. Move BB-8 onto the lowered platform, then switch to Poe Dameron. Attacking most objects created from Multi-Build bricks revert them to their component bricks, which means you can put them to use again.

When you destroy the motor here, the lift rises to its original position. Tag to Poe Dameron, then jump to grab the Gold Brick.

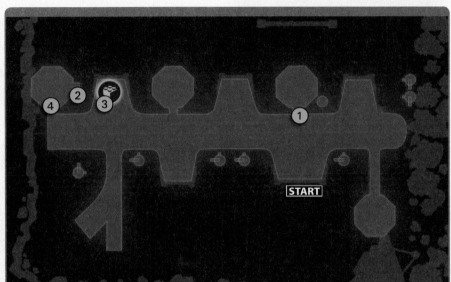

Move next to the pile of Multi-Build bricks and hold to the left while pressing the Build button. This new machine is an interface designed specifically for BB-8.

Tag to BB-8 and rotate the control stick in the indicated direction. When the gauge fills, BB-8 is launched to the X-wing's landing pad.

CLEARED FOR TAKE-OFF

Use the nearby astromech access ④ to begin a shape-matching puzzle. Rotate the larger piece so that the smaller piece inside aligns properly. Match two shapes to complete the puzzle and swing a crane's arm into position.

Tag to Poe Dameron and use the grapple handle at the end of the crane to join BB-8. Move to the location indicated by the blue light. Hop into the X-wing to bring up the Galaxy Map. Select Jakku to begin the adventure!

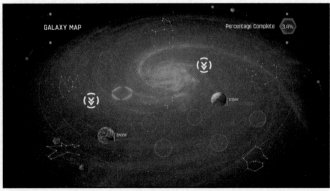

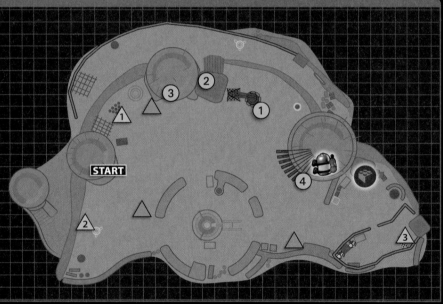

 = MINIKIT   = BARREL   ▲ = SPORTS MINIKIT   = RED BRICK

TRUE JEDI REQUIREMENT
80,000

STORY MODE CHARACTERS UNLOCKED (FREE)

 Poe Dameron

 FN-2187

 BB-8

VEHICLES UNLOCKED (FREE)

 Resistance X-wing (Poe)

 Rey's Speeder (and Microfighter)

 Poe's Blue X-wing (Microfighter)

COMPLETED MINIKIT VEHICLE

 First Order Dropship (and Microfighter)

Village Retreat

BB-8, POE DAMERON

ARM THE LOCALS— FIRST CACHE

With First Order forces attacking the village, it's no time to be delicate. Most villagers are running around in a panic and they need help. Smash everything in your search for two caches of weapons. The story automatically advances after you uncover the second cache of weapons (you can uncover them in any order), so grab the Minikits in the area first.

MINIKIT:
BARREL BUILDING

While arming the locals, build three barrels from bricks found throughout the village. The villagers use the barrels for cover.

MINIKIT:
RANDOM ACTS OF SPORTS

Smash the water jugs (location 1) set up like bowling pins. Two piles of bricks near a silver LEGO object become a basketball goal (location 2) and launch pad that sends BB-8 through the net. Finally, go into the fenced-in area (location 3). Build a ball dispenser with a power jack, then push the soccer ball into the goal.

Scan the crane between two dwellings ① to reveal a grapple handle. Tap the indicated button to pull down a pile of Multi-Build bricks. Build the object on the right first, a launch pad. It sends BB-8 up to the crane's basket.

Tear down the launch pad and use the Multi-Build bricks against the crane's base. Tag to Poe Dameron and move the basket by pressing the control stick in the indicated direction. Tag to BB-8 and complete the astromech access's ② shape-matching puzzle to restore power to the door below.

Tag to Poe Dameron and enter the building ③. Break down the objects inside and use the leftover bricks to rebuild a power jack. Switch to BB-8 and restore power to an outside device that pulls up a weapon cache from under the sand.

ARM THE LOCALS—SECOND CACHE

Look for a home with a large metal door ④ that's not far from the crane. Use salvaged bricks to restore a power jack. Restoring power draws out a twisty staircase. Ascend the stairs and enter the home.

Destroy everything inside the home. Most of the bricks are used to create a Gonk droid, which hops outside and becomes a rack of weapons.

Use the bricks near the window inside the home to construct a Minikit.

FAST BUILD

Break apart the objects on the ground next to a grass-awning-covered merchant's cart. Assemble the bricks you find into a stick-figure, which can go in two locations. Blast it and rebuild it at both spots.

First Order Assault

BB-8, DASHA PROMENTI, POE DAMERON

BATTLE THE FIRST ORDER

After the X-wing crash-lands, there's a quick firefight with a small contingent of stormtroopers. Avoid collecting studs that appear (unless they're about to vanish!) until after you take out the stormtroopers and increase your multiplier.

Target the grapple handle (5) and pull over the tower. Build a large blaster, then tag to BB-8 and connect with the power jack. The blaster clears a path ahead and reveals an ally, Dasha Promenti, who assists Poe Dameron in the upcoming Blaster Battle (6).

BLASTER BATTLE

Your first objective is to take out 15 stormtroopers. Focus on the ones out in the open for easier shots. Reinforcements are delivered by a troop transport after you eliminate the first group.

A scan spot pops up behind one of the barricades. Scan the side of the transport to reveal its power cells. Blast the cells to bring down the ship. To take down the shielded blast turret, move down the barricades until there's a clear shot at the target outside the shield. Hit it and the explosion wipes out the turret.

FIGHTING THROUGH FIRE

Dasha Promenti joins a group of villagers after they're freed from a squad of stormtroopers, leaving Poe Dameron and BB-8 alone again. Aim for the grapple handle ⑦ atop the shelter next to a water tower.

MINIKIT:
STORMTROOPER SHARPSHOOT

There's a solitary stormtrooper standing in the doorway of a hut behind a burning fence. Hit him with a ranged attack to earn a Minikit.

The right-hand build option is a swing for BB-8, which doles out a good amount of studs after BB-8 twirls around the top bar. Next, assemble a rotary control from the Multi-Build bricks. Tag to BB-8 and hold your control stick in the indicated direction to topple the water tower and extinguish some of the fire.

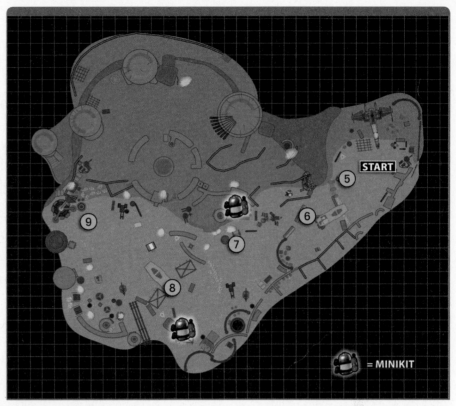

After a quick fight against some stormtroopers waiting on the other side of the fire, a troop transport lands nearby. After clearing out the First Order's forces, aim at the grapple handle atop the troop transport ⑧. Assemble an astromech access to send the transport on its way.

MINIKIT:
TRANSPORT INTERIOR

Attach a power jack on the side of the troop transport that lands across from the first one. Charging this power jack drops the front ramp. A Minikit is inside the transport.

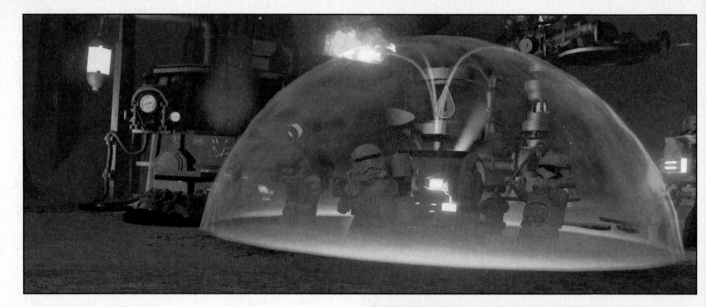

The stormtroopers beyond the troop transport ⑨ are a confident bunch equipped with a flamethrower and energy shield. Maintain a safe distance from the flames while breaking down the objects in the area.

When you uncover the Multi-Build bricks, choose the left option to create a large container of popcorn that tricks most of the stormtroopers into leaving the safety of their shield. Choose the right-hand option to construct a droid that tunnels underground and eliminates the energy field.

Water Tower Washout

There's more fire to extinguish here, and a local offers a hint on how to accomplish this with a nearby irrigator. Destroy the shield generator, which becomes Multi-Build bricks.

Repair the hoses on the left with the Multi-Build bricks. Bounce on the pad next to the villager until the barrel fills with water. Build a rotary control at the base of the water structure and move the barrel to the other platform.

Break down the rotary control and install a power jack on the large motor to the right. The water from the barrel shoots out and extinguishes the fire below. Either character's first step near the stormtroopers ends the chapter.

FREE PLAY:
ASSAULT ON JAKKU
Village Retreat

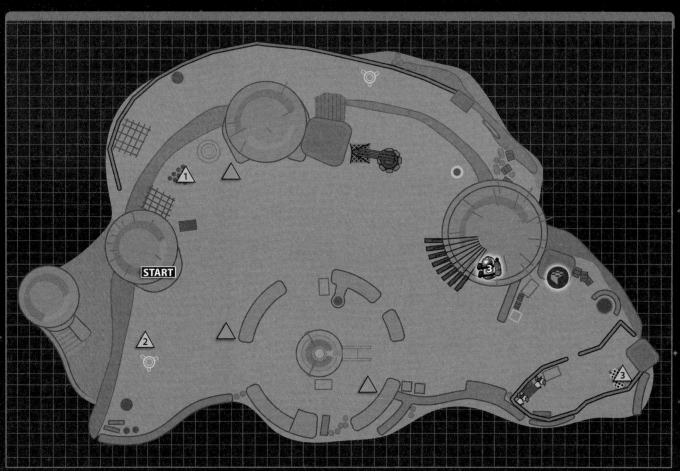

 = MINIKIT   ▲ = BARREL   ▲ = SPORTS MINIKIT   = RED BRICK

Minikit 1
While arming the locals, build three barrels from bricks found throughout the village.

Minikit 2
Smash the water jugs (location 1) set up like bowling pins. Two piles of bricks near a silver LEGO object become a basketball goal (location 2) and launch pad that sends BB-8 through the net. Finally, go into the fenced-in area (location 3). Build a ball dispenser with a power jack, then push the soccer ball into the goal.

Minikit 3
Use the bricks near the window inside the home to construct a Minikit.

FAST BUILD
Break apart the objects on the ground next to a grass-awning-covered merchant's cart. Assemble the bricks you find into a stick-figure, which can go in two locations. Blast it and rebuild it at both spots.

First Order Assault

Minikit 4

Destroy the three silver LEGO towers with an explosive attack from a character, such as Athgar Heece.

Minikit 5

After knocking over the water tower next to BB-8's swing, use the Force to shake the water tower's tank until the pieces of a Minikit fall out.

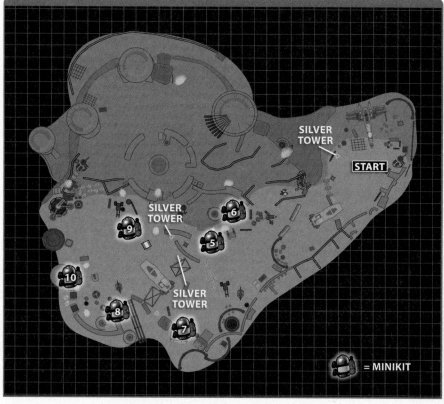

Minikit 6

There's a solitary stormtrooper standing in the doorway of a hut behind a burning fence. Hit him with a ranged attack to earn a Minikit.

Minikit 7

Attach a power jack on the side of the troop transport that landed during the fight. Charging this power jack drops the front ramp. A Minikit is inside the transport.

Minikit 8

Before tackling the shielded stormtroopers, dig around in the burning debris to reveal a dive pool. The dive pool leads to an underground storage area. Smash the objects in the basement. Build a Resistance terminal, which opens the safe with the Minikit inside.

Minikit 9

Bring in a character like Stormtrooper (Heavy) to blast open the gold LEGO chest near the shielded flametrooper.

Minikit 10

A strong character like Chewbacca is required to open the Strength Handles and get to the Minikit behind them.

HUB:
JAKKU

First Order Staging Area

FN-2187, POE DAMERON (PRISONER)

CHARACTERS NOW AVAILABLE FOR PURCHASE

 Constable Zuvio

 Dasha Promenti

 Flametrooper

 Ilco Munica

 Kinn Zih

 Ophi Egra

 Stormtrooper

NEW LEVEL UNLOCKED
None

POE THE PRISONER

Follow the guide studs through the burning remnants of the village. With Poe's hands tied and no BB-8, there's not much to do here besides pick up stray studs and check out the replay terminal.

REPLAY TERMINAL
Replay terminals allow you to return to previously-played chapters. They're not always necessary (you can often use the galaxy map), but many are conveniently placed next to the spots where you begin hub transit missions.

At the transport site ①, tag to FN-2187 and then interact with the First Order terminal. Tap the indicated buttons until each segment of the image is a stormtrooper.

A troop transport flies in from above and lands nearby. Walk up the ramp of the transport to continue to Star Destroyer Finalizer.

CHAPTER II:
ESCAPE FROM
THE FINALIZER

TRUE JEDI REQUIREMENT
120,000

STORY MODE CHARACTERS UNLOCKED (FREE)

 FN-2187 (Helmetless)

 Poe Dameron (Prisoner)

 Rey (Scavenger)

VEHICLES UNLOCKED (FREE)

 Special Forces TIE fighter (and Microfighter)

COMPLETED MINIKIT VEHICLE

 The Finalizer (and Microfighter)

Finalizer Hangar

FN-2187, POE DAMERON (PRISONER), R-3PO

PRISONER TRANSFER FROM CELL BLOCK 2187

Your destination is a staircase ❶ that descends into a recessed section of the floor. There's no hurry to get there, so have some fun slipping and sliding on the wet floor near the start point. If you attack any of the First Order forces, they'll fight back but you shouldn't have any problems handling them.

MINIKIT:
SECURITY DROIDS

Blast the small, white droid in the recessed area. Look for three more units exactly like i later. Destroy all four droids to earn a Minikit.

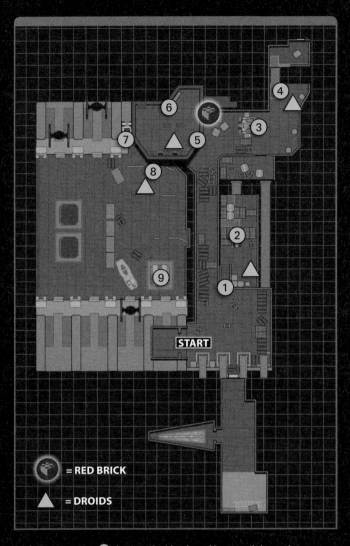

START

🔴 = RED BRICK

△ = DROIDS

PUT R-3PO TO WORK

Move past the terminal to a grapple handle attached to a container ④. Target the handle and tap the indicated button to pull down the container. Push the container into the break in the floor. Jump over the break and repeat the process of using a grapple handle to pull down a container and pushing into the break in the floor.

With a completed bridge over the break in place, smash the objects near the protocol droid storage pod. Use the bricks to awaken R-3PO from his shutdown. R-3PO can't jump, so if you didn't finish the bridge over the break in the floor earlier, you must do it now.

Return to the protocol access terminal ③ and interact with it as R-3PO. Select the colored patterns in the same order in which they appeared on the main screen. R-3PO wanders away as the ship takes off and crashes in short order, leaving your original pair of characters to deal with the fallout.

Blast the guards that investigate the crash. Fortunately, Poe Dameron's shackles are gone and he's managed to pick up a blaster. Smash the containers in the area to create a pile of Multi-Build bricks.

Push the container ② that's in the checkered lane until the path to a second much larger container beyond it is clear. The first container should end up against the wall. Both characters work together to push the larger container into a trench, so that it acts as a bridge.

Cross to the other side and destroy everything until you have enough bricks to build a lift. The way ahead is blocked ③ and only a protocol droid can help.

FAST INTERACT

Select the middle option for the Multi-Build bricks to form a bridge that connects to an alcove with a Red Brick.

ACQUIRE A TIE FIGHTER

Build the unit to the right first, which is a power source for a lift. Ride the lift up to the walkway, then hop on the narrow ledge against the windowed command center. Jump and grab the hanging bar (marked with a blue stud) near the end of the narrow walkway ⑤ to expose a triangular target.

Demolish the lift power source. Select the left option for the Multi-Build bricks to assemble an energy beam emitter. Interact with the emitter to destroy the windows above.

Quickly handle the guards that came down from the command center. Recreate the power source for the lift and ride it back up. Jump into the command center and eliminate the guards.

Tag to FN-2187 and complete the matching puzzle at the First Order terminal ⑥ to prepare a TIE fighter. Take the lift in the back of the room ⑦ to shift the scene to the hangar floor where you're invited to join a Blaster Battle.

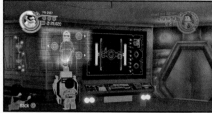

BLASTER BATTLE

Your initial objectives are five stormtroopers, and one heavy stormtrooper ⑧. The heavy stormtrooper has a health gauge (visible over his head) and fires in an arc. When the heavy stormtrooper starts firing, get behind cover. He needs a few seconds to start up again, so target him as soon as he stops shooting.

The stormtrooper on the right fires blindly over a barricade. To get a clear shot, move a character as far to the right as possible, then pop up and blast off his helmet.

Poe Dameron and FN-2187 advance to the next row of barricades. Eliminate another squad of six stormtroopers, this time supported by a shielded turret.

Move to the far left and pull on the grapple handle to cut off the power supply to the turret's shield. Blast the turret to advance again.

The next stop is in front of a giant turret ⑨, supported by an unending stream of stormtroopers. Tag to Poe Dameron and move to the left. Scan the turret's weapon arm, then blast the exposed power lines until the weapon arm explodes.

Before you go after the other arm, aim for the target-marked red canister on the far right. Move Poe Dameron to the scan location behind the new cover on the right. Blast the power lines to destroy the second weapon arm and end the Blaster Battle.

Run to the TIE fighter and board it. A damage meter pops up near the top of the screen. The TIE fighter flies itself around the hangar, leaving you in charge of shooting. Blast the other TIE fighters, troop transports, and turrets to get the damage meter to hit 100%.

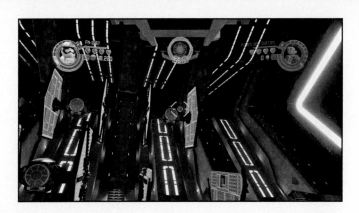

Star Destroyer Exterior

SPECIAL FORCES TIE FIGHTER

DESTROY 10 LARGE TURRETS, THEN A GIANT TURRET

There are 30 turrets on the exterior of this Star Destroyer (more about that soon), but you only need to get ten here. They're marked in red, and they're on top, along the sides, and even under the Finalizer. Shooting down TIE fighters boosts your multiplier, so don't neglect them.

MINIKIT:
SPECIAL FORCES TIE FIGHTERS

Shoot down five Special Forces TIE fighters (they're carrying proton torpedoes) before destroying the giant turret.

There are two sources of proton torpedoes: shooting down Special Forces TIE fighters, and the dispensers located near the ship's thrusters. Fly through the torpedoes to add them to your arsenal. Blast the screens first, then target the turret (marked with the same color as proton torpedoes) to destroy it.

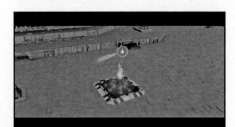

MINIKIT:
TIMED RUN

While destroying turrets, fly in the open gaps between the two decks of the Finalizer. Guide the TIE fighter into the purple sphere to start a countdown clock. Fly through the series of spheres, which ends in another purple sphere, before the clock hits zero.

MINIKIT:
TWENTY TURRETS

After the giant turret emerges, destroy 20 additional turrets.

A giant turret emerges from the hull. It's guarded by two energy screens and the only way to damage them is with proton torpedoes.

The next challenge is to evade incoming missiles and fighters while flying through rings of studs. Destroy the missiles and fighters to boost your multiplier (and make your journey a bit safer), but concentrate on picking up studs.

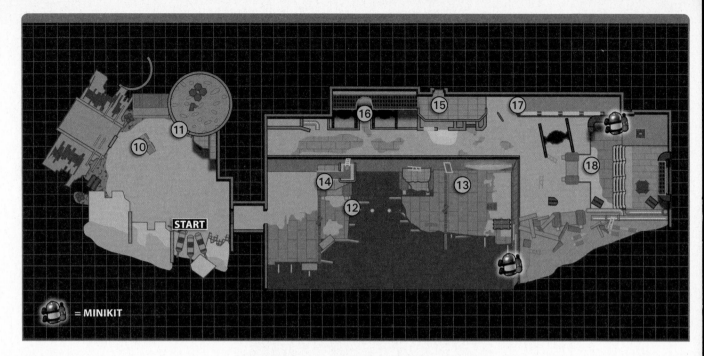

= MINIKIT

Jakku Graveyard

BB-8, REY (SCAVENGER)

FIGHT OFF TEEDOS

When you gain control of Rey, she's sandboarding down a dune. All you can do here is collect studs. To maximize your stud count, aim for the jumps. BB-8 joins the team when Rey ends her trip down the dune.

Battle the Teedos in the area and save the collection of studs for when your multiplier is built up. Use the bricks near where Rey landed to build a mini-sandcrawler. Let it drive around and it leaves trails of studs behind it. You can destroy it once for additional studs.

Use the Multi-Build bricks uncovered while battling the Teedos to free the luggabeast ⑩. The left-hand build option creates a droid with a mouse tail that frightens the luggabeast. The right-hand option is a giant carrot. Regardless of your choice, the luggabeast's rider is thrown.

Scan the back wall near the luggabeast to reveal a cracked brick doorway. Mount the luggabeast and break down the door. Tag to BB-8 and use the power jack to send a surge through parts of the crashed Star Destroyer.

STAR DESTROYER INTERIOR

Switch to Rey and jump to an orange hanging bar **11**, then into the dome. Step on the orange arrows, which indicate a flow of air that pushes Rey to another hanging bar.

Use the hanging bars to move to the right, then jump over to a final hanging bar that gives way under Rey's weight and reveals another power jack. Tag to BB-8 and restore power to the crashed Star Destroyer's doors.

Inside the Star Destroyer, approach the small platform on the left **12**. Tap the button flashing over your character's head to cross to the other side.

Destroy the objects in the area around Rey until you have the parts needed to rebuild a power source that goes against the wall **13**. You'll also uncover the parts for most of a Gonk droid.

MINIKIT:
HANGING OUT

There are two parallel pipes attached to the wall. Jump up to the pipes and shuffle to the right for a Minikit.

GET TO THE TOP

Target the empty yellow socket with Rey's staff. Use the twirl pole to reach a higher ledge. Step on the orange arrows to zip across the gap. Quickly tap the indicated button to maintain Rey's grip on the hanging bar, then hop up to safe ground.

Push the box of junk **14** over the edge. Build a launch pad from the bricks inside the box. Tag to BB-8 and zip up to a higher walkway. Roll down the walkway to an access hatch **15**. Go through the hatch to a room with an astromech access. Use the access to reveal a series of handholds Rey can use to meet up with BB-8, though the reunion is short-lived.

Use the grip walls **16** attached to the TIE fighter panels to ascend to a higher walkway (BB-8 is left behind). Slide under the barrier and use the orange arrows to zip over to a climb wall **17**. Climb to the top and slide under another barrier.

Drop down to the floor through the missing window. Attack the objects in the area until you reveal a stack of Multi-Build bricks **18**. Select the build option on the raised platform in the corner. The bricks become a spinner switch that Rey can turn and move a TIE fighter to form a bridge.

MINIKIT:
IN THE PIPE

After BB-8 joins Rey again, construct a launch pad from the Multi-Build bricks. It sends the droid into a broken pipe above.

To open the doors, construct a rotary control next to them using the Multi-Build bricks. After the doors open, step through with either character.

FREE PLAY:
ESCAPE FROM THE FINALIZER

Finalizer Hangar

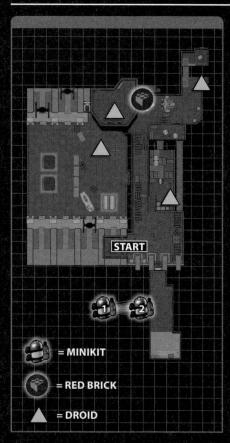

START

= MINIKIT

= RED BRICK

= DROID

Minikit 3
Blast the four small white droids in the area. The final droid is encountered during the Blaster Battle in the hangar.k.

FAST INTERACT
Select the middle building option with the Multi-Build bricks to form a bridge that connects to an alcove with a Red Brick.

Star Destroyer Exterior

Minikit 4
While destroying turrets, fly in the open gaps between the two decks of the Finalizer. Enter the purple sphere to start a countdown clock. Fly through the series of spheres, which ends in another purple sphere, before the clock hits zero.

Minikit 5
After a giant turret emerges, destroy 20 additional large turrets.

Minikit 6
Shoot down five Special Forces TIE fighters (they're carrying proton torpedoes) before destroying the giant turret.

Jakku Graveyard

Minikit 7
While the luggabeast is under your control, break the wall with a dark side Force user to open the way to a Minikit.

START

= MINIKIT

Minikit 8
Before entering the access hatch on the upper walkway, switch to a character wielding a lightsaber and cut through the door. Assemble the bricks behind the door.

Minikit 9
Look for a blue stud on a narrow ledge. After collecting it, move to the back wall and look for two pipes. Jump up to the pipes and move to the right to collect a Minikit.

Minikit 10
After BB-8 joins Rey again, construct a launch pad from the Multi-Build bricks. It launches the droid into a broken pipe above.

Minikit 1
Dark side Force powers are required to remove the debris blocking a door that leads to a behind-the-scenes area. Go through the door to enter a long, narrow room. Use the Force to tickle the Gonk droid in the back of the room.

Minikit 2
Dark side Force powers are required to remove the debris blocking a door that leads to a behind-the-scenes area. Go through the door to enter a long, narrow room.

Use dark side Force powers on objects to get building bricks. Use these bricks to build an object in the middle of the room; the Red Brick is in the object.

CHARACTERS NOW AVAILABLE FOR PURCHASE

 Chief Petty Officer Unamo

 First Order Fleet Engineer

 Officer Samitsu

 Petty Officer Thanisson

 Technician Mandetat

 TIE Pilot

 R-3PO

NEW LEVEL UNLOCKED
Lor San Tekka's Return

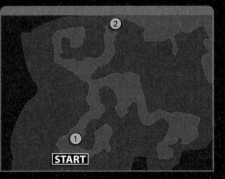

Jakku Sands

REY, BB-8

GET INTO NIIMA OUTPOST

Rey and BB-8 must cross a quicksand pit ①. A Teedo demonstrates why it's a bad idea to try to cross it on foot. Hop on Rey's Speeder, which hovers over the quicksand.

Your next destination is the outskirs of Niima Outpost, ② where an energy field blocks your progress. Attack the nearby junk to reveal a pile of Multi-Build bricks. Build the left machine first. It's an astromech access that BB-8 uses to position a socket above the archway.

Guide the Multi-Build bricks to the right, to construct a trampoline. Throw Rey's staff into the empty socket over the middle of the gate, then use the trampoline to reach the twirl pole over it. Jump from the twirl pole to the socket with Rey's staff, then on to the final twirl pole.

Tag to BB-8 and recharge the power jack. After both have been powered up, the energy field dissipates. Move your characters through the gate, then step into the column of blue light.

CHAPTER III:
NIIMA OUTPOST

TRUE JEDI REQUIREMENT
120,000

STORY MODE CHARACTERS UNLOCKED (FREE)

 Finn

 Rey

VEHICLES UNLOCKED (FREE)

 Millennium Falcon (and Microfighter)

COMPLETED MINIKIT VEHICLE

 Quadjumper (and Microfighter)

Niima Outpost

BB-8, FINN, REY

A TRIP TO THE BAZAAR

A short walk in the bazaar ends with a fight against a few squads of stormtroopers. When the coast is clear, tag to Rey and slide under the barricade ❶.

Fight the shovel-wielding stormtroopers, then smash the objects near the downed shuttle ❷. Choose the left option for the Multi-Build bricks, which become a large crossbow. Use the spinner switch to blast a path clear for Finn and BB-8.

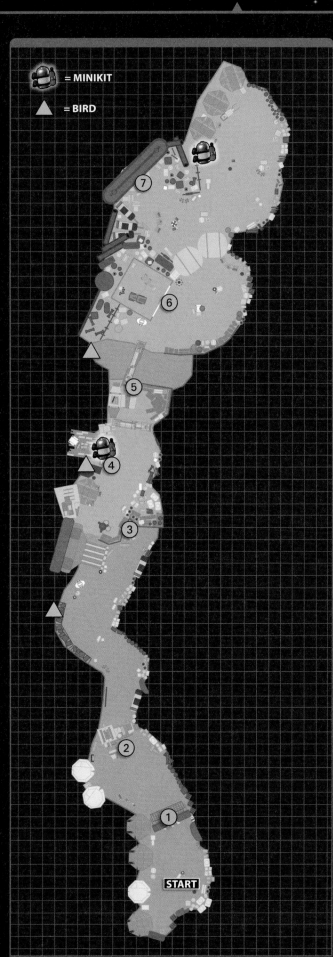

= MINIKIT

▲ = BIRD

7

6

▲

5

▲ 4

3

▲

2

1

START

After another quick battle against stormtroopers, construct a machine powered by a rotary control near the downed shuttle. Tag to BB-8 and use the machine to rip off the nose section of the shuttle.

Switch to Finn and use the First Order terminal to send the shuttle sliding down the dune. Follow it down the dune and send the Multi-Build bricks there to the left to create an energy shield emitter. The right-hand option is a combat training sphere launcher that helps against the stormtroopers.

MINIKIT:
WING IT

Look for a scavenger bird roosting on a broken wing in the distance. Target the wing and destroy it. There are two more wings in Niima Outpost, both marked by scavenger birds roosting on them.

TWIRL POLES TO THE TOP

A fresh wave of stormtroopers appears, and a few use the scaffolding to their advantage. If you chose to build the energy shield, pop out quickly to collect studs and hearts, but don't give your enemies an easy target.

Go to the other side of the depression and destroy all the junk near more robust scaffolding. Clear out the containers to reveal an access hatch ③. Send BB-8 through the hatch. Use the power jack not far from where you left Finn and Rey to spin a line of twirl poles in place.

Tag to Rey and target the empty socket with her staff. Swing over the twirl poles to meet up with BB-8. Build a ladder from the bricks near the scaffolding.

Target the grapple handle ④ between the conveyor belt and gate entrance. Tag to Finn, target the handle, then tap the button flashing over his head to start the conveyor line and reveal a target.

MINIKIT:
TREADMILL TREASURE

After starting the conveyor belt, hop up and run against the direction the belt is moving. You earn slightly larger rewards while running, including a Minikit.

Hitting the target sends a pile of bricks down the conveyor belt. Assemble a launch pad, then tag to BB-8. The pad launches BB-8 over a mechanical arm. Roll

up the ramp and use the astromech access to raise the arm.

EXIT STRATEGY? LUGGABEAST!

Move Rey on the white arrows, ⑤ which fling her over the gap. Attack the containers and debris and construct a turret from the bricks left behind. Blast the large mechanical arm to clear the bridge for BB-8 and Finn.

Attack the objects in front of the luggabeast pen ⑥. Assemble a Rotary Control. Lower the gate, then mount the luggabeast and smash the cracked bricks.

MINIKIT:
LUGGABEAST IS KEY

Follow the line of stalls to another cracked brick, off by itself. Crash through it with the luggabeast to reveal a Minikit.

Destroy the cracked brick block beyond the first two ⑦. Move any character beyond the gate to witness the First Order arriving in force.

Niima Bombardment

BB-8, FINN, REY, SN-1F4

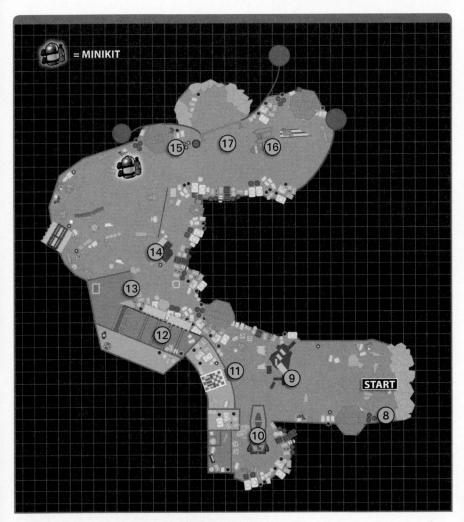

An object on the roof is too large for Finn alone to move. Construct a rotary control from the Multi-Build bricks in front of the door. Roll out a climb wall from behind the door. Send Rey up the wall.

Finn and Rey work together to push the large object off the roof. It drives an explosive canister through the climb wall. Shoot the target on the top of the canister to destroy the door.

GET TO THE SPACEPORT

Before moving to the spaceport, plant a garden under the water tower (8). There are bricks inside the crates in front of the tower that become a hose and valve. The flowers give off studs when they bloom and when they're smashed.

Attack the pile of metal (9) that looks like a salvaged satellite dish. The Multi-Build bricks can become either a rocket launcher (right-hand option) or turret (left option). Both options drive off the troop transport (10), but you need the turret to blast the gold LEGO objects that remain behind after the transport flees. The box with strength handles behind the transport must wait for Free Play, but there are plenty of studs you can collect immediately.

Additional Multi-Build bricks are available in front of the large door. Build a spinner switch next to the tall and narrow machine (11). Grapple up to the blue stud, then tag to Rey. Wind the switch to position the grapple handle where Finn can zip up to the roof.

COVERED WALKWAY COMBAT

Follow the enclosed walkway ⑫ to its end for a stormtrooper encounter. Shoot the target in the corner to knock loose the valve wheel needed to control the gate. Approach the control station with the character carrying the valve wheel and rotate your control stick to open the gate. Move ahead ⑬ to begin a Blaster Battle.

BLASTER BATTLE

Your first objective is to eliminate five stormtroopers and a heavy stormtrooper. To add to the challenge here, there's a shielded sniper on a tower.

A troop transport sweeps in with First Order reinforcements after you complete the first objective. You must take out 12 stormtroopers. A TIE fighter sweeps through the area after you clear out the twelfth stormtrooper.

Send BB-8 through the access hatch ⑭ uncovered by the TIE fighter. The astromech access controls powerful mounted guns. Target the gold LEGO object at the base of the tower with the shielded gunner.

With that threat gone, turn your attention to the sky. Shoot down three TIE fighters. To complete the final objective, blast the gold door on the troop transport.

WHAT A PIECE OF JUNK

Shoot the target ⑮ to reveal a SN-1F4 sifter droid. Take control of the droid and guide it to the mounds of sand scattered around the area.

MINIKIT:
UNDER THE SAND

Backtrack to the mound of sand closest to the point where your characters began in the area. Assemble a Minikit from bricks that appear.

After uncovering the Multi-Build bricks ⑯, send them to the left. Tag to BB-8 and use the rotary control to align the tracks. Next, build the Multi-Build bricks into an engine on the smaller machine on the tracks, which positions the larger machine, a missile launcher.

Take control of the missile launcher and shoot down six TIE fighters. The missile launcher kicks when fired, so you can't aim it like a blaster turret. Aim just under your target to score a hit.

The last TIE fighter shot down crashes into the gate ⑰. Go through the gate and board the Millennium Falcon.

Jakku Graveyard Flight

MILLENNIUM FALCON

TIE FIGHTER PURSUIT

You have limited control over the Millennium Falcon here. Focus on shooting down TIE fighters to boost your multiplier while flying through rings of studs.

MINIKIT:
CENTER OF THE ARCH

Watch for four arches that span the Millennium Falcon's course. Blast the solid center of each to earn a Minikit.

After breaking into the open, you are given the task of shooting down ten TIE fighters. Use the radar window to track their locations. There are rings of studs close to the ground scattered around the graveyard if you still haven't hit the True Jedi target.

MINIKIT:
RUSTED HULL SUPPORT

While hunting for rings of studs, look for a Minikit floating in the middle of a series of large, round hull supports.

MINIKIT:
BURIED IN THE SAND

Skim the surface and watch for red-colored walker wrecks half-buried in the sand. Blast three to get a Minikit.

After the tenth fighter falls, Rey diverts the Millennium Falcon through a narrow passage winding through the downed Star Destroyer. Focus on picking up additional studs and shooting down fighters while the trio makes their escape.

FREE PLAY: NIIMA OUTPOST

Niima Outpost

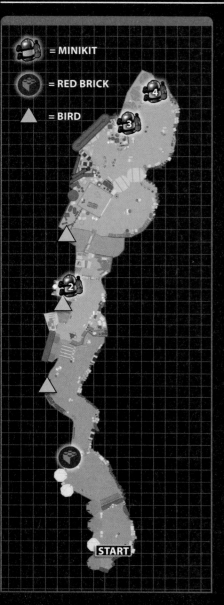

= MINIKIT

= RED BRICK

= BIRD

START

Minikit 3
Follow the line of stalls to another cracked brick, off by itself. Crash through it with the luggabeast to reveal a Minikit.

Minikit 4
In the area beyond the cracked brick, look for three droids buried in the sand. Use the Force to place the droids into the sled near "Crusher" Roodown.

STUDS X8
There's a silver LEGO container beyond the fencing, not far from the First Order terminal in the downed shuttle. Destroy the container, which is then rebuilt by a Niima local. After it flies off, a Red Brick floats down where you can collect it.

Niima Bombardment

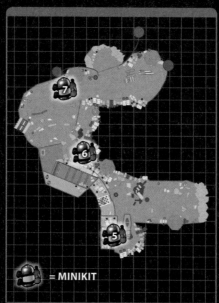

= MINIKIT

Minikit 5
After you drive off the troop transport, bring in a strong character to pull apart the container with the strength handles.

Minikit 6
Before starting the Blaster Battle (or after you finish it), blow up the silver LEGO object off to the right to fill a dive spot with water.

Minikit 7
Backtrack to the mound of sand closest to the point where your characters began in the area. Assemble a Minikit from bricks that appear.

Jakku Graveyard Flight

Minikit 8
Watch for four arches that appear shortly after you take control of the Millennium Falcon. Blast the solid center of each to earn a Minikit.

Minikit 9
While hunting for rings of studs, look for a Minikit floating in the middle of a series of large, rusted support rings.

Minikit 10
Skim the surface and watch for red-colored wrecks half-buried in the sand. Blast three to get a Minikit.

Minikit 1
Look for three scavenger birds roosting on broken wings. Blast each bird and wing to get the Minikit.

Minikit 2
After starting the conveyor belt, hop up and run against the direction the belt is moving. You earn slightly larger rewards while

HUB:
MILLENNIUM FALCON

Millennium Falcon Interior

BB-8, FINN, REY

CHARACTERS NOW AVAILABLE FOR PURCHASE

 Hobin Carsamba

 Hoogenz

 Monn Tatth

 Quinar

 Sarco Plank

 Taryish Juhden

 Unkar Goon

 Unkar Plutt

 Unkar Thug

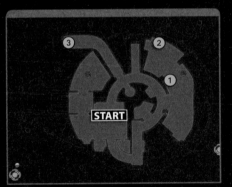

CLEAR OUT THE GAS

Guide BB-8 to the astromech access ➊ that opens the bulkheads. Unfortunately, the room beyond the bulkheads is filled with poisonous gas.

Tag to Finn and target the grapple handle at the back of the gas-filled room. Tap the button flashing over Finn's head to open the storage compartment and pull a gas mask across the room.

With the gas mask in place, walk through the gas to a valve handle ➋. Turn the handle by rotating your control stick. After the gas is vented from the room, tag to Rey and use the spinner switch near the astromech access to restore power to the Millennium Falcon. Return to the cockpit ➌.

TRUE JEDI REQUIREMENT

65,000

STORY MODE CHARACTERS UNLOCKED (FREE)

 Chewbacca (Wounded)

 Han Solo

VEHICLES UNLOCKED (FREE)

 Han's Freighter (Eravana)

 The Eravana (Microfighter)

 Guavaian Marauder (and Microfighter)

COMPLETED MINIKIT VEHICLE

 Imperial TIE Bomber (and Microfighter)

= RED BRICK

HAN SOLO, CHREWBACCA, BB-8 — START

FINN, REY — START

Freighter Battle

BB-8, CHEWBACCA, FINN, HAN SOLO, REY

DIVIDE AND CONQUER

Rey and Finn begin in a different spot than the rest of your crew for this chapter, which opens with Han Solo, Chewbacca, and BB-8 not far from a Blaster Battle. First, pull on the two grapple handles in the area to get a jump on your True Jedi goal.

Go around the corner ❶ and put Han Solo's quadnoculars to use. Scan the center of the large container to reveal silver LEGO bricks. Tag to Chewbacca and destroy the bricks with a thermal detonator.

BLASTER BATTLE

Take cover immediately. The enemies on the other side start firing as soon as the container blows up. The Kanjiklub gang members are relatively easy targets, but there's nothing Han Solo or Chewbacca can do about the turret. Hit six Kanjiklub gang members to shift the scene to Rey and Finn.

OVERLOAD THE TURRET

Tag to Finn and walk through the corridor filled with poison gas to reach a shut-off valve ❷. When the hallway is clear, move Rey on top of the white arrows, ❸ which fling her to a nearby platform.

Throw her staff into the empty socket near her landing spot. Swing between the twirl poles over the gap to another platform ❹. Smash the nearby containers. Assemble a spinner switch and turn it to move a bridge into place.

Move Finn across the bridge and turn down the short hallway that ends at a grapple handle ⑤. Pull the handle to expose a target. Blast the target to send a surge of energy that destroys the turret pinning Han Solo and Chewbacca.

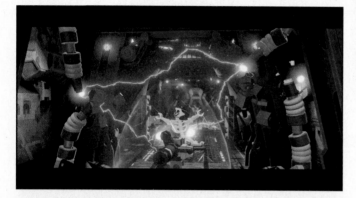

BLASTER BATTLE

Han Solo and Chewbacca advance forward but are stopped by a second, more powerful, shielded turret and rathtar tentacles ⑥ . You don't need to eliminate the Guavians guarding the turret, but keep track of them. The heavy gunner can dish out major damage. Toss thermal detonators at the silver LEGO locks on the floor grating. The now-free rathtar takes care of the rest.

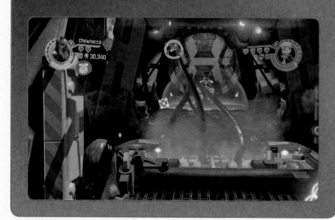

SEND A FUSE TO FINN AND REY

After the blast door closed behind the rathtar, there's only one way for Han Solo's group to go. Turn and hurry to the next room, which has a grapple handle and access hatch.

STUDS X2

Switch to Han Solo to open the storage locker with the grapple handle on its doors. A few pests spill out and attack, but they leave a Red Brick inside.

Send BB-8 through the hatch ⑦ and jump on the interface in the next room. The goal of the puzzle is to move the gates so that the green canister reaches the end.

To open a gate, trace the colored wire to its control point. The reticle on screen brightens when it's in position to open a gate. Open each gate as the cylinder reaches it. Spin the last control until the cylinder spills out near Finn and Rey.

Move Finn and Rey (control shifts to them automatically) to the cylinder ⑧ and break it open. Pick up the blue fuse from the ground and backtrack to the sparking junction box ⑨.

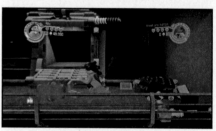

Install the fuse into the junction box to open the doors blocking both groups.

Unfortunately, it also cleared the way for a rathtar to reach Finn and Rey.

Freighter Chase

BB-8, CHEWBACCA, FINN, HAN SOLO, REY

RUN FIRST, FIGHT SECOND

A rathtar appears behind Finn and Rey and begins chasing them. Don't worry about the members of either gang that appear. Your only job is to keep ahead of the rathtar and collect as many studs as possible.

MINIKIT:
RUNNING FROM RATHTAR

When the perspective changes the first time during the rathtar pursuit, jump for the Minikit floating in the middle of the hallway. It's between the second and third arches.

The rathtar snags Finn just as the groups meet up. No one can move close to the rathtar yet (not counting Finn, obviously!), so start out by breaking all the objects in the room.

First, construct a shackle launcher with the Multi-Build bricks by sending them to the right-side option. Pinning one tentacle to the wall allows Chewbacca to reach the strength handles. Break apart the shackle launcher.

Rip the strength handles from the wall. Build a tentacle trap with those bricks. To trap another tentacle, choose the Multi-Build brick option directly in front of the rathtar.

The dancing hologram enrages the rathtar. The beast slams down its remaining free tentacle to shut it off, but the trap in front of the hologram catches it.

With both tentacles secured, assemble the final option with the Multi-Build bricks. Step up to the control panel to close the blast door and free Finn.

The exit is locked with two grapple handles. Put Han Solo and Finn in position to pull on them at the same time. Move through the newly-opened door to move on to the hangar.

Freighter Shutdown

BB-8, CHEWBACCA, CRAB DROID, FINN, HAN SOLO, REY

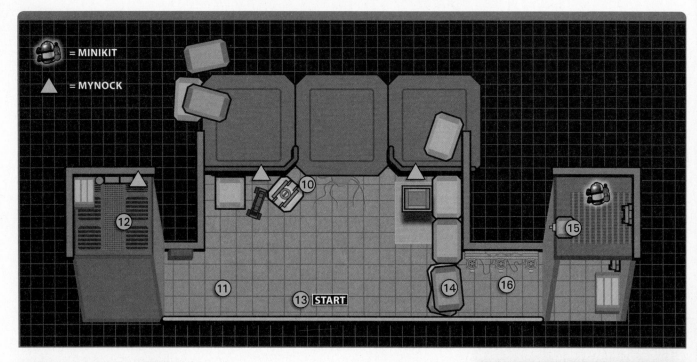

= MINIKIT

= MYNOCK

FIRST DELIVERY CONTROL PANEL

The rathtar isn't going anywhere, so build your multiplier by taking down the gang members in the hangar. Pick up all the studs you uncovered during the exchange of fire with the Kanjiklub members before your multiplier shrinks too much.

MINIKIT:
THREE MYNOCKS

Shoot the two mynocks clinging to fencing around the rathtar. The third mynock is above the climb wall.

When the rathtar grabs a yellow container, 10 hit the target on it. It explodes and showers a pile of Multi-Build bricks in the corner of the room 11. The order you build things doesn't matter, but both Rey and BB-8 must get up to the alcove.

The machine built against the shorter, protruding wall reveals a climb wall that Rey can climb to the top 12. The launch pad built in the corner near a large door sends BB-8 up to the same spot. Tag to Rey and use the spinner switch to roll out an astromech access. Switch to BB-8 and restart the conveyor belt.

A patrol of Guavians appears near the rathtar to investigate the disturbance. After you dispatch the gang members, the rathtar snags another explosive container.

Hit the target and use the bricks it leaves behind to make most of something ⑬. Unfortunately, there aren't enough bricks to complete it!

TRICKY TRAFFIC LIGHTS

After two containers explode in its grasp, the rathtar vents its frustration and knocks loose a panel on a cargo container. Move Han Solo or Rey to the proper spot in the corner and scan the top container ⑭.

Destroy the silver LEGO bricks with a thermal detonator from Chewbacca. Move Finn through the gas and use the grapple handle to pull down the container from its high perch ⑮.

Note the color of the lights in the middle of the large cargo container to the right and the wire housings on the wall behind the three spots where you can use the Multi-Build bricks ⑯.

Build the left-hand (red) unit first. Build the right-hand (green) unit next, and the center unit (yellow) last. If you build one out of order, you must start over with the red unit.

MINIKIT:
UPPER DECK

After completing the colored light puzzle, send BB-8 through the access hatch in the cargo container. He pops out on top of the container, next to a Minikit.

SECOND DELIVERY CONTROL PANEL

Use the bricks from inside the container to repair the crab droid. Send the crab droid to attack the rathtar. Build a lift control from the leftover bricks after the crab droid is crushed by the rathtar.

Assemble a rotary control that operates a lift. Send Chewbacca up to the top of the containers, where he can pull the strength handles to start the delivery system again.

The gangs can't resist the sound of a conveyor belt and make another appearance here. When they're gone, blast the yellow container the rathtar holds in its tentacle.

The bricks complete the construction started earlier. The finished item is a turret. Blast the rathtar and gang members to clear the path to the Millennium Falcon.

FREE PLAY:
THE ERVANA
Freighter Battle

START

A

A

2 3
1

= MINIKIT   A = CONNECTOR

STUD MAGNET
Open the storage locker with the grapple handle on its doors. A few pests spill out and attack, but they leave the Red Brick inside for you to collect.

Freighter Chase

Minikit 5
When the perspective changes during the rathtar pursuit, watch for a Minikit in the middle of the screen. It's floating in the air, so a well-timed jump is necessary to collect it.

Minikit 6
While Finn is held by the rathtar, use dark side Force powers to expose a dive spot. Send an aquatic character like Admiral Ackbar for a quick dip.

Freighter Shutdown

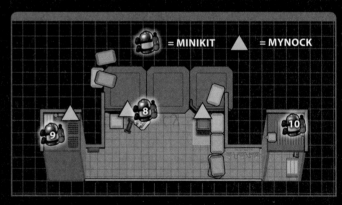

= MINIKIT   ▲ = MYNOCK

8

9   10

Minikit 1
After Finn clears the toxic gas, switch to a protocol droid like C-3PO and open a door to a new area with the protocol access terminal. Construct a First Order terminal from the remnants of the cargo containers in the room. When the rathtar appears, tap the button flashing over your character's head to escape its tentacles. When the rathtar departs, it leaves behind a Minikit.

Minikit 2
While collecting the first Minikit, open the large container under the fan with the Force. You can build a trampoline to get to the top of the container, or bring in a character that can double-jump.

Minikit 3
After collecting the first Minikit, the rathtar leaves behind parts for a power jack. Assemble the power jack, tag to BB-8, and charge it up. A nearby fan blows out pieces of a Minikit.

Minikit 4
After going through the access hatch, use the Force to pick up the large key and open the hatches next to the video monitor.

Minikit 7
Shoot the two mynocks clinging to fencing around the rathtar. A third mynock is above the climb wall Rey uses to reach the high ledge on the room's left side.

Minikit 8
After the first yellow container is destroyed, tear open the bars next to the rathtar with dark side Force powers.

Minikit 9
On the upper ledge near one of the mynocks, cut out the round door with a lightsaber.

Minikit 10
After completing the colored light puzzle, send BB-8 through an access hatch in the cargo container. He pops out on top of the container, next to a Minikit.

HUB:
MILLENNIUM FALCON

Forward Maintenance Bay

BB-8, CHEWBACCA, REY

CHARACTERS NOW AVAILABLE FOR PURCHASE

 Bala-Tik

 Crokind Shand

 Guavian Gunner

 Guavian Security Soldier

 Kanjiklub Gang Member

 Kanjiklub (Sniper)

 Razoo Qin-Fee

 Tasu Leech

 Volzang Li-Thrull

NEW LEVEL UNLOCKED
Rathtar Hunting

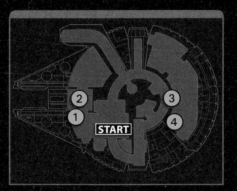

MYNOCK MYSERY

Move Chewbacca to the nearby strength handles **1** and pull them out to discover the problem with the Millennium Falcon. Step into the adjoining room **2** and clear out six mynocks.

With the mynocks out of the picture, move to a long room **3** with silver LEGO objects against a wall. Destroy the objects with Chewbacca's grenades, then build a rotary control **4** .

Tag to BB-8 and guide the top half of the malfunctioning part into place. Return to the room where things started off and step into the column of blue light.

CHAPTER V:
MAZ'S CASTLE

TRUE JEDI REQUIREMENT
100,000

STORY MODE CHARACTERS UNLOCKED (FREE)

 Rey (Takodana)

VEHICLES UNLOCKED (FREE)

 Takodana Cruiser (and Microfighter)

 Takodana Skipper (and Microfighter)

COMPLETED MINIKIT VEHICLE

 Imperial TIE Bomber (and Microfighter)

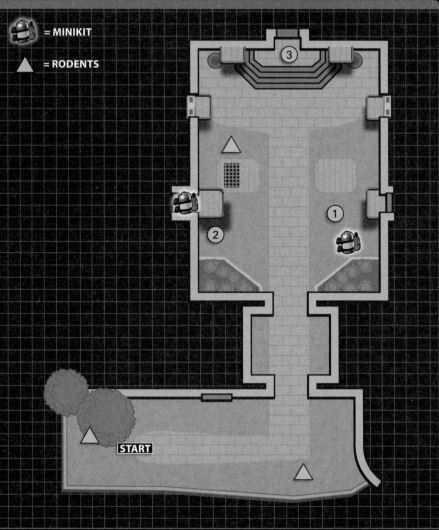

= MINIKIT

= RODENTS

Castle Approach

BB-8, FINN, HAN SOLO, REY (TAKODANA)

GUARD'S WAKE-UP CALL

There isn't much happening outside the castle. Investigate every nook and cranny for studs. When you're confident you have everything, move to the scan spot ① and inspect the nearby tower to reveal a grapple handle.

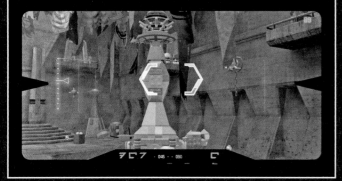

MINIKIT:
RODENT HUNTING

There are nine rodents (three appear together in three locations) lurking in the tall grass outside the castle. Flush them out and attack them.

Pull down the tower to pick up a collection of Multi-Build bricks. Choose to build the machine closer to the tree ② first. Tag to BB-8 and target the machine's power jack to activate it.

Send Rey up the climb wall and hop into the balcony. Knock over the planter. Build a downspout in the courtyard with its bricks.

MINIKIT:
RED WALL SCONCE

Shoot the red sconce on the wall (it's close to the scan location) and a Minikit falls out, in pieces.

MINIKIT:
ON THE BALCONY

After Rey ascends the climb wall, step into the alcove to collect a Minikit.

Repurpose the Multi-Build bricks into the machine closer to the downspout. Charge the power jack as BB-8 to splash the sleeping guard ③ with a blast of H2O.

The annoyed guard wakes up and pushes open a door. Follow him to get inside Maz's Castle.

Castle Hall

BB-8, FINN, HAN SOLO, REY (TAKODANA)

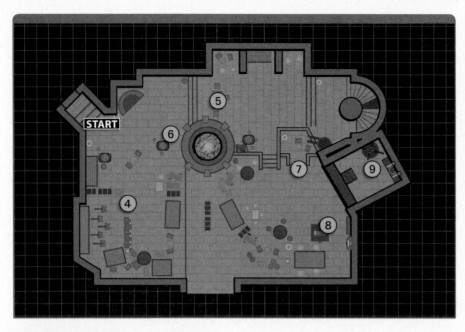

FINN NEEDS A RIDE

As Finn, go to the target range set up a short distance from where you took control. Speak with Sidon Ithano ④ who wants a demonstration of Finn's sharpshooting.

Set up behind the long table out front and shoot ten targets as they pop up before the time expires.

DWINDLING GROUP
Finn and Han Solo leave the group after you complete the blaster range and obtain the mug, respectively.

SERVE AN EXPLOSIVE MEAL

A group of Hassk ⑤ won't allow anyone up the stairs, so you must distract them. Scan the sawblade-shaped object above the window to reveal a power jack. Restoring power starts a fiery reaction that ejects Multi-Build bricks.

Construct a bellows at the end of the white hose ⑥. Jump on the hose and let it fall all the way to the ground. You want to pump air

through the hose to stoke the fire until a roasted bird lands on the nearby table. The Multi-Build brick option in the corner is a trampoline under a purple stud.

SOLO'S RED CUP OF COFFEE

Go up the newly-opened staircase, then over to the hot beverage shop ⑦. Destroy everything in front of the shop until there's a pile of Multi-Build bricks ready for use. Construct a spinner switch ⑧ that uncovers a nearby access hatch.

Tag to BB-8 and go through the hatch. Use the rotary control ⑨ to turn the pipes and restore the flow of liquid to the beverage prep area. Only green pipes can be turned. Tear down the spinner switch, then build a pipe above the cooktop to send the liquid into a mug, which Han Solo happily claims.

Castle Basement

BB-8, REY (TAKODANA)

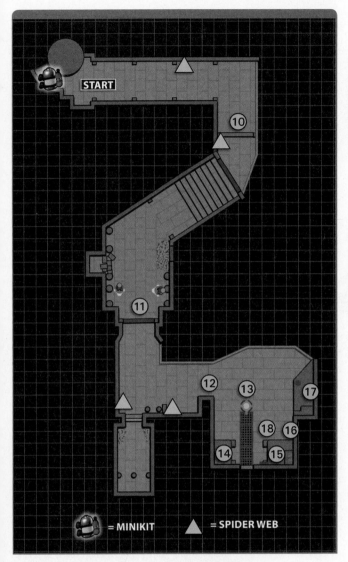

START

10

11

12   13   17

18   16

14   15

🤖 = MINIKIT   ▲ = SPIDER WEB

EXPLORE THE BASEMENT

The basement is dark. The low light causes Rey to move at a cautious pace. Everything in the basement is junk already, so swing wildly and collect as many studs as you can.

MINIKIT:
UP THE STEPS

As soon as you gain control of Rey, turn around and go up the curved staircase.

MINIKIT:
SPIDER WEBS IN CORNERS

Check the basement's ceiling often. Find and destroy four spider webs in the basement to earn a Minikit.

Where the hallway reaches a dead-end 10, look for a target around the corner. Break targets until you have enough bricks to build a rotary control. BB-8 must raise a nearby gate enough for Rey to slide under it. He must remain in place for the gate to stay raised.

The initial use for the Multi-Build bricks on the other side of the gate is to repair the

mechanism responsible for raising the gate. Choose the build option under the light, then turn the valve wheel to raise the gate.

Reassemble the Multi-Build bricks into an astromech access. After BB-8 completes the matching puzzle, a vine-covered section of the wall opens. Descend the stairs and get ready for a fight against barely functional droids. They come in two waves but are not a real threat.

TURN THE STATUES

Move ahead to the door covered by a chain ⑪. Assemble a spinner switch between the two large statues in front of the door. To open the door, both statues must face away from it.

Step on the green pad in front of either statue to change the light at the base of the statue to red. Step on the pad again to revert it to green. Statues with a green light perform a quarter turn each time Rey uses the spinner switch.

Use the winch until one of the statues faces away from the door. Step on the button in front of that statue (leave the other one green). Continue to turn the second statue until it's facing away from the door.

Tag to BB-8 and charge the power jack above the door to open it. Follow the hallway past a partially-obscured door made of silver LEGO bricks to enter the final room of the basement ⑫.

RESTORE TWO GEARS: GEAR 1

The game provides a quick overview of the area and its many gears. You must uncover and replace two gears near the door. Clean up the junk in the area, which leaves you with two piles of bricks.

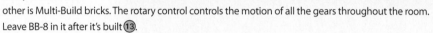

One pile becomes a rotary control. The other is Multi-Build bricks. The rotary control controls the motion of all the gears throughout the room. Leave BB-8 in it after it's built ⑬.

The Multi-Build bricks become a trampoline (of sorts) when directed against the wall to the right. Bounce Rey off it to reach a twirl pole above. Switch to BB-8 and change the positions of the gears to raise the twirl pole, which then allows Rey to swing to the next twirl pole and land near a climb wall ⑭.

Kick over the ladder on the corner of the roof. Climb to the top of the wall, then use the bottoms of the platforms to move to the other side of the room. When necessary, tag back to BB-8 and reposition the platforms by rolling around in the interface.

Jump from the last platform to the roof 15. Kick over a second ladder, then ascend the climb wall. If Rey falls from the climb wall, tag to BB-8 and lower it to where she can reach it. Switch back to BB-8 to raise it again while Rey clings to it.

Follow the climb wall to a set of handles 16. Watch closely for the button prompts to appear. Hit the button as quickly as you can when it appears. Walk across the narrow ledge and jump off near the tall light source.

Knock down the rope ladder. Attack the light 17 and rebuild it into a spinner switch, which opens a door below. Take out the decrepit droids and claim the gear.

RESTORE TWO GEARS: GEAR 2

Place the gear in one of the spots near the door. Take down the trampoline and direct the Multi-Build bricks to the left, where they become a spinner switch 18. Turn the winch to open the nearby door and pick up the second gear.

Place the gear in the other slot near the door. Knock down the spinner switch. Assemble the Multi-Build bricks above the door. Tag to BB-8, then move the gears to open the door. Go through the door to complete the chapter.

FREE PLAY: MAZ'S CASTLE
Castle Approach

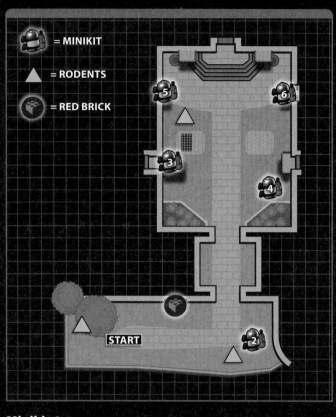

= MINIKIT

= RODENTS

= RED BRICK

START

Minikit 3
In the alcove on the balcony.

Minikit 4
Shoot the red sconce on the wall (it's close to the scan location) and a Minikit falls out, in pieces.

Minikit 5
Ascend the climb wall to the balcony. Jetpack over to the nearby balcony with a Minikit on it.

Minikit 6
After picking up Minikit 5, use the access hatch on the balcony to reach another balcony directly across from it.

Minikit 1
There are nine rodents (three appear together in three locations) lurking in the tall grass outside the castle. Flush them out and attack them.

Minikit 2
Jump into the dive pool to send out a Minikit in pieces.

STUDS X6
Break down the cracked block not far from the start point. A Red Brick is directly behind it.

Castle Basement

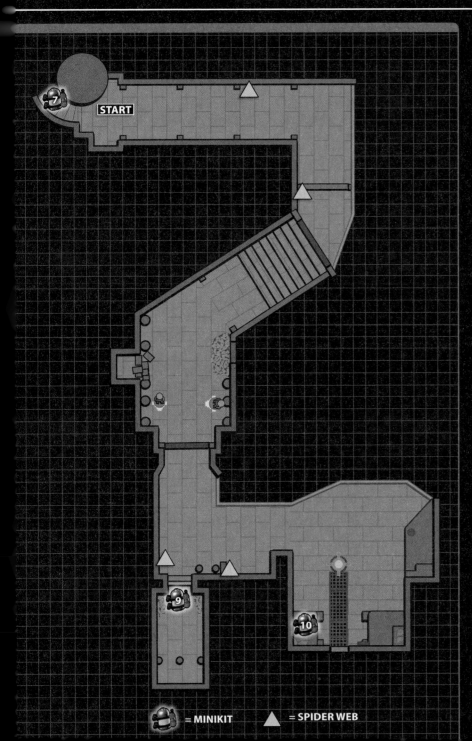

Minikit 7

As soon as you gain control of Rey, turn around and go up the curved staircase.

Minikit 8

Check the basement's ceiling often. Find and destroy four spider webs in the basement to earn a Minikit.

Minikit 9

Beyond the door opened by turning the two statues, plant an explosive device on the partially hidden wall made from silver LEGO bricks.

Minikit 10

There's one door in the room of gears that isn't operated by any of the devices inside. You must use dark Force to open the door and get to the Minikit inside.

= MINIKIT   = SPIDER WEB

HUB:
TAKODANA

Outside Maz's Castle

BB-8, REY (TAKODANA)

CHARACTERS NOW AVAILABLE FOR PURCHASE

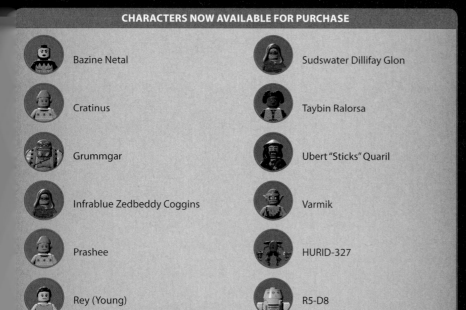

Bazine Netal	Sudswater Dillifay Glon
Cratinus	Taybin Ralorsa
Grummgar	Ubert "Sticks" Quaril
Infrablue Zedbeddy Coggins	Varmik
Prashee	HURID-327
Rey (Young)	R5-D8

NEW LEVEL UNLOCKED
None

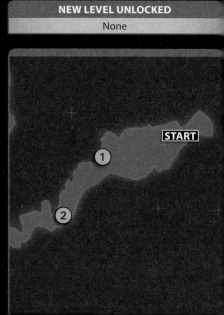

Outside Maz's Castle

BB-8, REY (TAKODANA)

OBJECTIVE

Rey and BB-8 need a new ship to get off-world, but first they must reach higher ground. Send Rey up the climb wall ➊. Go to the nearby spinner switch and turn it. BB-8 rides the lift to the top and hops out.

The way out of the valley is blocked by a vine-covered gate controlled by a rotary control. Switch to the droid and open the gate.

Go through the opened gate. It's a short walk to your destination ➋, with no other distractions. Pick up a few studs before you continue to the next chapter.

CHEWBACCA, HAN SOLO, FINN (TAKODANA), MAZ KANATA

TRUE JEDI REQUIREMENT
120,000

STORY MODE CHARACTERS UNLOCKED (FREE)

 Finn (Takodana)

 Maz Kanata

 Poe Dameron (Flight Suit)

 Snap Wexley

VEHICLES UNLOCKED (FREE)

 Poe Dameron's X-wing (and Microfighter)

COMPLETED MINIKIT VEHICLE

 Kylo Ren's Command Shuttle (and Microfighter)

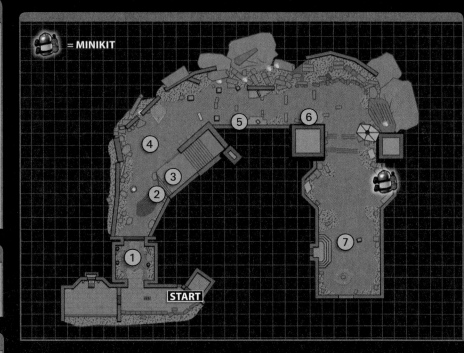

= MINIKIT

TURN BACK THE FIRST ORDER

Hold off on collecting the studs lining the corridor until after you build your multiplier during the fight around the first corner ①.

Cut through the doors, head outside, and get ready for a skirmish against a few stormtroopers. Look for metal bars at the base of a ledge ②.

Cut through the bars with the lightsaber to clear the path to an access hatch. Tag to Maz Kanata and go through the access hatch. Push the glowing crate ③ over the edge after repairing the track.

Bake a birthday cake from the Multi-Build bricks ④ by pushing to the right. The cake ruse takes down a number of stormtroopers. Reconstruct the Multi-Build bricks to the left to arm a thermal imploder and eliminate the remaining flametrooper. Your group quickly rushes ahead and takes cover.

BLASTER BATTLE

The First Order set up barricades and a few turrets in your path. Your first task is to take down a heavy stormtrooper, who is supported by standard stormtroopers. Knocking out the heavy stormtrooper is your sole objective here, so you don't need to bother with the others unless you want extra target practice.

After a TIE fighter strafes the area, your objective becomes handling five stormtroopers. The sniper and shielded turret put pressure on your group, but neither can be handled yet. Focus on taking down five other stormtroopers quickly.

Next up is another group of five stormtroopers, along with the sniper and shielded turret. A grapple handle ⑤ allows either Han Solo or Finn to gain the high ground. The sniper and the turret are vulnerable from the ledge. For the turret, ignore the stormtrooper operating it and target the gun.

The group advances again until another shielded gun is deployed against them. This one has better shielding and calls for another approach.

Move Han Solo into position to scan the base of the Rodian statue ⑥. The base is revealed to be silver LEGO bricks, an excellent target for Chewbacca's thermal detonators.

A pair of troop transports lands at the top of a wide stairway and deploys a horde of stormtroopers and a pair of flametroopers.

The flametroopers come out individually, but both bathe the area in fire. Their health is displayed over their heads, but don't get caught up in watching it and ignoring the health of your characters.

DEFEAT THE RIOT TROOPER

After the second flametrooper falls, mop up the remaining stormtroopers. Hop on the nearby gun emplacements for a bit of extra firepower.

MINIKIT:
DUAL GRAPPLE HANDLES

Look for a crate on a ledge on the top left of the breached wall. Target the two grapple handles to pull it down, then assemble the Minikit that was inside.

Break up the stormtrooper squad harassing two colorful individuals (7). A nearby door is blown open, and more stormtroopers pour into the courtyard.

When the last stormtrooper falls, a new enemy appears, a riot trooper.

Armed with a shock baton and shield, the riot trooper starts off the fight trading blows with your group. After taking damage, he jumps back and electrifies the ground around him. Stormtroopers appear and harass your group.

The Multi-Build bricks have three potential destinations. Any choice pulls the riot trooper off his perch and leaves him dazed. Attack him while he's vulnerable, but be ready to move before he attacks.

The riot trooper repeats his actions two more times. He takes damage, jumps away, generates an energy field on the ground, and summons stormtrooper support. Each time, you can choose any of the three Multi-Build options to knock him down. The fight ends with a brief duel against Finn, where you must tap the flashing button.

Takodana Skies

RESISTANCE X-WING (BLACK LEADER), RESISTANCE X-WING (BLUE SQUADRON)

STOP THE FIRST ORDER'S LANDING FLEET

The First Order initially deploys TIE fighters and Special Forces TIE fighters to combat the Resistance X-wings. Shoot down 15 TIE fighters to move on to the next objective.

MINIKIT:
BUOYANT TARGETS

There are four buoys in the bay. They're small targets, but they're fairly close together.

The next wave of targets consists of ten troop transports. The transports are more durable than TIE fighters, but have no defense other than TIE fighter escorts. You can blast them out of the sky, or strafe them on the ground after they land.

DESTROY ON CONTACT

A tower falls over in the courtyard after you shoot down the fifteenth TIE fighter. A Red Brick appears where the tower stood.

A Resistance command ship arrives on the scene and calls for assistance. Three flights of Special Forces TIE fighters are in pursuit.

Green arrows track the Command ship, while the TIE fighters in pursuit are red. There are additional TIE fighters in the air still, but you only need to shoot down the three flights pursuing the command ship to complete this chapter.

MINIKIT:
SHORE TARGETS

Three towers topped by parabolic antennae stand on the shoreline (two on one shore, the third across the way from them). You must use proton torpedoes to destroy them. Pick up proton torpedoes from Special Forces TIE fighters.

FREE PLAY:
BATTLE OF TAKODANA

Castle Corridors

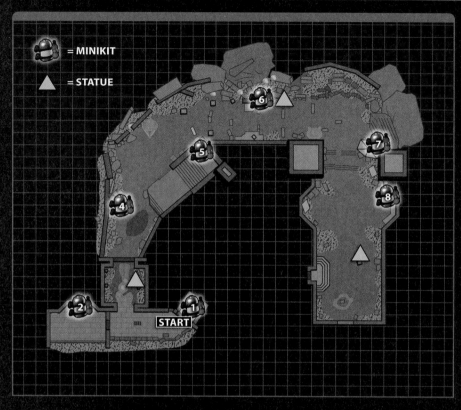

= MINIKIT

= STATUE

START

Minikit 1
Rip the lock from the door behind the start point with dark side Force powers. Cut through the door with a lightsaber.

Minikit 2
At the end of the first hallway, use the Force to open the door to a bedroom. Attack the chest on the ground to get to the Multi-Build bricks inside.

The left-hand and right-hand options for the Multi-Build bricks are power jacks that light up the paintings and drop studs. The rotary control at the foot of the bed drops the painting over the bed and reveals the Red Brick.

Minikit 3
Use Force powers to return three statues to their pedestals.

Minikit 4
Jump into the dive pool to bring out a Minikit.

Minikit 5
After going through the access hatch, scan the broken wall to reveal a crate made from silver LEGO bricks.

Minikit 6
You must return after wrapping up the Blaster Battle to break open this cracked block.

Minikit 7
After the Blaster Battle ends, use the Force to move the TIE fighter panel. The dive pool behind the panel has a Minikit in its waters.

Minikit 8
Look for a crate on a ledge on the breached wall's top left. Target the two grapple handles to pull it down, then assemble the Minikit that was inside.

Takodana Skies

Minikit 8
There are four buoys in the bay. They're small targets, but they're fairly close together.

DESTROY ON CONTACT
A tower falls over in the courtyard after you shoot down the fifteenth TIE fighter. A Red Brick appears where the tower stood.

Minikit 10
Three towers topped by parabolic antennae stand on the shoreline (two on one shore, the third across the way from them). You must use proton torpedoes to destroy them.

Ruins of Takodana

BB-8, CHEWBACCA, FINN (TAKODANA), HAN SOLO

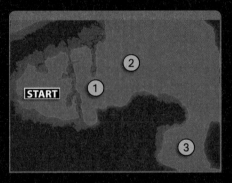

BACK TO THE MILLENNIUM FALCON

The path marked by the guide studs ends at a downed TIE fighter ❶. The TIE fighter blocks your progress, so blow it up with a thermal detonator from Chewbacca.

The next impediment is a giant tree ❷. Tag to Han Solo and scan the tree where the vines are thickest. Cut through the tree with Finn's lightsaber and continue along the path to the Millennium Falcon ❸. Board the ship to zoom off to your next destination.

CHAPTER VII:
THE RESISTANCE

TRUE JEDI REQUIREMENT
30,000

STORY MODE CHARACTERS UNLOCKED (FREE)

 General Leia

 C-3PO

VEHICLES UNLOCKED (FREE)

 Resistance Freight Transport (and Microfighter)

COMPLETED MINIKIT VEHICLE

 Rebel Alliance B-wing (and Microfighter)

Resistance Base

BB-8, C-3PO, FINN (TAKODANA), GENERAL LEIA

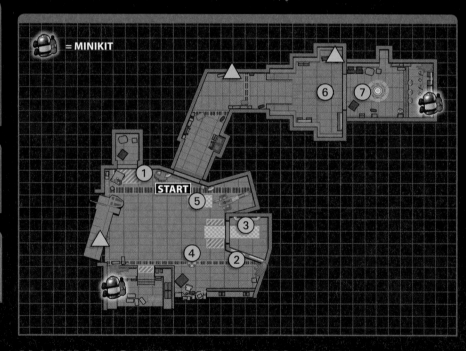

= MINIKIT

START

MANUAL OVERRIDE - STEP ONE

Take some time to explore the interior of the Resistance Base. Collect studs and pick up a few collectibles before you turn to the business of helping the Resistance against the First Order.

MINIKIT:
LOCKED UP

Near a map of the galaxy is a locker. Cut out the center of the locker with a lightsaber.

MINIKIT:
ASTROMECH ASSEMBLY

Build three astromechs from parts found throughout the base to earn this Minikit. The first batch of bricks is in a storage compartment on a command ship. Pull the grapple handle to open the compartment.

Use the Resistance Terminal down the hall from the large blast doors to get bricks for a second droid. The bricks for the final droid are in a crate near the door that leads to the command center.

When you're done exploring, tag to General Leia and interact with the Resistance terminal ① to open the smaller doors. Speak with the men who were behind the door. Target the group of four grapple handles and tap the indicated button to pull down the top container.

Hop up the containers to reach a hanging bar above the blast door. When it locks in place, power is restored to one side of the doors.

MANUAL OVERRIDE - STEP TWO

Move C-3PO to the protocol access terminal ②. Communicate with the terminal to open the large doors.

Cut through the power unit on the wall ③ with Finn's lightsaber and use the resultant bricks to repair the track on the ground. Push the large, frozen block down the track (it requires two characters to move it).

The Multi-Build bricks from the rack ④ repair two different parts of the ceiling track. Fix the left-most track first. Place BB-8 atop the rotary control and move the claw along the track so it's over the frozen block you just moved. You must move the Multi-Build bricks to repair the final stretch of the tracks.

After the claw picks up the block of ice, move it to the spot closest to the X-wing ⑤. You must move the Multi-Build bricks back to the first repair spot to complete the move.

Push the frozen block along the track until it's directly behind the X-wing. Connect BB-8 to the power jack to fire the X-wing's thrusters and melt the ice.

Assemble the now-thawed bricks into the missing power unit for the main blast doors. Jump up and hang on the bar to lower it into place. With both handles down, tag to BB-8 and target the power jack over the center of the doors.

BB-8 FILES A REPORT

Go through the blast doors and speak with the three Resistance officers, who will follow General Leia's actions. Move her to any of the four red lights on the platform ⑥ in front of the hangar door. When all four lights turn green, tag to BB-8 and hop on the rotary control.

Tap the multi-colored circles to spin the pipes. Restore the flow of air from both sides so they form a path through the middle pipe at the top. In the room beyond the door, stick with BB-8 and interact with the astromech access ⑦ to upload his data.

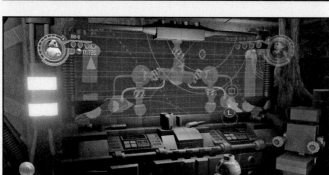

MINIKIT:
BACK WALL POWER JACK

Before uploading BB-8's data, hit the power jack on the back wall to reveal a Minikit in the room.

Resistance Hangar

BB-8, C-3PO, FINN (TAKODANA), GENERAL LEIA

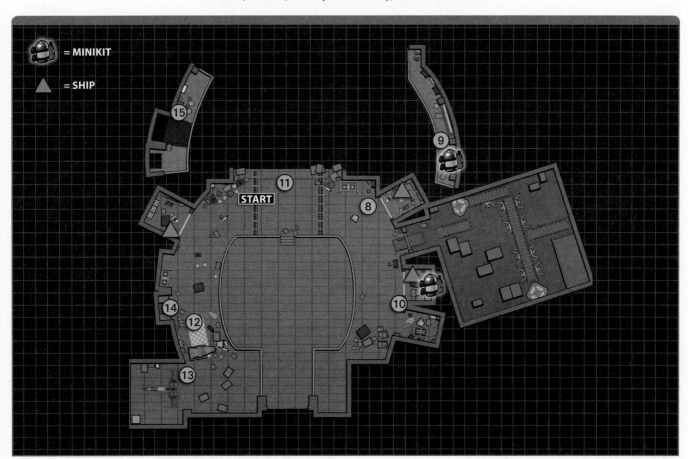

= MINIKIT

= SHIP

ICE CREAM AND COOKIES

Speak with Nien Nunb 8 as C-3PO. When the Sullustan lowers a lift from above, move everyone on it and ride it to the upper walkway. Assemble a rotary control 9 from the Multi-Build bricks you uncover in the area.

The rotary control is linked to a series of conveyor belts. Guide the gold LEGO crate through the system of conveyors until it comes through a door on the main floor.

--- MINIKIT: ---
WALL UNIT

Build a power jack against the wall with the Multi-Build bricks. Charge the jack, and bricks for a Minikit tumble out of the galaxy map terminal.

Only General Leia can open the Resistance Terminal 10 that has the trio of Resistance troops she needs to blast open the crate. Give them the command, then fire at the crate to get them started shooting.

Assemble the bricks into an ice cream dispenser. An overjoyed Nien Nunb drops an energy field on the storage room behind him. Break down all the objects inside the room and build a towing sled. Guide the sled to the lift in front of the Millennium Falcon 11.

MINIKIT:
BEHIND THE ENERGY FIELD

When the field drops to let out Resistance troops, go inside the room they vacated and collect the Minikit.

MINIKIT:
LEGACY VEHICLES

You must build three smaller versions of familiar vehicles from bricks you salvage here. The bricks for the first vehicle come from inside the room with the three Resistance troops. The second set come from the storage room next to Nien Nunb. The last vehicle is built with bricks found on the other side of the hangar, inside a room that is locked with a protocol droid terminal.

CONCUSSION MISSILES

Tag to General Leia and command the Resistance troops (who returned to their previous location) so they follow her to the other end of the hangar. Push the large engine 12 down the track. A large machine with two grapple handles then moves into place 13.

Target the handles with General Leia and Finn, then pull the machine to the ground. Rebuild the leftover bricks into a towing sled. Drive the sled in front of the Millennium Falcon and park it in the lift.

FUEL FOR THE FALCON

The lifts to reach half the upper walkway are broken. Clear out the debris in the shaft 14. Bounce up the grip walls as Finn, whose lightsaber allows him to cling to them. Guide C-3PO to the lift next to the grip walls.

Cut out the fuse 15 from the terminal, then place it into the empty terminal connected to the lift with C-3PO (don't worry about General Leia and BB-8, only C-3PO needs to reach the top).

Slide C-3PO to the second lift. Return the fuse to its original position, which brings the lift back to the upper walkway. Move C-3PO to the protocol droid terminal and use it to drop the energy field below.

Attack the objects in the room until the bricks for a towing sled are revealed. When the final sled is parked at the lift in front of the Millennium Falcon, the ship is ready to take off.

FREE PLAY:
THE RESISTANCE

Resistance Base

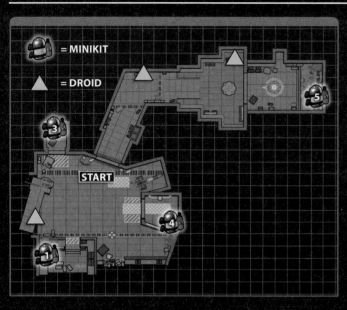

Minikit 2

Build three astromechs from parts found throughout the base to earn this Minikit. The first batch of bricks is in a storage compartment on a command ship. Pull the grapple handle to open the compartment. Use the Resistance terminal down the hall from the large blast doors to get bricks for a second droid. The bricks for the final droid are in a crate near the door that leads to the command center.

Minikit 3

After opening the door with a Resistance terminal, destroy the objects in the room with dark side Force powers.

Minikit 4

Melt the ice encasing the Minikit in the corner of the room. You need to either tag to a character with Immunity (Cold) or cut the power to the freezer unit before you can collect it.

Minikit 5

Before uploading BB-8's data, hit the power jack on the back wall to reveal a Minikit in the room.

Minikit 1

A locker is in the corner near the map of the galaxy. Cut out the center of the locker with a lightsaber.

Resistance Hangar

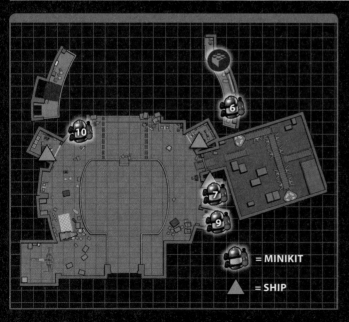

Minikit 7

When the field drops to let out Resistance troops, go inside the room they vacated and collect the Minikit.

Minikit 8

Build Y-wing (broken lift on left, behind door locked by upper level protocol droid terminal). Build A-wing (door locked by power jack, behind trio of Resistance soldiers). Build snowspeeder (door near Nien Nunb).

Minikit 9

Use the Force to restore an image on the back wall.

Minikit 10

From the upper walkway near the protocol droid terminal, toss a staff into the empty socket. Swing to the twirl pole and grab the Minikit. A jetpack-boosted jump can also reach the Minikit.

SUPER SLAP

Break through the cracked brick on the upper walkway near Nien Nunb. The access hatch behind the brick leads to a Red Brick on a platform overlooking the conveyor belt area.

Minikit 6

Build a power jack against the wall with the Multi-Build bricks. Charge the jack, and bricks for a Minikit tumble out of the galaxy map terminal.

HUB:
MILLENNIUM FALCON

Millennium Falcon Interior

CHEWBACCA, FINN (TAKODANA)

CHARACTERS NOW AVAILABLE FOR PURCHASE		NEW LEVEL UNLOCKED
		None

 Admiral Statura

 Caluan Ematt

 Goss Toowers

 Major Kolonia

 Nien Nunb (Classic)

 Resistance General

 B-U4D

 PZ-4CO

 R2-KT

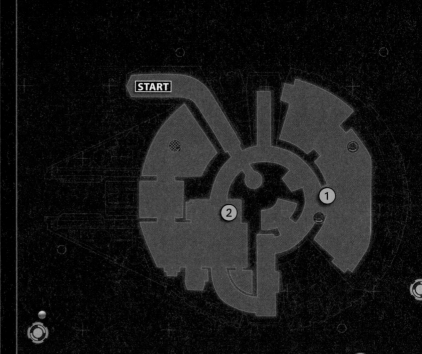

REROUTE POWER TO THE HYPERDRIVE

Follow the guide studs from the cockpit to the ship's power regulators ❶ . Prepare for a quick building and rebuilding challenge. Hit the grapple handle and pull it free from the wall. Before you put the Multi-Build bricks to work, you should understand what to do here.

Build the left option first, which drains the power from the shields and puts it in temporary storage. You must quickly destroy the first conduit you built and repurpose the Multi-Build bricks to create a new conduit in the center before the energy returns to the shields.

The energy drains away if the machine is left alone. Even with the conduit on the left destroyed, the energy in the storage tank will drain away.

As soon as the energy is transfered to the storage tank, blast the center conduit and build the conduit on the right. The hyperdrive energy indicator lights up when you're successful. Go to the navigational computer ❷ to take off for Starkiller Base.

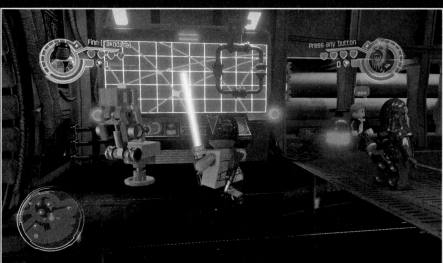

CHAPTER VIII:
STARKILLER SABOTAGE

Starkiller Crash Site

CHEWBACCA, FINN (TAKODANA), HAN SOLO (STARKILLER BASE)

STORY MODE CHARACTERS UNLOCKED (FREE)

 Han Solo (Starkiller Base)

 R3-A2

VEHICLES UNLOCKED (FREE)

 First Order Snowspeeder (and Microfighter)

 Snowspeeder Bike

COMPLETED MINIKIT VEHICLE

 Imperial AT-AT (Microfighter)

STARKILLER BASE APPROACH

You need to assemble a heat beam to melt the ice blocking the path ahead. The components for the heat beam are in two locations. Target the grapple handle and tap the indicated button for half the necessary bricks. The rest are behind the frozen metal door built ❶ into the side of the ridge. Use a lightsaber to cut open the door.

Construct the heat beam, then hop on the round platform attached to the back. The beam exposes a rock ❷ that calls for a thermal detonator from Chewbacca.

MINIKIT:
PROBE DROID DESTRUCTION

Shoot five probe droids. There are two at the crash site, while the rest are around the exterior of Starkiller Base.

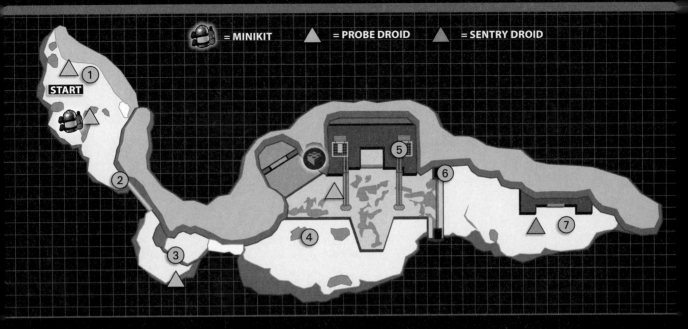

= MINIKIT   ▲ = PROBE DROID   ▲ = SENTRY DROID

START

① ② ③ ④ ⑤ ⑥ ⑦

MINIKIT:
BURIED IN SNOW

While clearing debris from the Millennium Falcon's crash site, break through pieces of snow to reveal bricks for a Minikit.

Cross the chasm on the narrow ledge. Target the dual grapple handles ③ with Han Solo and Finn to pull down the bricks you need to cobble together a makeshift ladder.

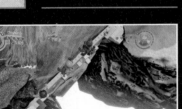

Tag to Chewbacca and pull out the strength handles from the side of the mountain. Tap the indicated button to leap between handholds across the chasm.

OVERCOME THE DEFENSES

Don't rush ahead to engage the First Order's guards. Build a snowball launcher (middle) or smoke machine (right) from the Multi-Build bricks ④ uncovered in the

Assemble the leftover bricks from the turret into a giant magnet, which exposes a pair of targets over the door. Hit the targets, then tag to Finn and use the grip walls behind the door to reach the roof. Build a grappling hook launcher ⑤ from the bricks there, then slide down the line to move beyond the energy field.

STUDS X4

Build a tall snowman by sending Multi-Build bricks to the location nearest the mountainside. Hop on the snowman's hat, then use the hanging bar to reach the ledge

Cut through the red power pylon ⑥ with a lightsaber, which drops the energy field and allows Han Solo and Chewbacca to join Finn. Switch to Chewbacca and

You must be quick with your Multi-Build brick destruction and reconstruction here. First, go with the left option on the ground. After you interact with it, a spark travels slowly up the wires. You must tear down the Multi-Build bricks and then move them to the top-center build option before the spark reaches it.

When the spark successfully travels to the panel on the opposite side of the doorway, the panels roll up to reveal a First Order terminal. Move all three characters to the lift to ride it up to the wall.

Starkiller Wall

CHEWBACCA, HAN SOLO (STARKILLER BASE), FINN (TAKODANA)

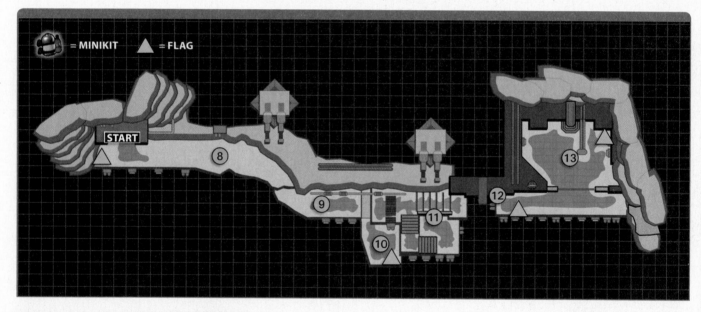

GET PAST THE TURRETS

The wall is heavily defended, so everyone moves in a careful crouch. Move to the snowy area and break apart the mounds of snow ⑧ to reveal Multi-Build bricks. The right-hand option is a slingshot. Once it's built, pull the grapple handle to take down a sentry in a nearby tower.

MINIKIT:
RAISE THE FLAG

Attack the metal spire next to the doorway, then rebuild it into a Resistance flag. There are three additional Resistance flags to raise in the area.

MINIKIT:
HAIRDRYER HELP

Choose the left option with the Multi-Build bricks to make a hairdryer that knocks free a boulder and Minikit.

With the sentry out of the way, your path past the turrets is clear. Drop off the ledge to land on a lower walkway. A sudden gas leak ⑨ temporarily holds back Han Solo and Chewbacca.

Send Finn through the gas. Hopping over the gap is a dead-end (poor mynock!) so slide down the ice to a lower level ⑩. Quietly eliminate the two guards and break apart the machine near them to reveal the valve wheel you need to shut off the gas above.

Ascend the red tube on the wall to return to the higher walkway. Descend the stairs to stay out of the turret's line of fire. Bash the droid in front of the strength handles ⑪ to get access to them.

Tear the strength handles from the wall. Build a mini snowspeeder from the bricks that came out with the handles. It distracts the turret, allowing you to move past it safely.

SHIELD ROOM ENTRY

Switch to Han Solo and use the grapple handle to cross the gap. Scan the pipes ⑫ directly overhead to reveal a target. Shooting the target opens a water pipe. The water that pours out freezes into a narrow bridge over the gap.

The next door is guarded by an energy shield, and is built from silver LEGO bricks. Pull both grapple handles above the door to lower the energy shield. A thermal detonator from Chewbacca will handle the rest.

Quickly dispatch the ill-prepared snowtroopers guarding the entrance to the shield room ⑬. Tag to Finn and interact with the First Order terminal. A defective droid becomes a pile of Multi-Build bricks near the fire.

The two build locations with these bricks are the same springboard in different spots. Assemble a trampoline, then jump up to hang from one of the handles. Leave that character in place. Break down the trampoline and rebuild it under the other handle. When both handles are pulled down, the door opens. Descend the ladder to enter the shield room.

Starkiller Shield Room

CHEWBACCA, FINN (TAKODANA), HAN SOLO (STARKILLER)

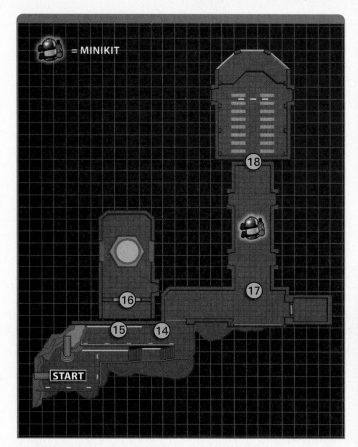

Release the strength handles to move Finn again. Switch to Finn and jump up to the higher grip handle. Eliminate the stormtrooper that emerges from the elevator door. Then go through the elevator to open a route for quick travel between floors.

FOLLOW FINN'S PLAN

Ascend the steps and walk past the scanner (14) in front of an energy-shielded doorway. Attack the objects in the area (15) until you have a pile of Multi-Build bricks.

The right-hand option is a power source for a lift. Move Finn on the lift, then another character atop the button that activates the lift. Tag to Finn and grab the grip handle.

Switch to another character and break down the lift power source, so it can be rebuilt as strength handles. Pulling the strength handles moves Finn to the center of a track. Hop over to the other grip handle that moved when Chewbacca pulled the strength handles.

Cut through the door ⑯ with Finn's lightsaber. The stormtroopers behind the door aren't prepared for a fight, so deal with them quickly. Destroy the lockers to get the bricks you need to build a hat dispenser.

Choose the white stormtrooper helmet and return to the scanner below. Take out the pair of soccer-loving stormtroopers beyond the security field. The end of the next hallway ⑰ marks the start of a Blaster Battle.

BLASTER BATTLE

The initial objective is to eliminate the heavy stormtrooper, but he's well-guarded by an energy screen. Hit the target over his head to reveal a grapple handle. Pull the grapple handle to take him out of commission.

A bridge appears over the hallway, with a horde of stormtrooper reinforcements. You must take out 12 total stormtroopers. To get to the ones on the bridge, toss a thermal detonator at the base of their energy field.

A shielded turret is your next objective. The explosion opens access to a scan location. Scan the pipes directly above the turret to reveal dual grapple handles. Pull the handles to drop the pipes on the turret and end the Blaster Battle.

MINIKIT:
ROLLING TARGETS

Tiny four-wheeled droids zip around the area where this Blaster Battle takes place. Hit four of them (during or after the Blaster Battle) to get a Minikit.

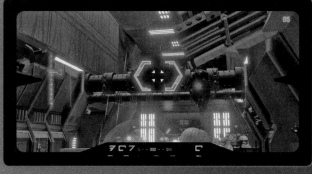

Assemble strength handles at the end of the hallway. ⑱ The strength handles open the door, which reveals Captain Phasma and a room set up for another Blaster Battle.

BLASTER BATTLE

Captain Phasma sends out stormtroopers and a probe droid to occupy you initially. She takes cover on an upper ledge. Watch for a prompt that indicates she's about to toss a thermal detonator. Cover won't help against it, so move everyone away from it before it explodes.

She moves to a side of the ledge and activates an energy screen. Two panels open under her position, exposing silver LEGO bricks. Tag to Chewbacca and toss a thermal detonator at the bricks. The explosion knocks out the generator and forces Captain Phasma to the opposite end of the platform.

Use another thermal detonator to destroy the second shield before the panels close. You must weather another round of stormtroopers and probe droids before they open again.

With both energy screens gone, Captain Phasma jumps into a large turret with two targets marking cooling ports on it. At first, both targets are hidden. Unfortunately, you can't simply wait behind a barricade for them to come into view. She fires rockets that you must blast out of the air before they reach anyone.

When the targets are exposed, shoot one quickly. The other becomes hidden again so you need to wait until it's exposed after another round of lasers and rockets from the turret. Hit the second target to destroy the turret.

Captain Phasma launches herself at Chewbacca. Tap the button flashing over his head to take her prisoner and end the chapter.

FREE PLAY:
STARKILLER SABOTAGE

Starkiller Crash Site

= MINIKIT   ▲ = PROBE DROID

START

Minikit 1
Shoot five probe droids. There are two at the crash site, while the rest are around the exterior of Starkiller Base.

Minikit 2
While clearing debris from the Millennium Falcon's crash site, break through pieces of snow to reveal bricks for a Minikit.

Minikit 3
Go through the access hatch near the energy shield. The Minikit is behind a frozen wall that's out of reach until you defeat the wampa in a fight. After winning the fight, cut open the frozen wall with a lightsaber.

STUDS X4

Build a tall snowman by sending Multi-Build bricks to the location nearest the mountainside. Hop on the snowman's hat, then use the hanging bar to reach the ledge.

Starkiller Wall

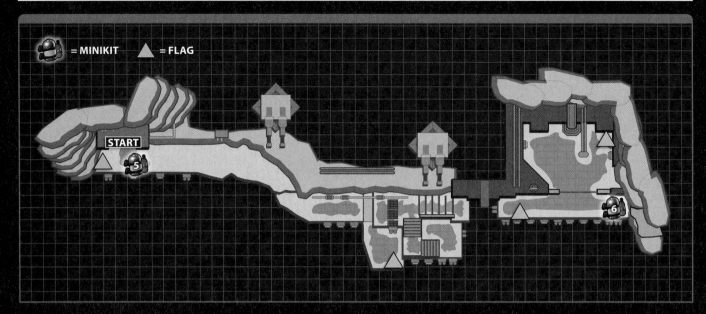

= MINIKIT   = FLAG

Minikit 4
Attack the metal spire next to the doorway, then rebuild it into a Resistance flag. There are three additional Resistance flags to raise in the area.

Minikit 5
Choose the left option with the Multi-Build bricks to make a hairdryer that knocks free a boulder and Minikit.

Minikit 6

Melt the ice covering the dive pool near the shielded silver LEGO door. It leads to a second dive pool on the mountainside.

Starkiller Shield Room

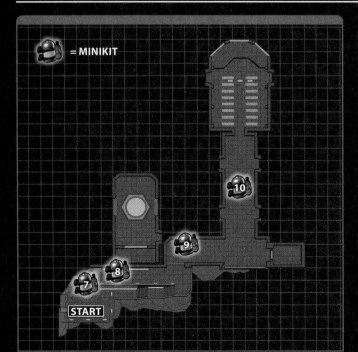

= MINIKIT

Minikit 7

Use the Force to open the panel with water splashing behind it.

Minikit 8

Build a launch pad from the Multi-Build bricks. Send BB-8 up to a rocky ledge with a Minikit.

Resistance Base

POE DAMERON (FLIGHT SUIT), SNAP WEXLEY

CHARACTERS NOW AVAILABLE FOR PURCHASE

 FN-2112

 Stormtrooper (Hot Tub)

 Snowtrooper

 Special Forces TIE Pilot

NEW LEVEL UNLOCKED
Trouble over Taul

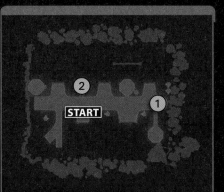

FIND A NEW ASTROMECH DROID

Snap Wexley and Poe Dameron are ready to take off, but one of their astromech droids is in dire need of repairs. The mechanic sends the pair in search of a new droid.

Follow the guide studs to the opposite end of the base ❶. Switch to Poe Dameron and scan the top crate to reveal dual grapple handles. Topple the crate by pulling on both handles at the same time.

The crate contains Multi-Build bricks, which represent parts of multiple astromech droids. The left option is R4-P44, a green unit. If you'd like a red droid, choose the center for Q7. R2-D3, a yellow astromech droid, is the right-side choice.

After making your selection, return to the launch pad ❷. Tag to your new astromech droid and interact with the astromech access. Match the shapes to prepare the X-wing for launch.

CHAPTER IX:
DESTROY STARKILLER BASE

Assault on Starkiller

RESISTANCE X-WING (BLACK LEADER), RESISTANCE X-WING (BLUE SQUADRON)

TRUE JEDI REQUIREMENT
100,000

STORY MODE CHARACTERS UNLOCKED (FREE)

 Finn (Junction Box)

 Rey (Junction Box)

VEHICLES UNLOCKED (FREE)

 Resistance X-wing (Blue Squadron)

 Resistance X-wing (Microfighter)

COMPLETED MINIKIT VEHICLE

 Imperial TIE Interceptor (and Microfighter)

TAKE THE LOW ROAD

Starkiller Base's defenses include TIE fighters, missiles, and large turbolaser turrets. Shoot down the TIE fighters and incoming missiles while flying between rings of studs.

MINIKIT:
CANYON ENTRANCE

Watch the right side of the canyon after flying into it. There's a Minikit inside a ring of studs.

ATTACK THE OSCILLATOR

There are four targets marked in light purple that must be destroyed. They're vulnerable only to proton torpedoes, which you can get from the dispensers on the surface of the oscillator, or from

The turbolaser turrets are vulnerable at the oscillator. Each one you destroy makes flying through the area a bit easier. There's no required order for taking down the targets, so go after the closest one after picking up a torpedo. Destroying the fourth target shifts the scene to Rey inside the base.

— MINIKIT: —
OSCILLATOR TIMED RUN

Fly through the purple sphere above the target tower to start a timed run. If you're having trouble completing the course in one piece, target any turrets nearby before starting a run.

Rey's Escape

REY, FN-1824

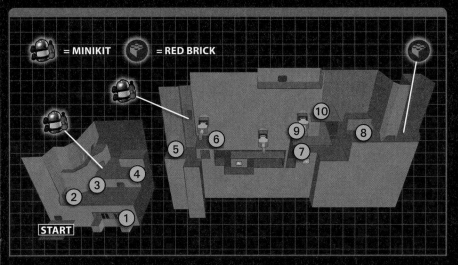

Break apart the First Order container ② and use the bricks from inside it to assemble a spinner switch. Lower the shorter bar down to FN-1824. Tag to the stormtrooper and grasp the bar, which automatically pulls him up to the ledge with Rey.

Pull the grapple handle near the door to extend a platform to the left ③. Switch to Rey and double-jump to the platform, then up again to the higher ledge with the patrolling stormtroopers.

UNWILLING ACCOMPLICE

When you gain control of Rey, aim for the empty socket against the wall. Jump to the staff, then wait for the ledge to extend outward. When it's in position, jump to it and then walk through the hidden hallway to a second ledge ①.

Climb up the ridged red tubing. To avoid the chatty stormtroopers, jump to the grip handles. Leap to the long hanging bar from the last grip handle, then go hand-over-hand all the way to the left and a second, much shorter hanging bar.

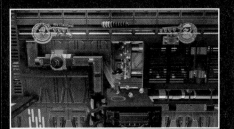

Attack the guards and objects scattered around the area. Attach the Multi-Build bricks as a power source on the machine to the right ④. After it positions a grapple handle, FN-1824 zips up to Rey's location.

MINIKIT:
HIDDEN FROM SIGHT

Send the Multi-Build bricks to the left to drop the energy shield over the open doorway. Pick up the two blue studs along with the purple stud and Minikit tucked out of sight.

WORKING TOGETHER, SEPARATELY

To get up to the next ledge, construct a ladder against the wall with the Multi-Build bricks. Target the grapple handle on the wall, which moves a second grapple handle into place above the nearby gap. Send FN-1824 across the gap. The First Order terminal ⑤ extends a bridge that allows Rey to cross.

Send Rey up the climb wall and hop off near the Gonk droid. Destroy everything and use the leftover bricks to complete the nearby track ⑥. Push the plug along the rebuilt track, into the socket. The gate blocking FN-1824's progress retracts, allowing him to move ahead.

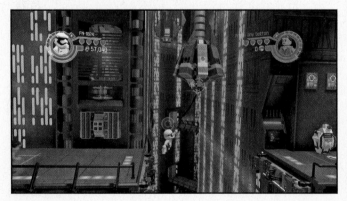

MINIKIT:
IN AN ALCOVE

Ascend to the top climb wall where there's a Minikit in an alcove.

Tag to Rey, then ascend the climb wall. Her progress is blocked by a lowered wall. As FN-1824 on the lower path, target the grapple handle and swing up to a higher walkway. Attack the large, red tubes, which become Multi-Build bricks.

Choose the right-hand option for the Multi-Build bricks first, which shifts the columns blocking the walkway above. After Rey moves ahead, break down the Multi-Build bricks and send them to the left.

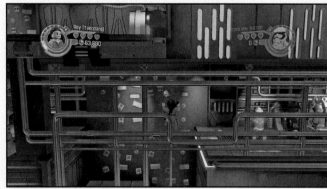

After Rey moves forward again, tag to her. Jump up and hang from the handle at the end of the blue tube. The doors in front of both FN-1824 and Rey slide open. An air current that originates from the lower level pushes your characters up to another higher ledge ⑦.

Attack the stormtroopers while they're distracted by an arcade machine. Turn the nearby lockers into the bricks necessary to restore power to the lift. Ride the lift up to the next walkway.

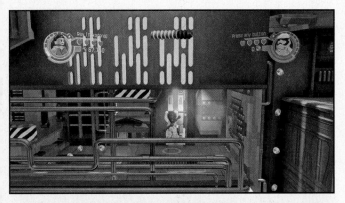

Tag to FN-1824 and swing across the gap ⑧ with a boost from the grapple handle. Eliminate the guards, then build a ladder of bricks salvaged from the nearby objects. Ascend the ladder, but he can't advance any more without a bit of help.

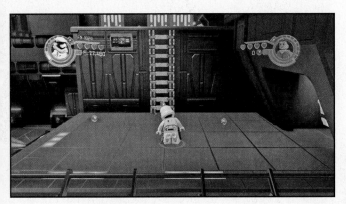

REGENERATING HEARTS

Before climbing the ladder, send FN-1824 through the almost-hidden doorway. Activate the First Order terminal to start five waves of stormtroopers. Defeat 15 total stormtroopers (each wave consists of three) to uncover the Red Brick.

Send Rey over the white arrows ⑨, which send her to the opposite side of the gap. Ascend the climb wall to the top, then look for the grip handles above.

The grip handles lead to another walkway. Rey is unable to use the First Order terminal here ⑩, but she can blast the target high on the wall around the corner. Hang from the bar that drops down to summon a droid that settles into FN-1824's range.

Swing across the gap, courtesy the grapple handle attached to the base of the sentry droid. Activate the First Order terminal, which moves an empty socket and a twirl pole into position. Toss Rey's staff into the socket, then swing over to a hanging bar under a climb wall. Ascend the wall, where Rey bids farewell to FN-1824 and meets up with a familiar crew.

Oscillator Interior

CHEWBACCA, HAN SOLO (STARKILLER BASE), SENTRY DROID

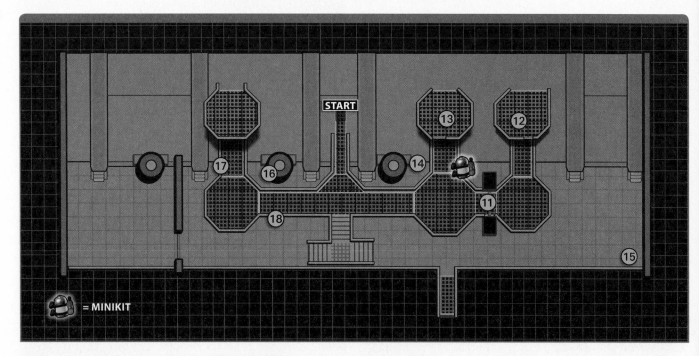

= MINIKIT

FIRST EXPLOSIVE CHARGE

A peaceful stroll down an empty hallway ends abruptly when Han Solo and Chewbacca emerge out into the open. The pair must plant explosives in four locations. You can tackle the four spots in any order.

Follow the walkway to the right until a red energy shield blocks the way (11). Shoot the targets on both sides of the frame to drop the energy shield.

Tag to Han Solo and swing up to the ledge (12) with a boost from the grapple handle. Scan above where the walls meet at an angle to reveal another grapple handle.

Swing over to a nearby platform (13). Break down the dark cylinder and use the leftover parts to complete the track. Push the container over the edge of the platform. The container that spills out is a silver LEGO object. Blow it apart with one of Chewbacca's thermal detonators, then use the remaining bricks to set the first charge.

SECOND EXPLOSIVE CHARGE

Hop over the side of the railing. Battle the stormtroopers that appear while moving toward the back wall (14). When you find a pile of Multi-Build bricks, turn them into strength handles by choosing the left build option.

Don't pull the handles yet. Go to the far corner of the base (15). A security droid calls for help. A large number of stormtroopers continue to appear until you silence the security droid, so make it your top priority. Salvage one of the yellow valve wheels from the three canisters, and return to the strength handles.

> ### FLOOR CLEANER
> If you want to keep the First Order base tidy, take the floor scrubber for a spin. Drive it over the four stains to earn a few extra studs while you're at it.

Pull out the strength handles, then tag to Han Solo. Place the valve wheel and then turn it to raise a container into the open space above the grating. Target the grapple handle and pull out the container, which holds the bricks needed to build another explosive charge.

MINIKIT:
DOWN THE HATCH

Add a power source above the small hatch to the right with the Multi-Build bricks to reveal the Minikit inside.

THIRD EXPLOSIVE CHARGE

Climb the central steps and turn past the door where Han Solo and Chewbacca entered the area. Stop when Han Solo takes note of a grapple handle (16). Pull on the

handle to spin the column and shake loose a pile of bricks. These bricks become an explosive charge when assembled against the column.

FOURTH EXPLOSIVE CHARGE

The final spot to plant charges is on the lower level. The first step is to recruit some help. Tag to Chewbacca, then pull the strength handles to get the Multi-Build bricks you need to free the Sentry Droid (17).

Aim the bricks at the top, right spot first. The shelf moves aside, and deposits Sentry Droid on the lower shelf. Switch the Multi-Build bricks to the lower, left location to drop Sentry Droid to the ground. It's now unlocked for use!

Move Sentry Droid to the nearby interface in front of a column (18). A part of the walkway slides open. A lift brings up a pile of bricks that become the final explosive charge when assembled against the column.

FREE PLAY: DESTROY STARKILLER BASE

Assault on Starkiller

Minikit 1
Watch the right side of the canyon after flying into it. There's a Minikit inside a ring of studs.

Minikit 2
Fly through the purple sphere above the target tower to start a timed run. If you're having trouble completing the course in one piece, target any turrets nearby before starting a run.

Rey's Escape

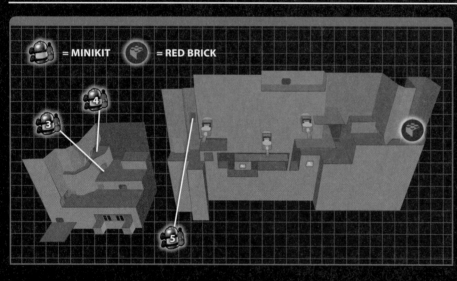

= MINIKIT   = RED BRICK

Minikit 5
Ascend to the top climb wall where there's a Minikit in an alcove.

REGENERATING HEARTS
Where Rey and FN-1824 are forced to split up the second time, look for a door on the lower ledge (where characters can swing across on a grapple handle).

Go through the almost-hidden doorway and switch to someone who can use First Order terminals. Defeat 15 stormtroopers (they appear in waves of three) to uncover the Red Brick.

Minikit 3
Send the Multi-Build bricks to the left to drop the energy shield over the open doorway. Pick up the two blue studs along with the purple stud and Minikit tucked out of sight.

Minikit 4

Use the Force to pull down a pipe from above and lay it across the gap. Cross over the gap on the pipe. Use dark side Force powers to tear open the door, then claim the Minikit inside.

Oscillator Interior

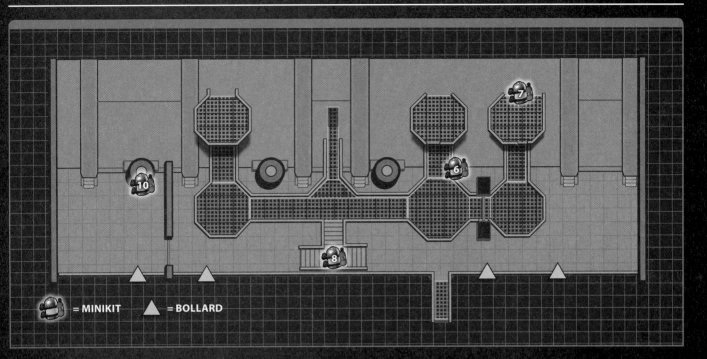

🎒 = MINIKIT   ▲ = BOLLARD

Minikit 6

Add a power source above the small hatch to the right with the Multi-Build bricks to reveal the Minikit inside.

Minikit 7

The protocol access terminal opens a hallway filled with green gas. A Minikit is in the back of the gas.

Minikit 9

Destroy four black bollards with lights on top of them. Three are in the main area. The fourth is behind the energy field opened by Sentry Droid.

Minikit 10

Use the Force to remove the cover of the Sentry Droid interface near the red energy field. Drop the field, then tag in a character that can destroy Gold LEGO objects to open the tower on the other side.

Minikit 8

An access hatch leads to an area under the central stairs, which contains a Minikit.

HUB:
STARKILLER BASE

Outside Starkiller Base

FINN (STARKILLER BASE), REY (STARKILLER BASE)

CHARACTERS NOW AVAILABLE FOR PURCHASE

General Hux

Jessika Pava

Kylo Ren (Hooded)

Lieutenant Mitaka

Nien Nunb

Stormtrooper Captain

Stormtrooper Combat Engineer

NEW LEVEL UNLOCKED
None

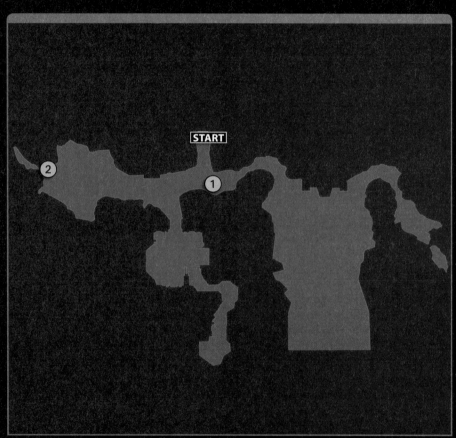

COMANDEER A SNOWSPEEDER

Finn and Rey start on a concrete landing pad with a narrow valley ahead. Follow the guide studs until a squad of snowtroopers attacks. After dealing with them, resume following the trail.

The destination is the snowspeeder ① Finn and Rey acquired earlier, but it's now guarded by First Order forces. It's a small group, so the fight should be over quickly.

Board the snowspeeder, which is armed with a heavy blaster. Don't slow to engage anything, just cruise through the area quickly. Drive until the trees become too narrow. Disembark the speeder and walk into the column of light to start The Finale.

CHAPTER X: THE FINALE

Oscillator Bombing Run

RESISTANCE X-WING (BLACK LEADER), RESISTANCE X-WING (BLUE SQUADRON)

TRUE JEDI REQUIREMENT
100,000

STORY MODE CHARACTERS UNLOCKED (FREE)

 Finn (Starkiller Base)

 Poe Dameron (D'Qar)

 Rey (Starkiller Base)

VEHICLES UNLOCKED (FREE)

 First Order TIE fighter (and Microfighter)

COMPLETED MINIKIT VEHICLE

 Starkiller Base (and Microfighter)

DESTROY THE OSCILLATOR

Before the Resistance can get at the oscillator, they need to clear the space above it. Destroy 20 TIE fighters while avoiding their laser fire and incoming missiles. Missiles are vulnerable to your weapons and leave a blue trail behind them, which allows you to track them.

MINIKIT:
TIMED RUN

Fly through the purple sphere to begin a timed run above Starkiller Base.

When a hole in the oscillator's defenses appears, Resistance forces hurry through it. Focus on blasting defenses and TIE fighters while guiding your X-wing through rings of studs.

After passing into the heart of the oscillator, the only objective is to cause as much damage as possible. Target the glowing red power lines to increase the percentage of damage done. When you hit 100% damage, the scene shifts to Finn and Rey.

MINIKIT:
GREEN TURRETS

During the flight into the trench run (and while flying through the trench), shoot five green turrets.

MINIKIT:
FIRST ORDER EMBLEMS

While inflicting 100% damage, look for three large First Order emblems on the walls. Press up and down to shoot the ones higher in your path.

MINIKIT:
RING OF STUDS

While in the trench run, watch for a minikit in a ring of studs. It pops up when flying through the spinning green turbines in the tunnel.

Starkiller Showdown

FINN (STARKILLER BASE), REY (STARKILLER BASE)

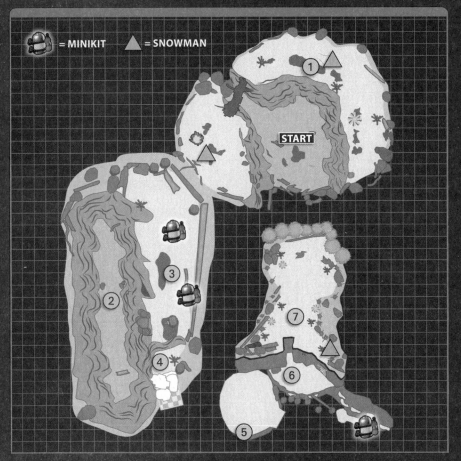

= MINIKIT   ▲ = SNOWMAN

DEFEAT KYLO REN

Keep a safe distance from Kylo Ren. Kylo Ren doesn't move quickly, but if he catches up to Finn, most of Finn's health will be gone quickly. Kylo Ren's defense is formidable. He blocks incoming blaster fire and melee weapon attacks.

You must wait for Kylo Ren to make a move. When he leaps into the air, press the button that appears to block his attack. Quickly tap the flashing button to push him away and inflict damage.

Build three snowmen while fighting Kylo Ren. Two of the three snowmen are built in the initial area. Break apart piles of snow as Rey to find what you need to build the first one.

After a few exchanges, Finn is caught with the Force and held in place. Tag to Rey, who is nearby. Wounds prevent her from moving quickly, but she's able to engage in combat with the snowtroopers who come after her.

Cross over the tree downed during the battle. Get to the pile of Multi-Build bricks ① and choose either option to distract Kylo Ren and free Finn. After another jumping attack is blocked, Finn loses his lightsaber. Get it to Rey by tapping the button that flashes over her head. The fight moves to a nearby location ②.

While fighting as Rey, block incoming attacks the same as before, but now attack Kylo Ren when he's dazed.

Kylo Ren shows off a new trick here. He leaps out of danger and orders snowtroopers to attack. This works out in your favor as they are more manageable enemies to handle and they may drop hearts to restore some of your health.

MINIKIT:

UP IN THE BRANCHES

The first in the line of three trees above where Kylo Ren confronts Rey has a Minikit on top. Pull the grapple handle with Finn to drop it where Rey can get it.

Continue to maintain a safe distance when possible and don't try to damage him outside of blocked attacks. Eventually, he freezes Rey and you are prompted to switch to Finn.

Target the grapple handle on the tree closest to Kylo Ren ③, which dumps a pile of snow on him. After shaking off the snow, he leaps to a pile of rocks and then flies off.

MINIKIT:

TARGET PRACTICE

Move close to the barricade above where the second half of the fight against Kylo Ren takes place. Fire at the droids as they emerge. After you hit six of them, you get a Minikit.

Chase Kylo Ren

Push the large object (two characters are required to move it) down the track ④. The ensuing avalanche changes the landscape dramatically. Rey hangs from a long bar ⑤ at the top of a climb wall. Move to the right to reach two twirl poles. Spin from the poles to reach a snowy ledge ⑥.

For Finn to reach the same spot, he uses grip handles and jump posts. The jump posts initially lead him away from the ledge where he meets up with Rey, but it's an easy trip back.

MINIKIT:

OVERCOMING HAZARDS

One path of jump points leads to an island covered in toxic gas. Go through the gas to reach a Minikit.

When the duo is together again, send Rey up the grip wall. There's a grapple handle for Finn. When they're together at the top, move into the clearing to face Kylo Ren again ⑦.

Repeat the same pattern as before. Maintain a safe distance and block Kylo Ren's incoming attacks. Only try to damage him when he's dazed. When his health is depleted, he attempts one last attack. Tap the button flashing over Rey's head to defeat him.

FREE PLAY: THE FINALE

Oscillator Bombing Run

Minikit 1
Fly through the purple sphere to begin a timed run above Starkiller Base.

Minikit 2
During the flight to the trench run (and while flying through the trench), shoot five green turrets.

Minikit 3
While in the trench run, watch for a Minikit in a ring of studs. It pops up shortly after the trench run begins.

Minikit 4
Blast three large First Order emblems on the walls where you're dealing 100% damage to the oscillator. Press up and down to shoot the ones higher in your path.

Starkiller Showdown

= MINIKIT = SNOWMAN = RED BRICK

Minikit 7
The first in the line of three trees above where the second half of the Kylo Ren fight takes place has a Minikit on top. Pull the grapple handle to drop it where your character can reach it.

Minikit 8
Move close to the barricade above where the second half of the fight against Kylo Ren takes place. Fire at the droids as they emerge. After you hit six of them, you earn a Minikit.

Minikit 9
Swing between grip handles until they change to jump points. One path of jump points leads to an island covered in toxic gas. Go through the gas to get the Minikit.

Minikit 10

On the snowy ledge, smash through the cracked brick to expose a Minikit.

COLLECT GUIDE STUDS

Use the Force to push a small snowball across the clearing. As it rolls, it increases in size and ends up next to a tree. Switch to a character with a jetpack, or who can double-jump, and leap on top of the snowball.

Minikit 5
Build three snowmen while fighting Kylo Ren. Two of the three snowmen are built in the initial area. Break apart piles of snow as Rey to find what you need to build the first one.

Minikit 6

Melt the ice covering the dive pool. Jump into the pool to pull out a Minikit.

HUB:
D'QAR

Resistance Base

REY (STARKILLER BASE), CHEWBACCA

CHARACTERS NOW AVAILABLE FOR PURCHASE

 Ello Asty

 General Leia (Formal)

 Kylo Ren (Unmasked)

 Lieutenant Bastian

 Snowtrooper Officer

NEW LEVEL UNLOCKED

Ottegan Assault

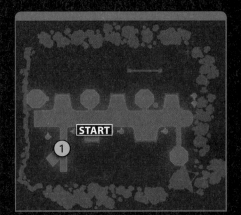

START

1

After the Resistance's victory over the First Order, D'Qar is in full celebration mode. However, there's another task ahead.

Armed with the knowledge of the whereabouts of Luke Skywalker, Rey, Chewbacca, and R2-D2 are ready to take off in the Millennium Falcon. All you need to do is guide them to the ship ❶.

EPILOGUE:
LUKE'S ISLAND

Luke's Island

CHEWBACCA, REY (RESISTANCE)

TRUE JEDI REQUIREMENT
30,000

STORY MODE CHARACTERS UNLOCKED (FREE)

 Rey (Resistance)

 R2-D2

VEHICLES UNLOCKED (FREE)

 Luke's Landspeeder (Microfighter)

COMPLETED MINIKIT VEHICLE

 Rebel Alliance A-wing (and Microfighter)

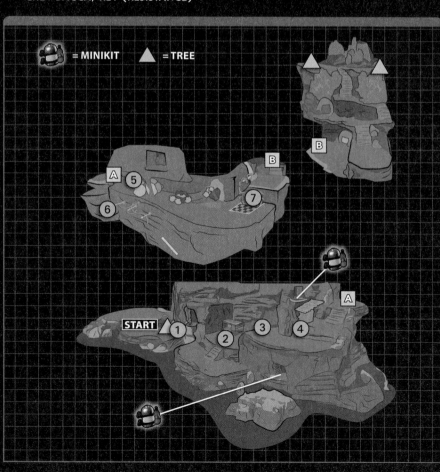

OBJECTIVE

Most of the activities you see around the landing area requires a return trip in Free Play. Step on the set of white arrows that push Rey across the gap ❶.

Move Rey to the scan spot. Scan the pile of rocks atop the mossy ledge against the hillside. Blast the revealed target to drop some rocks into the gap. Hop across the water on the narrow columns.

MINIKIT:
BREAK TREES

Before moving too far away from the Millennium Falcon's landing spot, shoot the small brown tree. There are two more to come during your ascent to the top of the nearby hill.

Send Rey past the stone steps and use the jump spot to clear the gap. A double-jump is necessary to reach the Minikit against the hillside.

With both characters over the gap, ascend the stone steps. Tag to Chewbacca, then rip apart the strength handles to reveal Multi-Build bricks ❷. Send them to the left to rebuild strength handles. Tag to Chewbacca and pull the handles to slide the large stone steps into place.

Tag to Rey (Chewbacca needs to maintain his hold on the strength handles) and jump up the steps. Toss her staff into the empty socket. Swing to the opposite ledge ❸.

The boulder on the track becomes stuck when Rey tries to push it. Tag to Chewbacca and break apart the strength handles. Build a weight under the spot where the rock's track curves upward.

Push the rock over the edge. Use the bricks to assemble a line of jumping spots, which allows Chewbacca to reach the upper ledge with Rey.

On the upper ledge, blast the target. Build strength handles with the bricks. Pull out the rock (4) that supports the structure above. Turn the new pile of bricks into a ramp that allows your characters to reach the next ledge.

Pull the strength handles to slide out another set of steps. Then Tag to Rey (Chewbacca can't let go of the handles) who finishes the trip to the top on her own.

MINIKIT:
TWIRL POLE

At the top of the stone steps, toss Rey's staff into the empty socket. Twirl up and over to the Minikit.

Continue along the path until a pile of boulders makes the path impassable (5). Pull the strength handles next to the blockage to retract the vines clogging the twirl poles below (6).

Tag to Rey, swing across the twirl poles and land on the narrow ledge beyond them. Hop quickly between the grip handles at the end of the ledge to reach a climb wall. Climb to the ledge where Chewbacca waits, but now Rey is on the other side of the rocks.

Backtrack to the blockage. Attack the debris against the hillside. Build a simple lever, powered by a spinner switch, from the leftover bricks.

With your characters reunited, push the vine-covered stone object over the edge (7). Then cross the narrow bridge.

FREE PLAY: LUKE'S ISLAND

Luke's Island

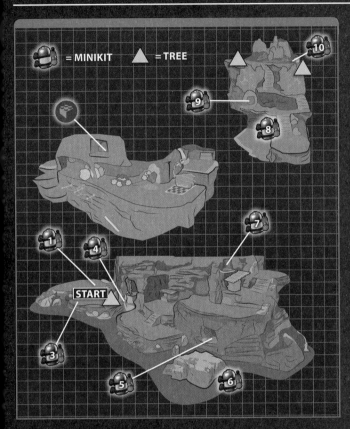

Minikit 5

Use the jump posts past the first stone steps to reach a stone outcrop. A double-jump, or jetpack, is necessary to reach the Minikit in a depression against the hillside.

Minikit 6

Use the jump posts past the first stone steps to reach a stone outcrop. Use the Force to retrieve a Minikit from the water.

Minikit 7

At the top of the stone steps, toss Rey's staff into the empty socket. Twirl up and over to the Minikit.

Minikit 8

Use the Force to remove rocks blocking a stone hut built in the mountainside.

Minikit 9

Destroy the gold LEGO brick door up a side path.

Minikit 10

Smash a cracked LEGO brick to reveal a Minikit behind it.

Minikit 1

Use the grapple handle on the container under the Millennium Falcon to pull it down and break it open.

Minikit 2

Attack three small brown trees to spook the birds roosting on them.

Minikit 3

The dive pool near the start point leads to a rocky outcrop in the water.

Minikit 4

Cut open the rocky door with a lightsaber.

THE FUNK AWAKENS

After clearing the rocks with the spinner switch, use dark side Force powers to clear the rocks in front of an access hatch. Go through the hatch to pick up the Red Brick on the ledge above.

POE TO THE RESCUE

Trash Compactor

ADMIRAL ACKBAR (RESISTANCE), BB-8, C-3PO, POE DAMERON (HELMETLESS)

TRUE JEDI REQUIREMENT
120,000

STORY MODE CHARACTERS UNLOCKED (FREE)

 Admiral Ackbar (Resistance)

 Poe Dameron (Helmetless)

VEHICLES UNLOCKED (FREE)

 Ackbar's Starfighter (and Microfighter)

COMPLETED MINIKIT VEHICLE

 Rebel Alliance Snowspeeder (and Microfighter)

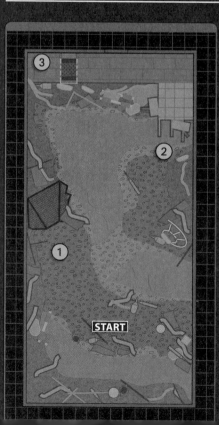

TRASH COMPACTOR CONFIGURATION 1

Dig through the trash in the compactor to uncover a pile of Multi-Build bricks ①. If you choose the closer build option, the dianoga is fed fish. The farther away option is a fishing rod. Regardless of which you build, the dianoga swims away and leaves your group alone in the compactor.

Cross the water at a shallow point and pull the dual grapple handles ② with Admiral Ackbar and Poe Dameron. Tag to Admiral Ackbar and jump into the dive pool.

The bricks he sends out become a launch pad that sends BB-8 over the deep water. Roll to the opposite end of the platform. The astromech access ❸ activates the walls, moving them closer together.

TRASH COMPACTOR CONFIGURATION 2

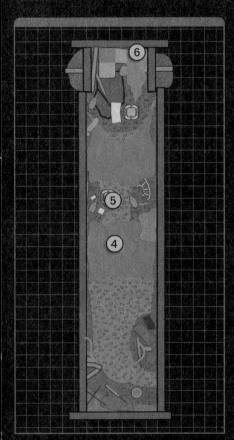

The dianoga resurfaces in a small pool of water ❹. Move BB-8 through the access hatch to rejoin the group. Open the overhead pipe with the grapple handle to uncover a stash of Multi-Build bricks. There are two ways to go with the bricks, but only one machine can be activated before the bricks fuse together.

Choose the left build option for an eye-poking machine. The machine on the right shocks the dianoga. Both machines are activated by BB-8, and both options are effective in driving away the dianoga.

Tag to Admiral Ackbar. Jump into the dive pool ❺, which leads to another pool beyond the impassable area. Jump to the hanging bar ❻ to widen the walls again.

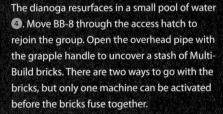

TRASH COMPACTOR CONFIGURATION 3

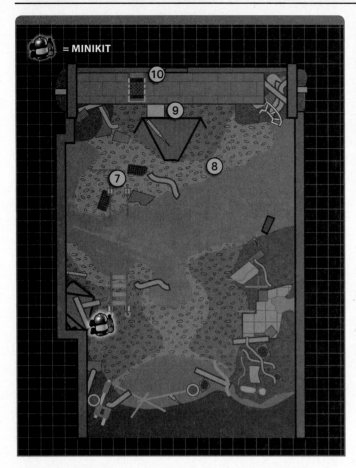

= MINIKIT

MINIKIT:

SEWAGE SWIM

After the bridge is pulled up from the muck, run Admiral Ackbar to where the rest of the group is waiting. There's a Minikit inside the dive pool behind them.

Stick with Admiral Ackbar to raise the bridge across the deep water. Attack the garbage ⑦ near the end of the bridge to collect the bricks necessary to build a spinner switch.

Destroy the junk near the rotary control ⑧. The machine built with the bricks controls the overhead garbage chute. Tag to BB-8 and move the chute from over the sludge so its trash falls where your group can put it to use. It's C-3PO's time to shine!

Wait until C-3PO moves to the platform ⑨ in the middle of the wall. Assemble the Multi-Build bricks in the spot closest to C-3PO. Hop on the button to raise the platform. Move C-3PO off the platform on to the raised area.

Break down the Multi-Build bricks and shift them to the center build position. Move C-3PO over the lowered bridge. Break down the Multi-Build bricks, then send them to the leftmost position. C-3PO rides the lift up. Use the protocol access terminal ⑩ to open the door. Go through the door to exit the trash compactor.

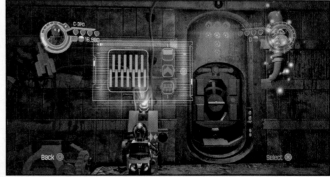

Hangar Battle

ADMIRAL ACKBAR (RESISTANCE), BB-8, C-3PO, POE DAMERON (HELMETLESS)

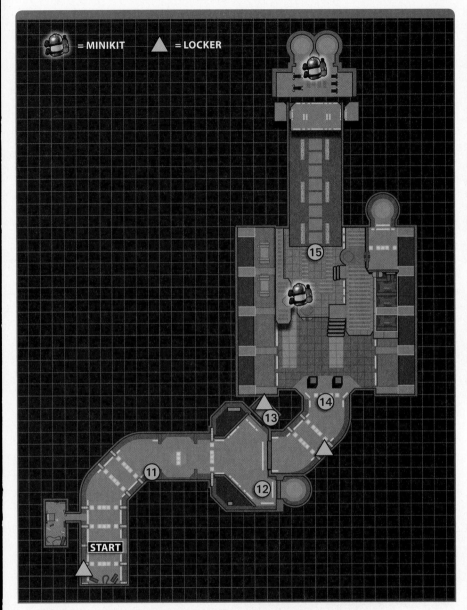

MINIKIT:
GRAPPLE HANDLE LOCKERS

Three lockers in the area can be opened by pulling on grapple handles. Open each one to free the tiny droid inside.

BATTLE THROUGH STORMTROOPERS

Eliminate the distracted stormtroopers. Advance down the hallway to an astromech access ⑪, which removes the energy shield blocking the path.

A larger unit of stormtroopers guards a door just ahead. While fighting them, assemble the Multi-Build bricks ⑫ against the door on the right. You can build either a floor waxer or a clothesline to help hold off reinforcements. You can switch freely between the clothesline and waxer.

The blast doors are locked with a scanner. The hat dispenser is in a nearby alcove ⑬ that opens when stormtrooper reinforcements exit it. Select the black helmet, then interact with the scanner to open the door. A Blaster Battle begins where the following hallway end ⑭.

BLASTER BATTLE

Take cover behind the columns as the First Order forces open fire. Your first task is to eliminate five stormtroopers and one heavy stormtrooper. There's nothing you can do about the shielded turret behind them, yet.

The next obstruction is a squad of stormtroopers. Your group moves closer to the turret, but its shielding is still too much for you to overcome.

As the tenth stormtrooper falls, your group splits up and moves around the turret. Blast the target on the generator powering the wampa's containment field (it's only visible from the raised walkway), and then enjoy the show.

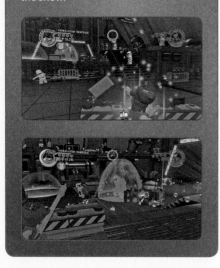

MOP UP DUTY

Take on the remaining stormtroopers while exploring the bay. Destroy the objects in the area to boost your stud count. Don't miss out on any collectibles! When you're ready to continue, go to the long lift at the end of the area (15).

MINIKIT:
UPPER DECK

Go through the access hatch hidden behind boxes on the end of the long lift (opposite the operating button). Spinning the rotary control drops three containers from the ceiling to the floor. Break open the containers to get a minikit.

MINIKIT:
ELEVATOR SHARPSHOOTER

While riding the lift down, past a First Order gymnasium, shoot the two targets on the wall above the aerobics class.

Add a push bar to the power rod with bricks salvaged from a nearby container. Push the rod into the wall socket to begin the ride down, where you are treated to a glimpse of what happens when First Order forces have some downtime. When the lift comes to a stop, those same First Order forces pour out of an elevator and attack. After eliminating the brightly-clad enemies, go into the opened elevator.

Asteroid Escape

ACKBAR'S STARFIGHTER, RESISTANCE X-WING (BLACK LEADER)

NAVIGATE THE ASTEROID FIELD

Your path is predetermined, so you should focus on nudging your ship through rings of studs and shooting down TIE fighters. C-3PO provides updates in his typical, understated fashion.

Admiral Ackbar notes an enormous asteroid ahead, which you fly into during a brief cutscene. There's less space to maneuver inside the asteroid, and the flying rocks have been replaced with mynocks.

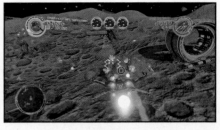

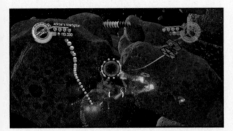

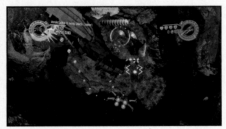

MINIKIT:
SMALLER CLUSTERS

Target three smaller gem clusters with proton torpedoes.

MINIKIT:
HOLLOWED OUT ASTEROID

When a large asteroid spins around and reveals hollowed out areas, dip down and fly through the Minikit surrounded by gold studs.

MINIKIT:
GOING GREEN

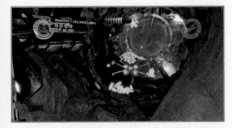

While flying through the mynock tunnel, shoot seven green growths attached to the rocky walls. There are exactly seven, so you can't miss any if you want to earn the Minikit. Plan on a few practice runs through the area before you can get all seven in the same pass.

CHARACTERS NOW AVAILABLE FOR PURCHASE

- General Hux (Leotard)
- Rancor
- Stormtrooper (Aerobics)
- Stormtrooper (Heavy)
- Wampa
- K-3PO
- R5-D8

DESTROY 20 TIE FIGHTERS

The surface of the asteroid includes violet gem clusters that are the key to escaping First Order pursuit. Before you can put them to use, you must shoot down 20 TIE fighters.

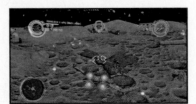

UNLEASH THE MYNOCKS

The next wave of enemies includes Special Forces TIE fighters, which carry proton torpedoes. There are also torpedo dispensers on the surface of the asteroid. Blast the three larger gem formations with proton torpedoes to unleash enough mynocks to cover your escape.

FREE PLAY:
POE TO THE RESCUE

Trash Compactor

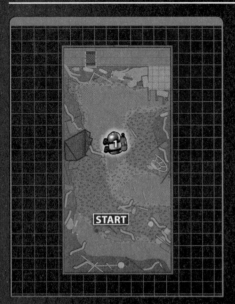

Minikit 1
Pull out the Gonk droid with the Force. Break it open to get the parts for a Minikit.

Minikit 2
After the bridge is pulled up from the muck, run Admiral Ackbar to where the rest of the group is waiting. There's a Minikit inside the dive pool behind them.

Hangar Battle

= MINIKIT

= LOCKER

= RED BRICK

Minikit 3
Three lockers in the area can be opened by pulling on grapple handles. Open each one to free the tiny droid inside.

Minikit 4
Destroy the silver LEGO pipes under the shielded turret.

Minikit 5

Use the Force to pull down the black First Order containers on the platform above the power rod. Jump up the remaining containers to get to the Minikit behind them.

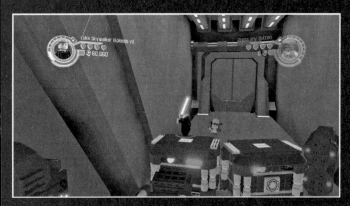

Minikit 6

Go through the access hatch hidden behind boxes on the end of the long lift opposite the operating button. Spinning the rotary control drops three containers from the ceiling to the floor. Break open the containers to get a Minikit.

Minikit 7

While riding the lift down, past a First Order gymnasium, shoot the two targets on the wall above the aerobics class.

INFINITE TORPEDOES

There's a door hidden behind pressurized tanks not far from where you begin in this area. Go through the door to reach Kylo Ren's room, which is filled with glowing red objects.

Tear apart everything in the room with dark side Force powers (only a TIE fighter and an X-wing will survive). A Red Brick will appear in the middle of the room.

Asteroid Escape

Minikit 8

When a large asteroid spins around and reveals hollowed out areas, dip down and fly through the Minikit surrounded by gold studs.

Minikit 9

While flying through the mynock tunnel, shoot seven green growths attached to the rocky walls. There are exactly seven, so you can't miss any if you want to earn the Minikit.

Minikit 10

Target three smaller gem clusters on the surface of the asteroid with proton torpedoes.

LOR SAN TEKKA'S RETURN

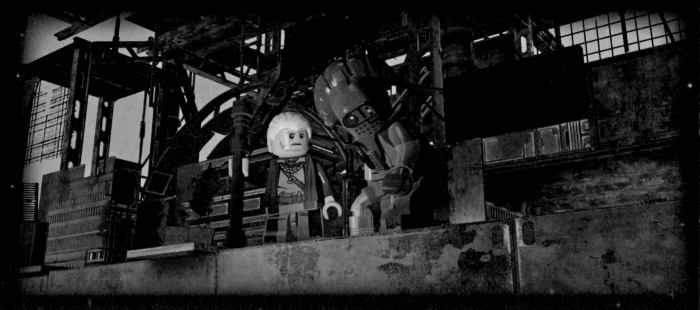

Kelvin Ravine

LOR SAN TEKKA, ATHGAR HEECE

OPEN THE BASE DOOR

Take advantage of the peaceful opening of this chapter by exploring the ravine. Build up your stud count by destroying the debris poking up from under the sand dunes.

MINIKIT:
WHACK-A-WORM

Four nightwatchers poke their heads above the sand. Hit each of the four to get a pile of bricks that assemble into a Minikit.

MINIKIT:
SAND SEARCHES

Shoot the target on the small machine against the wall of the canyon, just beyond the crashed ship. Follow the droid that emerges from within as it uncovers studs and the bricks for a Minikit from under the sand.

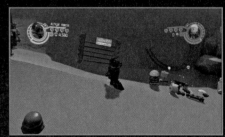

Locate the folded panel ❶ atop a machine that's missing a valve wheel. Go beyond it to reach the scavenger base. Search the base (there are a few scavengers guarding it) to find the necessary valve wheel ❷. You must destroy the machine to which the valve wheel is currently attached before you can claim it. Return to the machine with the folded panel and put the valve wheel to use.

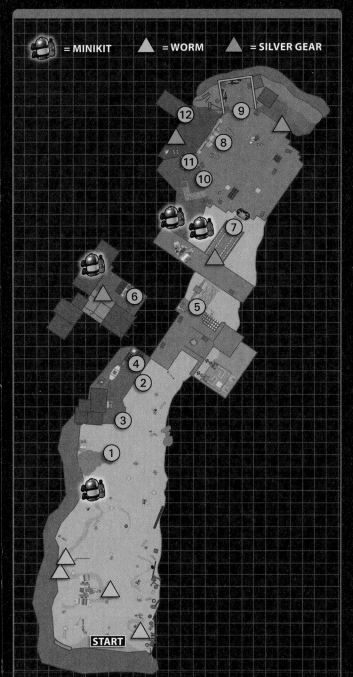

= MINIKIT   ▲ = WORM   ▲ = SILVER GEAR

START

Target the grapple handle as Lor San Tekka to pull open the door. Clear out the silver LEGO objects blocking the doorway with Athgar Heece's thermal detonator.

Tag to Lor San Tekka and crank the spinner switch ④, which opens the main doors to the base. The area behind the door is calm, but a gap ahead ⑤ allows blustery winds through, making it impossible to cross the bridge initially.

Tag to Athgar Heece. His jetpack allows him to reach the raised platform tucked into the corner of the ravine and the smaller platform on the outside of the scavenger base.

Walk along the narrow ledge and follow it around a corner. Hop off to the base's roof and smash everything. Build a ladder from the leftover bricks and drop it into place ③.

RAISE THE NET

Tag to Athgar Heece and hang on the twirl pole. Switch to Lor San Tekka (leave Athgar Heece in place) and turn the valve wheel.

Jump from the pole to the higher area. Look for a box of junk on a broken track ⑥. Repair the track with bricks salvaged from nearby debris. Push the box over the edge and build a spinner switch from its contents.

Turn the winch to move a catch net into place. Tag to Athgar Heece and jetpack over the gap. After a quick skirmish against scavengers, target the silver LEGO bricks on the derelict ship.

Three security droids settle in to the gap. Move Lor San Tecca across the gap by jumping between the droids, although he might do it on his own.

BREAKTHROUGH TO THE VILLAGE

Switch to Lor San Tekka and target the grapple handle ⑦. Pull down the TIE fighter panel to open the way to an open area with scavengers and hobbled luggabeasts.

Clear out the scavengers, then toss one of Athgar Heece's thermal detonators at the spinning cog ⑧ between the luggabeasts to set them free. Mount a luggabeast and bust through the two cracked blocks on either end of the area.

MINIKIT:
CRANK IT UP

Blow up the silver LEGO object on the roof; then jetpack up to the ledge with a Minikit.

MINIKIT:
SILVER LEGO GEARS

There are gears made from silver LEGO bricks attached to walls in four different spots inside the scavenger base. Hit each one with an explosive attack to earn a Minikit.

A droid emerges from above the cracked block on the right ⑨. Bounce on it to reach the small room above. Scan the panel on the back wall with Lor San Tekka, then destroy the exposed panel with a grenade from Athgar Heece. A surge of power shakes things up nearby.

Break through the cracked block on the left ⑩. Ascend the grip wall with Athgar Heece, then push the container of odds and ends over the edge.

MINIKIT:
BULLS-EYE

Walk away from the Spinner Switch found above the grip wall until you come upon a fence held in place by silver LEGO posts. Knock down the fence with grenades, then blast the target on the large turbine fan hanging from the wall. What you get from the wheel (studs, Teedos, or a Minikit) depends on where it stops. You get the Minikit when it points to the top image.

MINIKIT:
NARROW LEDGE

Drop over the edge not far from the spinning wheel to land on a narrow ledge. You may have seen this Minikit after crossing the windy gap.

Build a ladder from the bricks in the container. Send Lor San Tekka up the ladder and over to the spinner switch ⑪. After completing the tasks behind both cracked bricks, the center structure (where the leader was holed up) tumbles to the ground.

Construct two bouncing gears from the bricks that fell out of the fallen platform. Bounce to the handholds, which your characters employ to reach to the highest area. Go through the doorway ⑫ to continue to the village.

CHARACTERS NOW AVAILABLE FOR PURCHASE

Bobba Jo		Teedo
Constable Zuvio		EGL-21 "Amps"
"Crusher" Roodown		GTAW-74 "Geetaw"
Davan Marak		SN-1F4

FREE PLAY:
LOR SAN TEKKA'S RETURN

Kelvin Ravine

= MINIKIT

= SILVER GEAR

= WORM

= RED BRICK

Minikit 1
Four nightwatchers poke their heads above the sand. Hit each of the four to get a pile of bricks that assemble into a Minikit.

Minikit 2
Shoot the target on the small machine against the wall of the canyon. Follow the droid that emerges from within as it uncovers studs and the bricks for a Minikit from under the sand.

Minikit 3

Charge the power jack on a wrecked ship with BB-8.

Minikit 4

Cut through the round fan-shaped hatch next to the valve handle.

Minikit 5

An astromech access near the windy gap raises a row of thick bars.

Minikit 6

Bring in Admiral Ackbar for a quick dip in the dive pool, just inside the scavenger base.

Minikit 7
Blow up the silver LEGO bricks on the roof; then jetpack up to the Minikit.

Minikit 8
There are gears made from silver LEGO bricks attached to walls in four different spots inside the scavenger base. Hit each one with an explosive attack to earn a Minikit.

Minikit 9
Walk away from the spinner switch found above the grip wall until you come upon a fence held in place by silver LEGO posts. Knock down the fence with explosives, then blast the target on the large turbine fan hanging from the wall.

Minikit 10
Drop over the edge not far from the target. Grab the Minikit on the narrow ledge below.

STUDS X10

After building the spinner switch to raise the catch net, run parallel to the windy gap. Continue down a few levels until you see a blue robot and a power jack.

Charge the power jack in the lower area to activate two boxing battle droids. Hit the matching colored bag in front of the robot to cause it to punch. Land enough punches to knock back the other droid's head to score a point. Score three points with either droid to get a Red Brick. The droids reset after one scores three points, so you can play with them as much as you like.

RATHTAR HUNTING

Rathtar Caverns

CHEWBACCA (TWON KETEE), HAN SOLO (TWON KETEE), VAROND JELIK

TRUE JEDI REQUIREMENT
65,000

STORY MODE CHARACTERS UNLOCKED (FREE)

 Chewbacca (Twon Ketee)

 Han Solo (Twon Ketee)

 Varond Jelik

VEHICLES UNLOCKED (FREE)

 Prana Predator

 Prana Ship (Microfighter)

 Radon-Ulzer Podracer

COMPLETED MINIKIT VEHICLE

TREACHEROUS WATER

Don't blink or you may miss Varond Jelik's crack team of rathtar hunters vanishing during the early stages of exploring the caverns. Also, don't be eager to follow them into the watery area ahead. Blast the flora filling the area outside the cavern's entrance to score some studs first.

MINIKIT:
SKELETAL ASCENT

Toss Varond Jelik's staff into the empty socket above the cavern entrance. Swing across the twirl poles to a ledge with a grapple handle and pile of bones. Break apart the bones and build a ladder from its spine. Send Han Solo up the ladder and pull the grapple handle free from the rocky wall.

MINIKIT:
GOLDEN PETALS

Shoot ten golden flowers hanging from the ceiling while wading through the water inside the cavern. Blast the first two as you enter the water, and the last two above where the water ends.

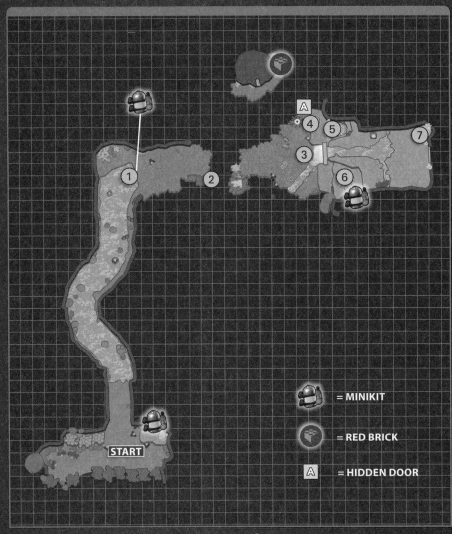

= MINIKIT

= RED BRICK

Ⓐ = HIDDEN DOOR

START

As the rathtar retreats, it leaves behind Multi-Build bricks. Build the climbing wall against the ledge first. After Varond Jelik climbs to the top, tear down the climbing bits. Assemble a droid that opens an umbrella to divert the waterfall.

Cross under the droid and push the purple crystal ④ over the edge. Build a flowery lift from the bricks that appear after the crystal breaks open. Move Han Solo and Chewbacca on the lift to reach the ledge with Varond Jelik.

Tag to Chewbacca and pull the strength handles ⑤ to reveal a flowery trampoline. Bounce to the higher ledge, then cross under the waterfall to a ledge filled with purple flowers.

Wade through the water to reach dry land at the end ①. Break through the nearby translucent pink cap to create a stud fountain. When the path appears to hit a dead-end ②, break down the skeleton and convert it into a bridge.

Move everyone over the bridge. Target the grapple handle overhead to pull down the stem of a flower, which becomes a trampoline. Your competitors from the Solculvis pop up here, to introduce themselves.

FIRST RATHTAR ENCOUNTER

Look for a blue stud in front of a waterfall ③. After scanning the waterfall, a rathtar attacks. Tap the button flashing over your character's head to escape the beast.

FAST FORCE

Where the flower lift drops off your characters on the higher ledge, there's a hidden door in the rocks. Go through the door to reach a stony path that leads to a Red Brick.

SECOND RATHTAR ENCOUNTER

Attack the flowers ⑥ to uncover Multi-Build bricks. Selecting the build option directly ahead fills the alcoves with sweet treats that bring out insects that act as handles. Jump up and over the ledge by tapping the button that flashes over the head of your character. Be ready for a quick firefight at the top.

MINIKIT: CUPCAKE CLIMBING

The Multi-Build bricks become cupcakes when sent into the alcoves on the right. Hop up the handles to reach the Minikit at the top.

Scan the area near the large yellow flowers ⑦ in the back of the cave to flush out a rathtar. Just like the previous encounter, tap the button flashing over the captured character's head to escape the rathtar's clutches.

After the beast flees, build strength handles from the bricks left behind. Slide down the slimy ramp to reach the loading area.

Loading Area

CHEWBACCA (TWON KETEE), HAN SOLO (TWON KETEE), VAROND JELIK

= MINIKIT ▲ = FLOWER

STEAL FROM SOLCULVIS

The action kicks off as soon as you gain control of your rathtar-hunting party. Duck behind cover quickly and settle in for a Blaster Battle.

BLASTER BATTLE

You must first blast ten members of the Solculvis crew, and one robust heavy gunner standing atop the rathtar trap. There's nothing you can do about the shielded turret yet. The color of helmets doesn't matter for the countdown.

Most of the Solculvis crew members are around the rathtar cage. A few are in the rocks on the opposite side of the valley.

MINIKIT:
GOLDEN PETALS

During the Blaster Battle, target five glowing flowers scattered around the enemy units. Hit all five to get a Minikit.

Move Han Solo to the scan location ⑧ that appears after taking down the enemies. Scan the dark disc atop the ridge to reveal a grapple handle. Pull on the handle to unfurl a ladder.

Chewbacca ascends the ladder and moves to the end of the barricades ⑨. Target the rathtar cage with a thermal detonator. The creature smashes the shielded turret.

Mop up the last few stragglers of the Solculvis crew. If you missed any blue bulbs earlier, use them now to shorten these fights. First up is five general troops, and one heavy gunner. Then defeat a third group of five, this time joined by a large battle droid.

The fighting agitates the rathtar, who knocks a crate down to the valley floor and spills a pile of bricks. Assemble a miniature Millennium Falcon from the bricks. The tiny Millennium Falcon flies around and completes your task.

MINIKIT:
TOP SHELF

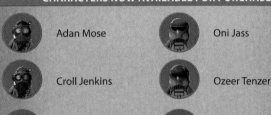

Before you assemble the small Millennium Falcon, pull down the container with the grapple handle on it from the ledge.

CHARACTERS NOW AVAILABLE FOR PURCHASE		
Adan Mose		Oni Jass
Croll Jenkins		Ozeer Tenzer
Gaff Kaylek		Zylas

FREE PLAY:
RATHTAR HUNTING

Rathtar Caverns

= MINIKIT

= RED BRICK

A = HIDDEN DOOR

FAST FORCE
Where the flower lift drops off your characters on the higher ledge, there's a hidden door in the rocks. Go through the door to reach a stony path that leads to a Red Brick.

Loading Area

= MINIKIT   ▲ = FLOWER

Minikit 1
Tear away the rocks covering a cave mouth with dark side Force powers.

Minikit 2
Toss a staff into the empty socket above the cavern entrance. Swing across the twirl poles to a ledge with a grapple handle and pile of bones. Break apart the bones and build a ladder from its spine. Send a character with a grapple gun up the ladder and pull the grapple handle free from the rocky wall.

Minikit 3
Shoot ten golden flowers hanging from the ceiling while wading through the water inside the cavern. Blast the first two as you enter the water, and the last two above where the water ends.

Minikit 4
Go through the access hatch just after first rathtar escape (in the waterfall).

Minikit 5
Multi-Build bricks become cupcakes when sent into the alcoves on the right. Hop up the handles to reach the Minikit at the top.

Minikit 6
Jump into dive pool just before the second rathtar encounter (on top of waterfall).

Minikit 7
Before starting the Blaster Battle, use the Force to open the yellow flower's petals.

Minikit 8
Target the gold LEGO stalactite hanging from a hollow in the mountainside (above the yellow flower).

Minikit 9
During (and after) the Blaster Battle, look for five glowing flowers scattered around the Solculvis units. Hit all five to get a Minikit.

Minikit 10
Before you assemble the small Millennium Falcon, pull down the container with the grapple handle on it from the ledge.

THE CRIMSON CORSAIR

Landing Site

PRU SWEEVANT, QUIGGOLD, SIDON ITHANO

DROP THE SHIELD

There's a wall of gold LEGO bricks ❶ that keeps enemies away initially, leaving you free to explore the area and collect studs. When you're done, tag to Quiggold and blast through the gold LEGO bricks and eliminate the stormtroopers on the other side of them.

MINIKIT:
IN THE SHIP

Pull open the ship's cargo hatch with the grapple handle.

MINIKIT:
BEHIND THE SHIP

Turn around at the start of the level. Knock down the rock attached to the cliff face with gold LEGO bricks to plug the geyser.

MINIKIT:
CRYSTAL LIZARD HUNTING

Blast three crystal lizards found in the area. The first is under a thruster pod of the ship at the starting point.

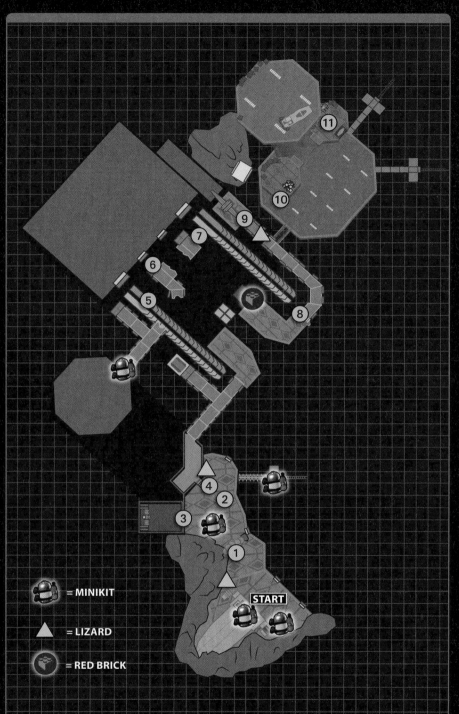

= MINIKIT

= LIZARD

= RED BRICK

DRILLING DOWN

The left option for the Multi-Build bricks is a drilling droid. It punches through the concrete and pulls up a Minikit.

BALANCE BEAM

Step off the edge of the concrete across from the staircase that was covered in electricity. Carefully move out to the Minikit at the walkway's end.

Eliminate the stormtroopers inside the building. Build another set of strength handles against the shield generator. Pull on the strength handles to expose the generator, which is built from silver LEGO bricks.

Tag to Pru Sweevant and destroy the generator with a thermal detonator. Break down the Multi-Build bricks, then cap the energy geyser on the right with them. Electricity lingers on the steps, making them impassable, until that happens.

With the stormtroopers out of the way, tag to Sidon Ithano and target the grapple handle. The yellow machine ❷ becomes a pile of Multi-Build bricks when pulled apart.

Assemble strength handles against the door ❸ with the Multi-Build bricks. Switch to Quiggold and pull on the strength handles to destroy the door to the shield generator building.

GET TO THE LANDING PAD

Ascend the staircase (4). Battle stormtroopers through the windowed walkway. Don't worry about the giant fan until you return in Free Play, but the stormtroopers guarding it investigate your crew when they emerge from the windowed walkway.

Destroy the long gear shaft made of silver LEGO bricks (5) with a thermal detonator. A droid emerges from the blast doors and hovers overhead. Switch to Sidon Ithano and target the grapple handle under the droid.

MINIKIT:
ROOFTOP CONTAINER

Follow the upper walkway to a large storage container with a grapple handle on its door. Pull open the door and claim the Minikit inside.

Swing across to another broken section of the upper walkway with an assist from a grapple handle-equipped droid. Go to the white arrows (6) that send Sidon Ithano over the gap. Drop down to the concrete walkway.

Rebuild the door controls by directing the Multi-Build bricks (7) to the spot in the corner on the left. The blast doors open and trios of droids emerge from it. When the droids stop in place, Pru Sweevant and Quiggold can hop across the gap using the droids.

Tag to Quiggold to clear the path ahead (8). The stormtroopers across the gap deactivate the bridge. Clear out the debris blocking access to an access hatch (9).

Send Pru Sweevant through the access hatch, which leads to a ledge above. Toss a thermal detonator at the silver LEGO device to send a makeshift bridge below. The final lizard is on this broken walkway as well.

STEAL A TROOP TRANSPORT

The bridge isn't stable, so the first person to cross it slips off. Quickly tap the flashing button to get back up. The others can hurry across without a worry, except for stormtrooper fire.

Stormtroopers shuttled in on floating platforms form a greeting party (10), and you must defeat a dozen of them. After the twelfth stormtrooper falls, a microfighter is assembled on a landing pad and sent after your crew.

It's constructed from gold LEGO bricks, making it Quiggold's target. When the mini TIE fighter is rebuilt with silver LEGO bricks, it's Pru Sweevant's turn to shoot it down.

A final platform swoops in, but it's caught in plasma and crashes. Switch to Sidon Ithano and jump to the landing pad. Move to the right edge of the platform, then target the grapple handle above.

Swing over to the landing pad to the left (11). Rebuild the lift's engine so that Quiggold and Pru Sweevant have a way to get up on the platform. Scan the back of the landing pad. Target the silver LEGO gears with a thermal detonator to remove the energy shields on the support columns.

Scan the right-hand shaft to reveal a door built from gold LEGO bricks. Remove the bricks, then toss a thermal detonator at the silver LEGO bricks behind it.

Cobble together strength handles from the bricks leftover after the explosion. Rip open the left shaft to expose another column of silver LEGO bricks. The troop transport slides down until its new crew takes over and flies off.

CHARACTERS NOW AVAILABLE FOR PURCHASE	
Blass Tyran	Stormtrooper Sergeant
Oskus Stooratt	Wi'ba Tuyill

FREE PLAY: CRIMSON CORSAIR
Landing Site

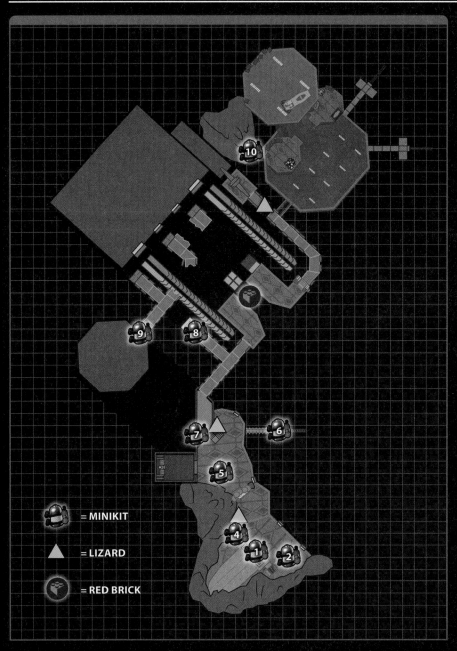

= MINIKIT

= LIZARD

= RED BRICK

Minikit 4
Shake loose a Minikit from the thruster pod with the Force.

Minikit 5
The left option for Multi-Build bricks is a drilling droid. It punches through the concrete and pulls up a Minikit.

Minikit 6
Step off the edge of the concrete across from the staircase that was covered in green gas. Carefully move out to the Minikit at the end of the walkway.

Minikit 7
The First Order terminal beyond the gas-filled walkway operates a vending machine that dispenses one Minikit.

Minikit 8
Dark side Force powers are required to rip off the cover of the large fan and expose the Minikit behind it.

Minikit 9
Follow the upper walkway to a large storage container with a grapple handle on its door. Pull open the door and claim the Minikit inside.

Minikit 10
After the platform carrying stormtroopers crashes, get up to the landing pad and tag in a character with Force powers. Pull the platform with the Minikit down to the ground.

IMPERIAL INACCURACY
Send the Multi-Build bricks to the right of the energy field. After the energy field fades, clear out everything to reveal the Red Brick.

Minikit 1
Pull open the ship's cargo hatch with the grapple handle.

Minikit 2
Turn around at the start of the level. Knock down the rock attached to the cliff face with gold LEGO bricks to plug the geyser.

Minikit 3
Blast three crystal lizards found around the area.

TROUBLE OVER TAUL

Corvette Interior

CAPTAIN PHASMA, FN-2199, 0-MR1

STORY MODE CHARACTERS UNLOCKED (FREE)

 Captain Phasma

 FN-2199

 0-MR1

VEHICLES UNLOCKED (FREE)

 Sterdic Star (and Microfighter)

 Vulptereen 412 Podracer

COMPLETED MINIKIT VEHICLE

 Imperial Shuttle (and Microfighter)

TAKE COVER

This chapter opens with a bang! Resistance soldiers open fire immediately. There's nothing to pick up before engaging in the Blaster Battle, so take cover as quickly as possible.

BLASTER BATTLE

Your first objective is to clear 18 Resistance soldiers from the corridor. After the first few fall, your party pushes forward. Keep Captain Phasma on the left-hand side, where she can make use of the scan location that pops up.

Scan the silver door with a valve wheel on the right-hand wall to reveal gold LEGO bricks. Target those bricks with Captain Phasma's blaster rifle to clear out the remaining Resistance forces.

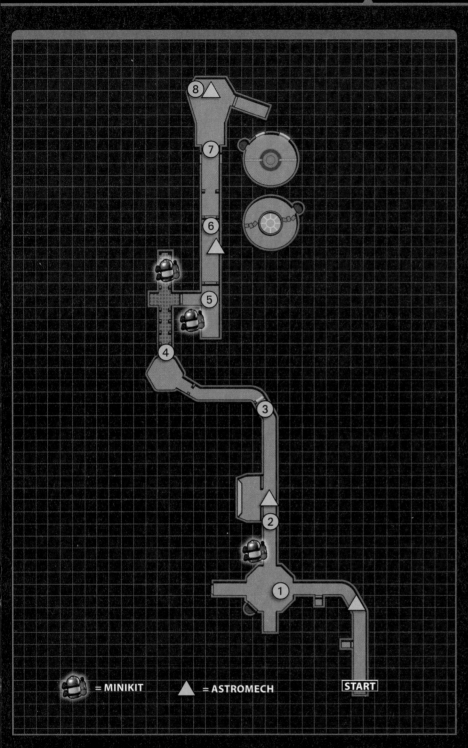

= MINIKIT   ▲ = ASTROMECH   START

MINIKIT:
DESTROY ALL ASTROMECHS

Watch for four astromechs scurrying around the interior of the car. The tricky one to find is in the final hallway up in the ceiling.

MINIKIT:
JANITORIAL PROTOCOL

Tag to 0-MR1, then input the correct sequence on the protocol access terminal to open the door to the janitor's supply closet.

The path ahead ends at a fire ②. Switch to FN-2199, whose Riot Baton can break through cracked bricks, and open a path around the flames.

Switch to Captain Phasma. Target the grapple handle next to the monitor and shake loose the bricks needed to build a protocol access terminal. After 0-MR1 matches the inputs correctly, a fire suppression system kicks in and clears out the flames blocking the path.

Get to the Bridge

The following hallway is clear of enemies. Blow open the gold LEGO blast door ③ at the end with Captain Phasma's rifle. Resistance forces wait for you at an open area at the end of the next hallway segment. Blast the blue control panels on either side of the energy field blocking a doorway to shut it off.

SEARCH THE SHIP

Hurry down the hall that's empty, save for a lone astromech droid. Explosive decompression ends a potential encounter with Resistance soldiers before it begins ①.

There's nothing else to do in this open area until you return in Free Play. Follow the hallway on the right after crushing any Resistance soldiers who appear.

BLASTER BATTLE

Stepping through to the following hallway ④ starts up a wild ride where the walls and ceiling take turns serving as the floor.

Each time the floor spins, your objective changes. First, eliminate five Resistance soldiers. The next turn pushes your target number to 15. The final obstacle is a Resistance trooper hauling a heavy blaster.

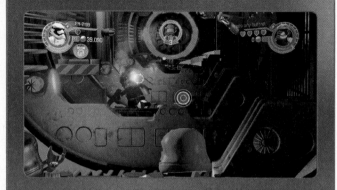

MINIKIT:
HULL SPINNING

Watch for a gold LEGO object on a wall while battling through the spinning hallways. Target it after the first spin. You can't come back to get it.

The last spin deposits your group in a hallway ⑤. Don't be fooled by the relative calm. The way ahead becomes increasingly hazardous.

MINIKIT:
CRACKED BLOCK BACKTRACK

Return down the hall, away from the blast doors, for another cracked block. There's a Minikit in the room behind the cracked block.

At the next closed door ⑥, scan the panel on the right to reveal a cracked brick. Break open the brick to expose a grapple handle for Captain Phasma to pull. Explosive decompression tears out part of the hull ahead.

In order to continue safely toward the bridge, target the grapple handle on the ceiling and pull the building bricks to where your group can put them to use. Turn the valve wheel on the new control panel to restore the hull's integrity.

Continue forward to the door that leads to the bridge ⑦. Open the door with the protocol access terminal. Send in Captain Phasma to dispose of the Resistance soldiers and destroy the central computer in order to scan the computer bank on the left side of the bridge ⑧.

CHARACTERS NOW AVAILABLE FOR PURCHASE

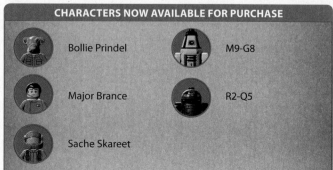

Bollie Prindel

M9-G8

Major Brance

R2-Q5

Sache Skareet

FREE PLAY:
TROUBLE OVER TAUL

Corvette Interior

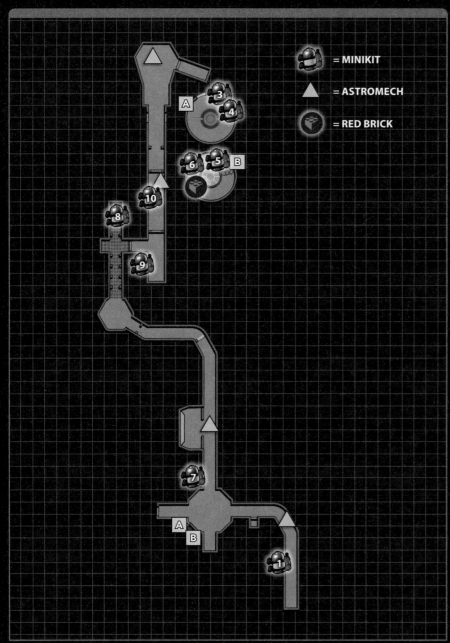

Minikit 3
The Resistance terminal opens an access ladder. Ascend the ladder and sit in the gunner seat to start a minigame where you shoot meteors.

Minikit 4
In the same room as the meteor minigame, melt the ice surrounding the Minikit.

Minikit 5
Descend the access ladder opened by the Resistance terminal. Extricate the Minikit from the wiring with dark side Force powers.

Minikit 6
Use the Force to shake loose the bricks to build a Minikit from a vending machine.

Minikit 7
Open the door to the janitor's supply closet with the protocol access terminal.

Minikit 8
Watch for a gold LEGO object on the wall while battling through the spinning hallways.

Minikit 9
Return down the hall after the tumbling battle for a cracked block. There's a Minikit in the room behind the cracked block.

Minikit 10
Use the Force to pull down the Minikit from the wrecked ceiling.

COMBAT BAR REGEN

Descend the access ladder opened with the Resistance terminal. The Red Brick is protected by coolant pouring from a broken pipe. Only a character with Immunity (Cold), such as a droid, can get it.

Minikit 1
Toss an explosive device at the silver LEGO door where the Blaster Battle ends to open a storage closet. Destroy the crate that falls out to reveal the bricks required to build this Minikit.

Minikit 2
Watch out for four astromechs scurrying around the interior of the car. Blast them all to get a Minikit.

Ottegan Pursuit

FIRST ORDER COMMAND SHUTTLE, SPECIAL FORCES TIE FIGHTER

TRUE JEDI REQUIREMENT
175,000

STORY MODE CHARACTERS UNLOCKED (FREE)

 Kylo Ren

VEHICLES UNLOCKED (FREE)

 Ottegan Defense Ship

 Ottegan Defense Fighter (Microfighter)

COMPLETED MINIKIT VEHICLE

 Imperial TIE fighter (and Microfighter)

CITY STRIKE

The action starts with Kylo Ren and Captain Phasma flying through a city built on floating islands. They are in pursuit of a shielded Resistance transport. You have limited control over where your ships fly, so focus on destroying the Resistance vessels to boost your multiplier while collecting studs.

MINIKIT: THREE TRANSPORTS

Non-shielded transports pop up in this initial area, including two that appear when the chapter begins. Shoot down three of these transports to earn a Minikit.

MINIKIT: INNER RIM

When you briefly leave the city and fly through the inner rim, grab the Minikit floating in a ring of gold studs.

SHOOT DOWN 15 FIGHTERS

Captain Phasma notes the Resistance ships are trying to escape. You gain more control over your ships and must shoot down 15 fighters. The Ottegan Defense Fighters are protecting the dwellings built atop floating islands, but they're not robust vehicles. One to two shots are enough to destroy them.

MINIKIT:
TIMED RUN

Start a timed run by flying through the purple sphere between the floating islands. You must fly through the series of spheres before the timer expires.

DESTROY FIVE SIEGE ENGINES

Resistance X-wings appear on the scene just as the Ottegan forces roll out siege engines, and Kylo Ren couldn't be happier. Only the proton torpedoes released by dispensers and carried by the X-wings are capable of destroying the siege engines.

Pick up torpedoes placed on top of the floating islands indicated by pink arrows. With a torpedo in tow, fly toward a pink target, which indicates a siege engine. When a siege engine is in range, tap the indicated button to launch the proton torpedo at it. Take out the five siege engines in this way.

CHASE THE COMMAND TRANSPORT

Destroying the final siege engine flushes out the command transport. It begins with 100% shielding, but each time you hit it, the number drops by 20. When its shielding hits 0%, it's forced to land.

Don't lose track of the other Resistance fighters while focusing on the transport. The X-wings and Ottegan Defense Fighters are still gunning for your ships.

Ottegan Surface

CAPTAIN PHASMA, KYLO REN

OVERCOME THE DEFENSES

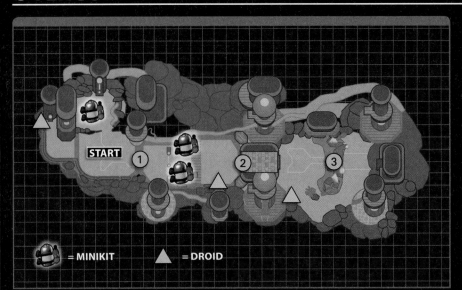

START   ①   ②   ③

= MINIKIT   ▲ = DROID

To reach the now-crashed command transport, you must overcome a few defensive measures. First, there's a sturdy wall ① to destroy. Before you can get to the wall, you must defeat 15 Resistance soldiers.

A hovering missile launcher appears next. Tag to Kylo Ren and use the Force to toss around missiles for fun. When that becomes tiresome, shoot the missile launcher with one of its own missiles. It crashes into the wall's power source with an impressive explosion.

PHASMA'S FIGHTER

Open the cockpit on Captain Phasma's Special Forces TIE fighter with the Force.

GOIN' FISHIN'

The right-hand option with the Multi-Build bricks is a fishing pole that retrieves a Minikit.

MISSILE MISDIRECTION

Take control of an incoming missile and guide it into the wrecked ship made from silver LEGO bricks.

TARGET PRACTICE

Shoot down three green droids flying above the fighting. They won't appear until after you defeat the initial 15 Resistance soldiers.

Clear away the remnants of the wall with the Force to get a sneak preview of what lies ahead. The next line of defense is a wall guarded by two turrets and toxic gas. Keep Kylo Ren clear of the gas, then manipulate the left turret to blast the wall.

The Resistance has a strong presence at this wall, so work as quickly as you can. Tag to Captain Phasma, whose blaster overheats the gold LEGO base of a tower in front of another wall. When assembled in front of the wall, the Multi-Build bricks become a motor that brings up a rack of explosive canisters made from gold LEGO bricks.

Use the Force to position a canister in front of the wall ahead. Blast the canister with Captain Phasma's blaster until it explodes and takes out the wall.

The final wall ② is guarded by blaster turrets atop towers, and the door is locked with four grapple handles. Your first task is to handle the turrets.

Blast the gold LEGO locks on the large wooden barrels to shake them loose. Grab the barrels with the Force and slam them into the turrets.

A First Order troop transport lands long enough to disembark a trio of stormtroopers. Captain Phasma can command the stormtroopers to assist in opening the door and its four grapple handles.

A large chunk of debris blocks the far end of a short hallway. Switch to Kylo Ren and cut a hole in it with his lightsaber.

CAPTURE THE OTTEGAN COMMANDER

When Kylo Ren and Captain Phasma breach the wall, the Ottegan Commander ③ deploys a shield and a rocket launcher. He's also protected by a few Resistance and Ottegan soldiers.

To crack the Commander's defense, target the gold power node cover on the right with Captain Phasma's blaster. The left-hand power node cover calls for dark side Force powers.

After removing the covers, grab incoming rockets using the Force and guide them into the exposed power nodes, which are made from silver LEGO bricks. Resistance reinforcements drop in after each node is destroyed.

With both nodes destroyed, the Commander's shield fails. He closes the hatch on his ship, but Kylo Ren can easily rip it off and pull the Commander to the ground.

CHARACTERS NOW AVAILABLE FOR PURCHASE

Kaydel Ko Connix

Pamich Nerro Goode

Trentus Savay

Ottegan Acolyte

Praster Barrun

Ottegan Warrior

Praster Ommlen

FREE PLAY: OTTEGAN ASSAULT

Ottegan Pursuit

Minikit 1
Unshielded transports pop up in this initial area, including two that appear when the chapter begins. Shoot down three of these transports to earn a Minikit.

Minikit 2
When you briefly leave the city and fly through the inner rim, grab the Minikit floating in a ring of gold studs.

Minikit 3
Start a timed run by flying through the purple sphere between the floating islands. You must fly through the series of spheres before the timer expires.

Ottegan Surface

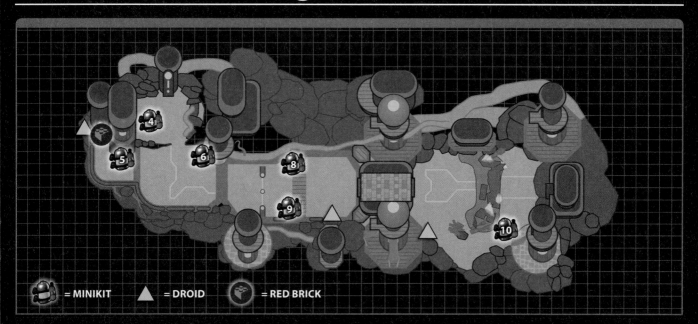

= MINIKIT   ▲ = DROID   = RED BRICK

Minikit 4
Open the cockpit on Captain Phasma's Special Forces TIE fighter with the Force.

Minikit 5
The Resistance terminal behind the starting point opens the rattling door next to it.

Minikit 6
Jump into the dive pool in front of the first defensive wall.

Minikit 7
Shoot down three green droids flying above the fighting. They won't appear until after you defeat the initial 15 Resistance soldiers.

Minikit 8
Target the silver LEGO bricks inside the wrecked ship at the end of the third defensive wall. You can also use the Force to guide a missile from the defense droid into it.

Minikit 9
The right-hand option with the Multi-Build bricks here is a fishing pole that brings up a Minikit.

Minikit 10
While confronting the Ottegan Commander in his ship, send a character immune to toxic gas, such as Finn, through the green cloud to pick up the Minikit behind the wreckage.

EXPLOSIVE BOLTS

Go around the building behind the starting point. Target the cracked block with a character like FN-2199 and smash it open. Go inside the door and pick up the Red Brick.

HUB:
D'QAR
Points of Interest

D'Qar is a large Resistance base. At the medical building, you can view the characters you've unlocked after collecting carbonite and create your custom characters. If you prefer to purchase your Red Bricks from a person rather than through a menu, he's near the back of the command center.

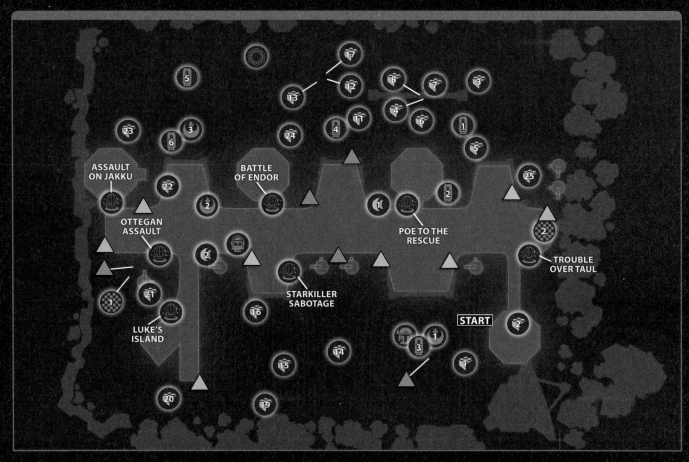

COLLECTIBLES	
Gold Bricks: 42	Carbonite: 6

RACES
Race 1: Requires Poe's Blue X-wing (Microfighter)
Race 2: Any Microfighter

TERMINALS	
The Battle of Endor	Trouble over Taul (50 Gold Bricks Required)
Assault on Jakku	
Starkiller Sabotage	Ottegan Assault (60 Gold Bricks Required)
Luke's Island	
Poe to the Rescue (10 Gold Bricks Required)	

 = CARBONITE

= REPLAY TERMINAL

= BOUNTY HUNTER

= FIRST ORDER

= GENERAL QUEST

= PROTOCOL DROID

= RESISTANCE

= GOLD BRICK

= GONK DROID

= GENERATOR

= SATELLITE DISH

 = RACE

Carbonite

CARBONITE 1

Unlocks Gray Squadron Pilot
Skills needed: Lightsaber, Immunity (Cold)

In the cantina, cut through the glass door with a lightsaber. Switch to a character able to handle the cold, like a snowtrooper, to get inside the freezer.

CARBONITE 2

Unlocks Admiral Ackbar (Classic)
Skills needed: Agile/Jet pack, Aquatic

Double-jump or jet pack from the landing pad for Ackbar's Starfighter to the nearby fuel storage tank. There's a dive pool atop the tank with carbonite inside.

CARBONITE 3

Unlocks Princess Leia (Classic)
Skills needed: Astromech, Force Powers

Inside the command building, interact with the astromech access to generate a hologram. Use the Force to move carbonite from inside the hologram to where you can collect it.

CARBONITE 4

Unlocks A-Wing Pilot
Skills needed: Grapple Gun (x2)

Switch to two characters with grapple guns and enter the barracks. Pull open the locker next to a bed.

CARBONITE 5

Unlocks Rebel Fleet Trooper
Skills needed: Charge Up, Sharpshooter

Go to the shooting range. The power jack starts up a target in the back of the range. Hit the target three times and it drops carbonite. Don't fire until the target pauses its movement.

CARBONITE 6

Unlocks Zev Senesca
Skills needed: Silver LEGO

Visit the shooting range and plant an explosive on the silver LEGO containers mixed in with the munitions.

Gold Bricks

GOLD BRICK 1

Skills needed: Sharpshooter

Shoot three mynocks off an antenna above the command center. The Gold Brick pops up in a nearby hangar. The cutscene that plays after the satellite moves shows you where to go.

GOLD BRICK 2

Skills needed: Charge Up

Smash the containers in front of the quadjumper engine to get the bricks needed to attach a power jack to the engine. Charge the jack to get the Gold Brick.

GOLD BRICK 3

Skills needed: Gold LEGO, Aquatic

Get to the roof of the cantina. Switch to a character that can destroy gold LEGO bricks and destroy the large chest. A quick dip in the now-exposed dive pool yields a Gold Brick.

GOLD BRICK 4

Skills needed: None

Walk on the pipe connecting two buildings. The Gold Brick is between two short obstacles.

GOLD BRICK 5

Skills needed: BB-8

On the cantina roof, smash 16 sets of cylinders colored like BB-8. The countdown restarts at 15 seconds each time a set is smashed.

GOLD BRICK 6

Skills needed: BB-8

In the field behind Admiral Ackbar's starfighter, destroy nine cylinders in under 15 seconds.

GOLD BRICK 7

Skills needed: Thaw LEGO

Bring a character with a flamethrower to thaw out the hapless Resistance technician standing in front of a freezing mist.

GOLD BRICK 8

Skills needed: Cracked LEGO

Break open the cracked LEGO in the field behind Admiral Ackbar's starfighter.

GOLD BRICK 9

Skills needed: Don't use an astromech droid!

Rebuild five Gonk droids.

GOLD BRICK 10

Skills needed: Don't use an astromech droid!

Tear down and rebuild three generators.

GOLD BRICK 11

Skills needed: Force Powers

Use the Force to move the mini X-wing on the ceiling of the barracks until it flies off and comes back to destroy the mini Deathstar.

GOLD BRICK 12

Skills needed: None

The scanner next to the locked doors at the back of the barracks can only be opened by someone wearing Princess Leia's hair. Break down the dark column on the other end of the doors. Build a hat dispenser and select Leia's hair.

GOLD BRICK 13

Skills needed: None

Jump and pull down the hanging bar near a commode surrounded by green gas.

GOLD BRICK 14

Skills needed: Protocol Droid

Use the protocol droid terminal in either the command center or medical building to open a tunnel between them. A Gold Brick is inside the tunnel.

GOLD BRICK 15

Skills needed: Resistance

The Resistance terminal in the medical building is attached to an x-ray machine. Whoever picks up the Gold Brick inside the machine is in for a jolt!

GOLD BRICK 16

Skills needed: Force Powers

At the entrance to the medical building, shock awake the sleeping pilot by using the Force on the nearby medical device.

GOLD BRICK 17

Skills needed: Silver LEGO

The flower garden on top of the barrack's roof needs watering. Move to the next roof via a grassy walkway. Blow up the silver LEGO container on the roof. Return to the flower garden with the valve wheel needed to turn on the water.

GOLD BRICK 18

Skills needed: BB-8

Power up five satellite dishes with nearby rotary controls.

GOLD BRICK 19

Skills needed: Force Powers

A Resistance pilot made a mess with his rooftop picnic atop the medical building. Use the Force to float three objects in the tall grass back to him.

GOLD BRICK 20

Skills needed: Quadnoculars, Silver LEGO

Scan the generators behind the Millennium Falcon. Plant a thermal detonator to destroy the revealed silver LEGO bricks.

GOLD BRICK 21

Skills needed: Charge Up

Charge the power jack in front of the Millennium Falcon.

GOLD BRICK 22

Skills needed: BB-8

You probably collected this Gold Brick before Poe Dameron took off for Jakku. If you missed it then, use the launch pad to get up to it now.

GOLD BRICK 23

Skills needed: BB-8

At the end of the landing pads, smash 17 sets of cylinders colored like BB-8. The countdown restarts at 15 seconds each time a set is smashed.

GOLD BRICK 24

Skills needed: Grapple Gun

Pull the grapple handle on the vent behind the blue X-wing's landing pad.

GOLD BRICK 25

Skills needed: Gold LEGO

Blast open the gold LEGO spire near the fuel tanks.

Quests

QUEST—BOUNTY HUNTER

Skills needed: Scan

Caluan Ematt in the command building wants to idenfity a First Order spy. Investigate the band playing in the cantina. After identifying the spy, you must defeat two Unkar goons and two Unkar thugs.

QUEST—FIRST ORDER

Skills needed: None

The disguised First Order spy needs someone to fly a stolen X-wing back to Starkiller Base. You must first complete a sphere course. Unfortunately, she neglected to inform the First Order about her plan, so the Starkiller Base defenses will fire on you! After completing the course, shoot down 20 TIE fighters.

QUEST—GENERAL 1

Skills needed: None

Agree to help the X-wing pilot and the scene shifts to the same area as the final battle in Poe to the Rescue. Shoot down 20 marauders, who often use the mynocks as cover.

QUEST— GENERAL 2

Skills needed: None

After accepting the quest, your crew flies to Arthon. Two groups of raiders are attacking the floating cities. For the first wave, shoot down 15 Jakku scavengers. The second wave is bulkier ships. Shoot down ten, while also tangling with additional Jakku scavengers.

QUEST— PROTOCOL DROID

Skills needed: None

A protocol droid is necessary to speak with the pilot in green outside the command building. Your task is to destroy three radio-controlled TIE fighters while operating an X-wing microfighter.

QUEST— RESISTANCE 1

Skills needed: None

General Leia needs a crack commando team to infiltrate Starkiller Base and obtain something of vital importance. To reach your objective, you must complete a Blaster Battle against First Order snowtroopers and stormtroopers. Go through the large opened door behind them to collect your prize.

QUEST—RESISTANCE 2

Skills needed: None

A Resistance officer is concerned with the toughness of his soldiers. He wants someone to spar with three groups of five troops. The groups are increasingly more skilled. The first group is novices, while the final group is seasoned veterans.

QUEST—RESISTANCE 3

Skills needed: None

Speak with the trainer inside the shooting range. The targets pop up and drop down quickly, so you need to be ready to hit them as soon as they appear. Shoot ten targets to complete the quest.

HUB:
JAKKU
Points of Interest

The main hubs of activity on Jakku are Tekka Village (which was destroyed during Assault on Jakku) and Niima Outpost. Get to know these locations, as you will be traveling between them often.

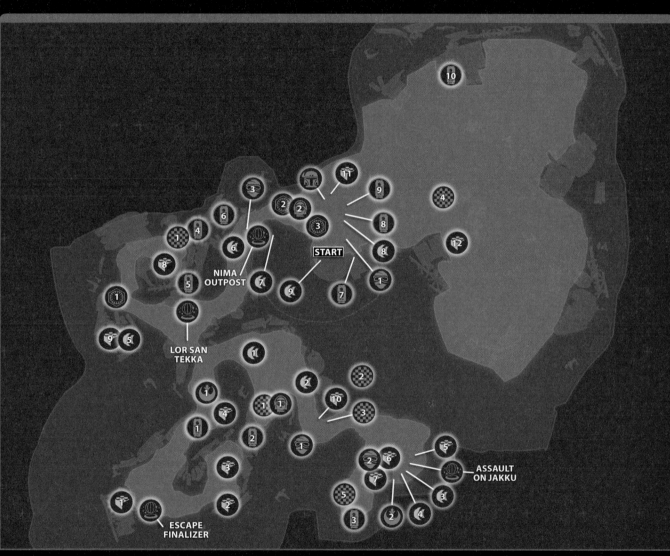

NIMA OUTPOST

START

LOR SAN TEKKA

ASSAULT ON JAKKU

ESCAPE FINALIZER

COLLECTIBLES	
Gold Bricks: 54	Carbonite: 10

TERMINALS	
Assault on Jakku	Niima Outpost
Escape from the Finalizer	Lor San Tekka's Return (20 Gold Bricks Required)

RACES	
Race 1: Any Microfighter	Race 4: Any Microfighter
Race 2: Any Microfighter	Race 5: Any Microfighter
Race 3: Any Microfighter	Race 6: Any Agile Character

= CARBONITE

= GENERAL QUEST

= RACE

= BOUNTY HUNTER

= RESISTANCE

= REPLAY TERMINAL

= PROTOCOL DROID

= SCAVENGER

= FIRST ORDER

= GOLD BRICK

Carbonite

CARBONITE 1

Unlocks Padmé Amidala
Skills needed: Gold LEGO

Destroy the gold LEGO bricks near the quicksand pit. The revealed grip handles lead to a small platform suspended from the roof.

CARBONITE 2

Unlocks Greedo
Skills needed: Grapple Gun,
**   Force Powers**

Use the grapple handle attached to the scaffolding to land atop the scaffolding. Now use Force powers to knock over a white case that has carbonite inside.

CARBONITE 3

Unlocks Emperor Palpatine
Skills needed: Aquatic

Jump into the dive pool.

CARBONITE 4

Unlocks Obi Wan Kenobi (Classic)
Skills needed: Agile, Lightsaber,
**   Immunity (Toxic)**

Jump to the two hanging bars to reach a walkway on the scaffolding near an ice cream dispenser. Ascend the climb wall, then cut through the door with a lightsaber. The carbonite is inside a cloud of green gas.

CARBONITE 5

Unlocks Jawa
Skills needed: Grapple Gun (x2),
**   Gold LEGO, Immunity (Toxic)**

You need two characters with grapple guns to open the door, but there's a second door behind it, made from gold LEGO bricks. The carbonite is inside a cloud of green gas.

CARBONITE 6

Unlocks Anakin Skywalker (Podracer)
Skills needed: None

Defeat 12 Unkar goons to obtain a valve wheel. Take the wheel to the door in the back to open it.

CARBONITE 7

Unlocks Bith
Skills needed: Astromech,
**   BB-8**

Break apart the spare parts near the Millennium Falcon, which contain Multi-Build bricks. Build an astromech access on the wall, which knocks down a pipe. Rebuild the astromech access into a power jack on the pole.

CARBONITE 8

Unlocks Boba Fett
Skills needed: None

To bypass the scanner in the central building of Niima Outpost, break apart the large containers and construct a hat dispenser. Choose the stormtrooper helmet and return for a scan.

CARBONITE 9

Unlocks Tusken Raider
Skills needed: Force Powers

Use the Force to brush grime from carbonite hanging on a wall inside the central building of Niima Outpost.

CARBONITE 10

Unlocks Luke Skywalker
**   (Episode IV)**
Skills needed: None

The lonely carbonite beyond Niima Outpost is inside the wreck of a large ship, near the rancor.

Gold Bricks

GOLD BRICK 1

Skills needed: Force Powers, Aquatic

Use Force powers to build a ladder. Climb to the scaffolding, which has a dive pool in the back.

GOLD BRICK 2

Skills needed: Silver LEGO

Use explosives to clear away the blockage made from silver LEGO bricks.

GOLD BRICK 3

Skills needed: Force Powers

Pull the droid from under the sand with Force powers.

GOLD BRICK 4

Skills needed: Grapple Gun

Aim for the grapple handle to pull down a destroyed turret.

GOLD BRICK 5

Skills needed: Quadnoculars, Lightsaber, First Order

Scan the door of the hut to reveal cut lines. Operate the First Order terminal inside the hut to obtain the Gold Brick.

GOLD BRICK 6

Skills needed: Force Powers

Rebuild the village's communication array with the Force.

GOLD BRICK 7

Skills needed: Charge Up

Break apart the container outside the raised hut. Send the Multi-Build bricks against the house to make a power jack, which opens up the hut. Rebuild the Multi-Build bricks into a trampoline. Eliminate 15 Womp Rats inside the home.

GOLD BRICK 8

Skills needed: None

Fight through the Teedo resistance, then climb a ladder attached to scaffolding. Bounce on the trampoline to reach the next level. Hop up the jump points to reach the top. Grab the Gold Brick and zipline back down.

GOLD BRICK 9

Skills needed: Cracked LEGO

Break through the cracked brick door. Walk up the ramp behind the door to reach the Gold Brick.

GOLD BRICK 10

Skills needed: Jetpack

Jump from the end of the ramp and jetpack into the Gold Brick floating high in the air.

GOLD BRICK 11

Skills needed: Force Powers, Charge Up

Use the Force to clear junk from the two power jacks around the door to the central building of Niima Outpost. A ship swoops in and drops a crate nearby. The crate has a Gold Brick inside.

GOLD BRICK 12

Skills needed: Dark Side Force Powers

To reach the Gold Brick behind Niima Outpost, tear down the tower with dark side Force powers.

Quests

QUEST— BOUNTY HUNTER 1

Skills needed: None

Defeat 20 thugs on Takodana (transport there is automatic), then take down Grummgar.

QUEST— FIRST ORDER 1

Skills needed: Astromech Droid

First Order transmitter dishes are under attack by Resistance saboteurs. Find three transmitters and drive away the saboteurs attacking them. Destroy the crates near the transmitter, which contain the bricks needed to build astromech access points.

QUEST— FIRST ORDER 2

Skills needed: Quadnoculars

Find three spies disguised as stormtroopers.

QUEST—FIRST ORDER 3

Skills needed: None

This is a flying mission that takes place in the Jakku Graveyard. While piloting a TIE fighter, shoot down 15 old Rebellion fighters. A wave of five B-wings is up next. The other fighters are still around, but only B-wings count toward your total.

QUEST—GENERAL 1

Skills needed: BB-8

Guide BB-8 through an agility course before the timer hits zero.

QUEST—GENERAL 2

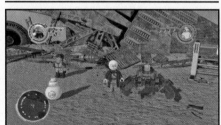

Skills needed: None

Test drive a Podracer by guiding it through highlighted checkpoints before the timer hits zero. Each checkpoint you reach increases your timer by ten seconds.

QUEST—GENERAL 3

Skills needed: None

Near a dive pool, build a giant mobile of lights that brings nightwatchers to the surface. Hit ten heads to give the villager a good night's sleep.

QUEST—GENERAL 4

Skills needed: None

The bloggin racer can't train with his prized mount and asks for help. Hop on his surprisingly small mount and complete a timed course around the center of the village.

QUEST—GENERAL 5

Skills needed: None

Scavengers have stolen a bloggin. Defeat 15 scavengers in the nearby Teedo area to reclaim the man's prized pet.

QUEST—GENERAL 6

Skills needed: None

Complete a timed run around a Star Destroyer with active defenses. After completing the run, shoot down ten TIE fighters.

QUEST—GENERAL 7

Skills needed: None

After accepting the quest, a pile of Multi-Bricks appears. You can build a fast speeder with poor handling (right-hand choice), or a slower speeder with good handling (left-hand choice). After making your choice, complete a timed race.

QUEST—GENERAL 8

Skills needed: None

Unkar Plutt wants an item of historical significance (he claims) retrieved from scavengers. Engage in a Blaster Battle to claim the AT-ST.

QUEST— GENERAL 9

Skills needed: None

Complete a timed race around Takodana Skies.

QUEST— PROTOCOL DROID 1

Skills needed: Quadnoculars, Jetpack

To retrieve the X-wing pilot suit, scan the crash site directly across from the alien who gave the quest. The scan reveals the three pieces you need, as well as a field of explosive mines. The safest way to reach the parts is to jetpack over the top of the mines.

QUEST— PROTOCOL DROID 2

Skills needed: Astromech, BB-8

Go to the back of Tekka Village. Break apart the orange and white object, which becomes Multi-Build bricks. Build a rotary control between the large solar panels and align the panels. Rebuild the bricks into an astomech access on the control panel, which diverts power into a nearby ice cream machine.

QUEST—RESISTANCE 1

Skills needed: None

Fly in an X-wing around the Finalizer and shoot down 15 TIE fighters. The second wave is 10 Special Forces TIE fighters. Standard TIE fighters remain in the area, but only Special Forces fighters count.

QUEST—RESISTANCE 2

Skills needed: None

The First Order intercepted a vital shipment of ice cream. The shipment is at Niima Outpost, where you must defeat 20 stormtroopers to secure the prize.

QUEST—SCAVENGER 1

Skills needed: Thaw LEGO

Before you can get this quest, you need to melt the ice block covering the Tuanul Villager. Track down the steelpecker birds, which are not far from the Escape from the Finalizer replay terminal. Defeated birds drop the parts needed to complete the quest.

QUEST—SCAVENGER 2

Skills needed: BB-8

The parts the villager wants are near the quicksand area. Build a rotary control not far from the ice cream machine. The rotary control moves a magnet attached to a crane arm, which pulls the necessary parts from under the sand.

QUEST—SCAVENGER 3

Skills needed: None

Defeat 16 Teedos (15 in an initial wave, then a fight against their leader). Pick up the Rodian Scavenger's missing part after the battle ends.

QUEST—SCAVENGER 4

Skills needed: None

Pick up sweet treats for a Tuanul Villager in Niima Outpost.

HUB:
TAKODANA

Points of Interest

Water makes up a good portion of Takodana's map. Characters who end up in the water are returned to shore. However, microfighters are able to zoom over the water, allowing you to reach the area's islands. To return to land while piloting a microfighter, look for naturally-occurring ramps.

COLLECTIBLES	
Gold Bricks: 35	Carbonite: 8

RACES
Race 1: Any Microfighter
Race 2: Use Rey's Speeder (Microfighter)
Race 3: Any Microfighter

TERMINALS
Maz's Castle
Battle of Takodana
Crimson Corsair (40 Gold Bricks Required)

 = CARBONITE

 = GENERAL QUEST

= RACE

= REPLAY TERMINAL

= PROTOCOL DROID

= SCAVENGER

= BOUNTY HUNTER

= RESISTANCE

= FIRST ORDER

= GOLD BRICK

Carbonite

CARBONITE 1

Unlocks Qui Gon Jinn
Skills needed: Cracked LEGO
Smash the cracked brick.

CARBONITE 2

Unlocks Obi Wan Kenobi (Episode III)
Skills needed: Aquatic
Jump into the dive pool near the shore of the lake.

CARBONITE 3

Unlocks Rebel Commando
Skills needed: First Order
Use the First Order terminal to open the large container.

CARBONITE 4

Unlocks Yoda
Skills needed: Staff, Agile
A spinner switch in the ruins raises a platform. To reach the carbonite, ascend the climb wall.

CARBONITE 5

Unlocks Queen Amidala
Skills needed: Lightsaber
Cut through the door next to GA-97 with a lightsaber.

CARBONITE 6

Unlocks Princess Leia (Ewok Village)
Skills needed: None
Go up a staircase that ends with a button on a landing. Move one character on the button, which opens the door. Send your other character through the door to get the carbonite.

CARBONITE 7

Unlocks Stormtrooper (Classic)
Skills needed: Grapple Gun (x2)
A troop transport at the edge of the ruins has two grapple handles on its front ramp. Pull both handles at the same time to open the ramp.

CARBONITE 8

Unlocks Teebo
Skills needed: Grapple Gun, Force Manipulation
Pull the grapple handle above Grummgar to wake him. Defeat him in a fight, then use Force powers to open his bed.

Gold Bricks

GOLD BRICK 1

Skills needed: Force Powers

Use the Force to bloom five sprouts lining the path.

GOLD BRICK 2

Skills needed: None

Ride the zipline down to the lake.

GOLD BRICK 3

Skills needed: Staff, Agile

Build a trampoline under the twirl poles near the Millennium Falcon. Throw a staff into the empty socket, then bounce up and swing between the poles to reach the Gold Brick.

GOLD BRICK 4

Skills needed: Command (Resistance), Grapple Gun

Open the cockpit of a TIE fighter that crashed into the trees with an assist from a trio of Resistance soldiers.

GOLD BRICK 5

Skills needed: Gold LEGO

Blast the gold LEGO rocks at the base of the boulders blocking the path beyond the downed TIE fighters.

GOLD BRICK 6

Skills needed: BB-8, Grapple Gun, Force Manipulation

Raise three banners in the clearing near Maz Kanata and Grummgar.

GOLD BRICK 7

Skills needed: None

Look for hanging bars on the wall. Move to the left for the Gold Brick.

GOLD BRICK 8

Skills needed: None

Destroy five empty pedestals and rebuild them into statues.

GOLD BRICK 9

Skills needed: BB-8

Destroy the crate to the right of the crashed X-wing. Assemble the BB-8 zorb switch free the downed fighter.

GOLD BRICK 10

Skills needed: Force Powers

Shake the Gold Brick from the box atop the tree stump with the Force.

GOLD BRICK 11

Skills needed: Force Powers

Build a fishing rod and reel on the small dock. Use the Force to reel in a Gold Brick and bring it ashore.

GOLD BRICK 12

Skills needed: Grapple Gun

Pull the grapple handle to open the chest.

GOLD BRICK 13

Skills needed:
Cracked LEGO

Smash the cracked LEGO rock.

GOLD BRICK 14

Skills needed: Gold LEGO

Melt the statue crafted with Gold LEGO bricks to get a Gold Brick.

GOLD BRICK 15

Skills needed: BB-8

Smash 36 sets of cylinders colored to match BB-8 before the timer expires. Destroying a cylinder resets the timer to 20 seconds.

GOLD BRICK 16

Skills needed: BB-8

Smash 39 sets of cylinders colored to match BB-8 before the timer expires. Destroying a cylinder resets the timer to 20 seconds.

Quests

QUEST— FIRST ORDER

Skills needed: None

To reclaim the riot baton, look for Mi'no Teest in the clearing beyond the gold LEGO blockade and downed TIE fighter. Defeat ten of his cronies first, then take him down.

QUEST— GENERAL 1

Skills needed: None

You're given control of a ship flying in the Jakku Graveyard. Your first task is destroying five pieces of scrap, which don't shoot back. Next up is taking out ten Jakku Scavengers, which do shoot back, so be careful!

QUEST— GENERAL 2

Skills needed: None

Recreate the Battle of Yavin in Microfighter form. Shoot down six TIE fighters, four AT-ATs, and six Advance TIE fighters.

QUEST— GENERAL 3

Skills needed: None

Shoot down 20 Takodana skippers over the Takodana skies.

QUEST—PROTOCOL DROID 1

Skills needed: None

Defeat seven stormtroopers in the clearing up the path from the Millennium Falcon.

QUEST—PROTOCOL DROID 2

Skills needed: None

Protect Bazine Netal from four members of Kanjiklub.

QUEST—RESISTANCE

Skills needed: None

Pru Sweevant wants to deal another blow to the First Order. Use any microfighter to shoot down nine microfighter TIE fighters flying over the lake.

QUEST—SCAVENGER 1

Skills needed: None

Retrieve three artifacts from soldiers of Solculvis. You must defeat nine of them in a Blaster Battle.

HUB:
MILLENNIUM FALCON
Points of Interest

While the Millennium Falcon has the fewest collectibles of any hub, it does offer a challenge found nowhere else: Dejarik Battle.

DEJARIK BATTLE

Dejarik Battle pits four beasts from holochess against waves of enemies. You can swap between the giant Mantellian Savrip, the diminutive M'onnok, Kintan Strider, and Molator. When you complete Dejarik Battle, this quartet becomes available for use in Free Play.

COMPOSITION OF WAVES	
Wave I	15 Teedo
Wave II	9 stormtroopers and a flametrooper
Wave III	9 stormtroopers and Captain Phasma
Wave IV	9 bounty hunters and Varmik, then HURID-327
Wave V	9 stormtroopers and Kylo Ren
Wave VI	9 Kanjiclub and Guavians, then a rancor

There are 65 total enemies to defeat, and your offensive options are limited to punches and the general melee special attack when your Combat Bar is ready. The lack of ranged attacks is the toughest obstacle for you to overcome. A good rule of thumb is to save your Combat Bar attacks to take out enemies carrying blasters.

Work quickly to collect the shower of studs that pops up at the end of each wave. Attack the giant stud that appears after you complete the final wave for another bonus.

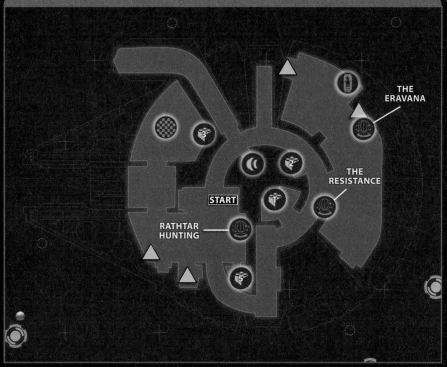

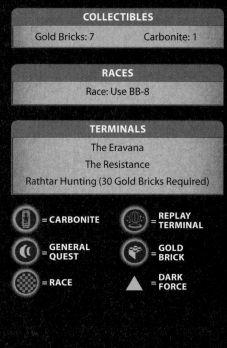

COLLECTIBLES	
Gold Bricks: 7	Carbonite: 1

RACES
Race: Use BB-8

TERMINALS
The Eravana
The Resistance
Rathtar Hunting (30 Gold Bricks Required)

= CARBONITE   = REPLAY TERMINAL

= GENERAL QUEST   = GOLD BRICK

= RACE   = DARK FORCE

Carbonite

CARBONITE 1

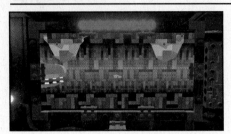

Unlocks Han Solo (Classic)
Skills needed: BB-8
Break apart the objects in the room near the terminal for The Eravana. Build a BB-8 interface, which allows you to play a video game. You must avoid the hazards and Exogorth to reach open space.

Gold Bricks

GOLD BRICK 1

Skills needed: Immunity (Toxic), Resistance
In a room filled with gas, turn the valve wheel to clear it out. Interact with the Resistance terminal to drop a Gold Brick from above.

GOLD BRICK 2

Skills needed: Immunity (Cold)
To thaw out the Gold Brick, bring in a character unfazed by cold who can also turn the valve wheel. Snowtroopers are a good choice.

GOLD BRICK 3

Skills needed: None
Clear out the debris in the corner near the race start point.

GOLD BRICK 4

Skills needed: Dark Side Force Powers
Use dark side Force powers to open four storage compartments found around the ship.

GOLD BRICK 5

Skills needed: Force Powers
The door next to the Rathtar Hunting replay terminal must be opened with Force powers. You don't need to defeat the training droids that spill out before you claim the Gold Brick.

Quests

QUEST—GENERAL 1

Skills needed: None
Descend the ladder to enter one of the Millennium Falcon's gun turrets. Blast ten asteroids to earn a Gold Brick.

HUB: STARKILLER BASE

Points of Interest

Other than the First Order base (where the action begins), the busiest area of Starkiller Base is the wide open parade grounds. Most races use some part of the parade ground, so become familiar with the area's layout and the location of the ships there.

STARKILLER DESTRUCTION

Starkiller Destruction is unlocked after you obtain 249 gold bricks. In Starkiller Destruction, you fly the Starkiller Base in a solar system and destroy planets. Use the Starkiller Destruction bonus level to build up a fortune in studs.

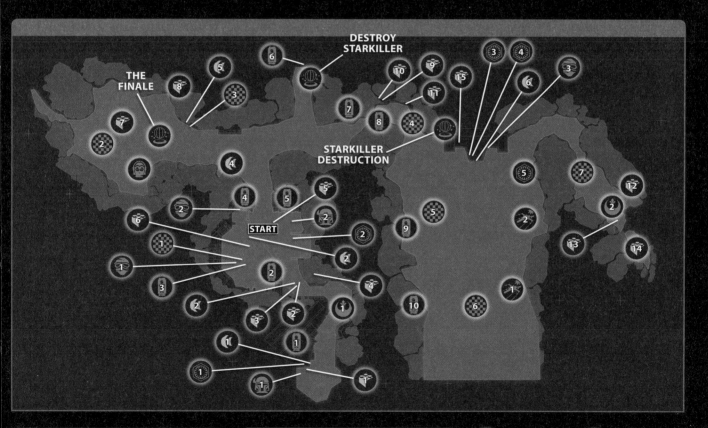

COLLECTIBLES
Gold Bricks: 55   Carbonite: 10

TERMINALS
Starkiller Sabotage
Destroy Starkiller Base
The Finale
Starkiller Destruction
(after collecting 249 Gold Bricks)

RACES
Race 1: Any Microfighter
Race 2: Use Wampa
Race 3: Any Microfighter
Race 4: Use First Order Snowspeeder Microfighter
Race 5: Any Microfighter
Race 6: Use Poe Dameron's X-wing Microfighter
Race 7: Any Microfighter

= CARBONITE
= GENERAL QUEST
= SCAVENGER
= BOUNTY HUNTER
= RESISTANCE
= RACE
= REPLAY TERMINAL
= PROTOCOL DROID
= SKIRMISH
= FIRST ORDER
= GOLD BRICK

Carbonite

CARBONITE 1

Unlocks Imperial Royal Guard
Skills needed: Cracked LEGO
Break through the cracked block near the TIE fighter landing pads. Eliminate the auto-guns before you enter the hall containing the carbonite.

CARBONITE 2

Unlocks Darth Maul
Skills needed: Agile
Reach the top of the wall by jumping between handles. Leap from the small platform to a pair of twirl poles that end at an even smaller platform under more handles. The handles lead to a platform with white arrows. Ride the air current from the arrows around a corner and the carbonite.

CARBONITE 3

Unlocks Count Dooku
Skills needed: Grapple Gun, BB-8
Use the grapple handle high up on the building at the north entrance to the main base to get up to the roof with with a turbolaser turret on top. Build a rotary control, which attaches to the turret. Blast the roof of a building across the courtyard to drop the carbonite to the ground.

CARBONITE 4

Unlocks Luke Skywalker (Stormtrooper)
Skills needed: Dark Side Force Powers, Charge Up
Rip the covering off a power jack atop an energy-shielded door with dark side Force powers. Power down the shield with the power jack.

CARBONITE 5

Unlocks Han Solo (Stormtrooper)
Skills needed: None
To reach the carbonite behind the energy shield, get a Kylo Ren helmet from the nearby hat dispenser and interact with the scanner.

CARBONITE 6

Unlocks Death Star Trooper
Skills needed: None
Destroy everything on the ledge with the Destroy Starkiller Base replay terminal. Assemble a mini TIE fighter and mini X-wing. After their brief battle, they leave behind carbonite.

CARBONITE 7

Unlocks TIE Interceptor Pilot
Skills needed: Thaw LEGO
Use the grip handles to reach a rocky ledge with a block of ice surrounding carbonite.

CARBONITE 8

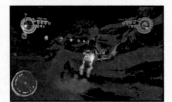

Unlocks Scout Trooper
Skills needed: Jetpack, Gold LEGO
From the ledge with the frozen carbonite, jetpack across the gap to the snowy area with gold LEGO rocks. Clear the rocks to open a steam vent. Ride the steam into the carbonite.

CARBONITE 9

Unlocks Anakin Skywalker
Skills needed: Force Powers, Aquatic
Use the Force to move the X-wing wreckage and uncover a dive pool. Hop into the pool to pull out carbonite.

CARBONITE 10

Unlocks Snowtrooper (Classic)
Skills needed: Cracked LEGO
Smash open the entrance to the cave to get to the carbonite inside.

Gold Bricks

GOLD BRICK 1

Skills needed: Quadnoculars, Agile

Scan the wall to reveal handholds. Scale the wall to reach a higher ledge. Ascend the ladder to enter the Command Tower with two quests and a Gold Brick.

GOLD BRICK 2

Skills needed: Thaw LEGO, Aquatic

Melt the ice covering the dive pool under the ramp.

GOLD BRICK 3

Skills needed: Grapple Gun (x2)

Pull both grapple handles at the top of the ramp to open a hatch.

GOLD BRICK 4

Skills needed: Small Access

An access hatch on the wall leads up to a ledge with a Gold Brick.

GOLD BRICK 5

Skills needed: Astromech

Power down the energy dome blocking access to the Gold Brick with the astromech access.

GOLD BRICK 6

Skills needed: Dark Side Force Powers

Tear open the hatch to the troop transport with dark side Force powers.

GOLD BRICK 7

Skills needed: None

Destroy five snowmen in the trees.

GOLD BRICK 8

Skills needed: Thaw LEGO

Melt the ice encasing the Gold Brick on a small, snowy ledge.

GOLD BRICK 9

Skills needed: Quadnoculars, Lightsaber

Scan the red bars to reveal cut lines. Cut through the bars with a lightsaber.

GOLD BRICK 10

Skills needed: Grapple Gun

Use the grapple handle to reach a snowy ledge atop the large doorway.

GOLD BRICK 11

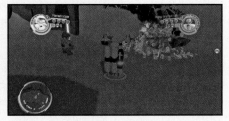

Skills needed: Thaw LEGO

Melt the ice encasing the stormtrooper and a First Order Snowspeeder Microfighter.

GOLD BRICK 12

Skills needed: Agile

Crack the rock near the steam vent and use the bricks to build a climb wall. Follow the snowy path to the edge.

GOLD BRICK 13

Skills needed: None
Pick up the Gold Brick on the narrow bridge spanning the gap.

GOLD BRICK 14

Skills needed: None
Defeat nine stormtroopers digging under the Millennium Falcon.

GOLD BRICK 15

Skills needed: BB-8
As BB-8, break 39 canisters before the timer expires. Each canister destroyed resets the timer to 20 seconds.

Quests

QUEST— BOUNTY HUNTER 1

Skills needed: Quadnoculars, Agile
To obtain this quest, you must reveal a climb wall with a scan, then climb a ladder. The quest sends you to the skies above Ottegan, where you must shoot down 20 Guavian Marauders.

QUEST— BOUNTY HUNTER 2

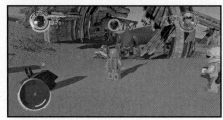

Skills needed: None
This quest leads to outside Niima Outpost on Jakku (the travel is automatic). Defeat the rancor in a fight to earn a Gold Brick. The rancor is a formidible enemy best fought with a blaster, from a safe distance.

QUEST— FIRST ORDER 1

Skills needed: None
Accepting General Hux's mission results in a trip to the Resistance base on D'Qar. Clear out Resistance forces in a Blaster Battle. Go into the barracks to eliminate the remaining Resistance soldiers and claim the base mascot.

QUEST—FIRST ORDER 2

Skills needed: First Order
In order to get in the room to fix the hot tub, use the nearby First Order terminal. Break the object in front of the hot tub to get a pile of Multi-Build bricks. Assemble the bricks into a power unit at three different locations in any order to complete the repair.

QUEST—FIRST ORDER 3

Skills needed: None
Recreate the Battle of Hoth by piloting a Rebel Alliance Snowspeeder Microfighter on the parade grounds. Destroy 10 Imperial Microfighters (AT-AT or TIE fighter) to complete the task.

QUEST—FIRST ORDER 4

Skills needed: None
Captain Phasma set up a training area in the parade ground. Take up a position behind a barricade and blast ten targets.

QUEST—FIRST ORDER 5

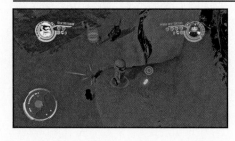

Skills needed: Grapple Gun
To help with marching in unison, the commander wants music. Get the music disc from the ledge just behind him.

QUEST—GENERAL 1

Skills needed: None

Fly in the sky above the oscillator and shoot down 15 Prana fighters attacking the First Order location. After the fifteenth fighter drops, a group of Guavian ships appears and you must shoot down seven of them. The battle becomes chaotic with three groups flying around, so learn to pick out targets by the color of their laser cannon fire.

QUEST—GENERAL 2

Skills needed: None

Follow the path up the ramp to a landing pad with two TIE fighters. Blast seven mynock from the TIE fighters or on the ground.

QUEST—GENERAL 3

Skills needed: None

Shoot down 15 Resistance X-wings over the oscillator. The next objective is to destroy five Resistance Command ships.

QUEST—GENERAL 4

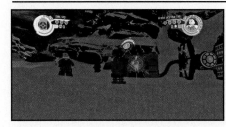

Skills needed: Charge Up

Follow the TIE Pilot's advice and repair the TIE fighter with the power jack. To earn the Gold Brick, run the TIE fighter through a timed course on the parade grounds.

QUEST—GENERAL 5

Skills needed: None

This snowball fight takes place under Blaster Battle rules. Set up behind a barricade and hit snowtroopers when they pop up from behind their barricades. Knock out ten snowtroopers to earn a Gold Brick.

QUEST—GENERAL 6

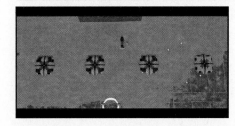

Skills needed: Command (First Order)

Note the order the platforms light up. Gather up the stormtroopers and guide them to the platforms in the same order. Stand on any of the red buttons to show the stormtroopers what to do.

QUEST—PROTOCOL DROID

Skills needed: None

Follow the R2 unit down the hill and protect it from a droid shakedown. Defeat 12 droids to earn a Gold Brick.

QUEST—RESISTANCE 1

Skills needed: Quadnoculars, Silver LEGO

Barricades have been set up near three troop transports. You must destroy all three transports to free the prisoners. Target the explosive canisters in front of the left and right transports to blow them up. Move to the far right-hand barricade and scan the center transport. Target the explsove canister with a thermal detonator to complete the task.

QUEST—RESISTANCE 2

Skills needed: Quadnoculars, Silver LEGO

After agreeing to help the trapped pilot, back up to the Scan spot and center on his cage. Toss an explosive to remove the silver LEGO bars. Defeat the Wampa after it comes out to investigate the noise.

QUEST—SCAVENGER 1

Skills needed: Quadnoculars, Grapple Gun (x2), Small Access

You must find missing sanitation equipment scattered around the base. Scan next to the quest giver for the first piece of equipment. Go through the access hatch near the energy-shielded doorway to get another. Destroy the equipment rack to the left of the dual grapple handles for the final pieces.

QUEST—SCAVENGER 2

Skills needed: First Order

For this quest, you must collect a variety of helmets. One helmet is at the top of a line of grip handles next to a large door. Two are behind First Order terminals (Kylo Ren's room and a facility north of the main base). For the six snowtrooper helmets, defeat a dozen mynocks near the Destroy Starkiller Base replay terminal.

QUEST—SCAVENGER 3

Skills needed: First Order, Small Access

Go directly north of the First Order base where a mouse droid zips into a building. Interact with the First Order terminal to drop the energy field. Go through the access hatch to reach the roof and take Captain Phasma's weapon from the tiny droid.

COLLECTIBLES CHECKLISTS

Story Mode Collectibles

MINIKITS

PROLOGUE: THE BATTLE OF ENDOR		
Got It?	#	Notes
	1	Multi-Build brick trampoline at start
	2	Use the Force on an insect hive
	3	Multi-Build brick lift
	4	Make musical instruments for Ewoks
	5	Blast three rock piles from an AT-ST
	6	Open an AT-ST hatch with three Rebellion soldiers
	7	BB-8 flies a ship to safety in a minigame
	8	Go through an access hatch while battling the Emperor
	9	Destroy five turbolaser towers
	10	Destroy the three blue pylons above the power core

CHAPTER I: ASSAULT ON JAKKU		
Got It?	#	Notes
	1	Build three barrels in Village Retreat
	2	Go bowling, shoot BB-8 like a basketball, and score a soccer goal
	3	Inside a raised home
	4	Destroy three silver LEGO towers during First Order Assault
	5	Use the Force on a downed water tower tank
	6	Sharpshoot a stormtrooper in a hut
	7	Dive pool near shielded stormtroopers
	8	Gold LEGO chest near flametrooper
	9	Pull strength handles on a hut

CHAPTER II: ESCAPE FROM THE FINALIZER		
Got It?	#	Notes
	1	Tickle the Gonk droid's feet with the Force
	2	Destroy four white droids
	3	Build a bridge under the command center
	4	Timed run that starts between decks of the Finalizer
	5	Destroy 22 large turrets
	6	Shoot down five Special Forces TIE fighters
	7	Behind red sparkling bricks; use dark side Force powers.
	8	Cut through a door with a lightsaber
	9	Hanging at the end of parallel pipes
	10	Send BB-8 up to a broken pipe

CHAPTER III: NIIMA OUTPOST		
Got It?	#	Notes
	1	Shoot three scavenger birds roosting on broken wings
	2	Restart the conveyor belt, then use it as a treadmill
	3	Behind a cracked brick near the buried droids
	4	Pull three droids from the sand with the Force
	5	Open a container with strength handles
	6	On a roof reached through a dive pool
	7	Under a mound of sand, uncovered by SN-1F4
	8	Blast the center of four arches
	9	Floating in a ring of studs
	10	Destroy three red-wrecks in the sand

Minikits continued on next page.

MINIKITS (CONTINUED)

CHAPTER IV: THE ERAVANA

Got It?	#	Notes
	1	Escape a rathtar in a the area beyond the protcol terminal
	2	On top of a container in the area beyond the protocol terminal
	3	After collecting the first Minikit, assemble a power jack to power a fan
	4	Use the Force to unlock a hatch with a key
	5	Floating in the air during Freighter Chase
	6	In a dive pool while Finn is held by a rathtar
	7	Shoot three mynocks
	8	Use dark side Force powers to open bars near the rathtar
	9	Cut through a door on a high ledge with a lightsaber
	10	Atop a cargo container near a colored light puzzle

CHAPTER V: MAZ'S CASTLE

Got It?	#	Notes
	1	Flush out and defeat nine rodents
	2	Dive pool in the courtyard
	3	In the alcove on the balcony
	4	Shoot the red sconce on the wall
	5	Jetpack between balconies
	6	Use an access hatch to travel between balconies
	7	Back up the curved stairs
	8	Destroy four spider webs
	9	Behind the silver LEGO segment of the wall
	10	Use the Force to open a door in the gear room

CHAPTER VI: BATTLE OF TAKODANA

Got It?	#	Notes
	1	Open a door with dark side Force powers and a lightsaber
	2	Use rotary control beyond the door opened with the Force
	3	Return three statues to their pedestals
	4	Dive pool outside the castle
	5	Scan a wall to reveal silver LEGO bricks
	6	Return to a cracked block after a Blaster Battle
	7	In a dive pool behind a TIE fighter panel
	8	Dual grapple handles on a crate
	9	Shoot four buoys in the water
	10	Hit three towers with proton torpedoes

CHAPTER VII: THE RESISTANCE

Got It?	#	Notes
	1	Cut open a locker with a lightsaber
	2	Rebuild three Astromech droids
	3	Destroy objects with Dark Force Destruction
	4	Melt the ice and get past the cold
	5	Use the power jack before BB-8 uploads the data
	6	Build a power jack near the galaxy map terminal
	7	In a room behind an energy field
	8	Rebuild three Rebellion fighters
	9	Use the Force to restore an image
	10	Empty socket and twirl poles

CHAPTER VIII: STARKILLER SABOTAGE

Got It?	#	Notes
	1	Destroy five Probe droids
	2	Under the snow at the crash site
	3	Through an access hatch, then fight a wampa
	4	Raise four Resistance flags
	5	Build a hairdryer
	6	Melt the ice from a dive pool
	7	Use the Force to open a panel
	8	Launch BB-8 up to a rocky ledge
	9	Score a goal by guiding a soccer ball into a net with the Force

CHAPTER IX: DESTROY STARKILLER BASE

Got It?	#	Notes
	1	While flying through the canyon, watch the right side for a ring of studs
	2	Complete a timed run while flying
	3	Hidden in a small room locked with an energy field
	4	Use the Force to build a bridge over a gap
	5	At the highest point of a climb wall
	6	Assemble an engine from Multi-Build bricks
	7	Behind toxic gas and a protocol access terminal
	8	Under the central stairs, through an access hatch
	9	Destroy four black bollards
	10	Blast the gold LEGO bricks from the side of a tower

CHAPTER X: THE FINALE

Got It?	#	Notes
	1	Timed run above the oscillator
	2	Destroy five green turrets
	3	In a ring of studs on the left
	4	Destroy three First Order emblems
	5	Build three snowmen while fighting Kylo Ren
	6	Melt the ice from a dive pool
	7	Grapple handle on the middle three while fighting Kylo Ren
	8	Blaster Battle target practice on sentry droids
	9	On a small island, behind toxic gas
	10	Behind a cracked brick on a snowy ledge

EPILOGUE: LUKE'S ISLAND

Got It?	#	Notes
	1	Pull down a container with a grapple handle
	2	Scare birds off three trees
	3	Dive pool leads to a small outcrop
	4	Cut open a rocky door with a lightsaber
	5	Jetpack or double-jump to an alcove
	6	Use the Force to pull junk from the water
	7	Empty socket and twirl poles
	8	Use the Force to remove rocks from a doorway
	9	Behind gold LEGO door
	10	Behind cracked LEGO brick

MINIKITS (CONTINUED)

POE TO THE RESCUE

Got It?	#	Notes
	1	Use the Force to pull up a Gonk droid
	2	Inside a dive pool
	3	Open three lockers with grapple handles
	4	Silver LEGO pipes under a turret
	5	Behind First Order containers moved with the Force
	6	Dropped from the ceiling by a rotary control
	7	Hit two targets while riding a lift
	8	In a hollowed out asteroid
	9	Shoot seven green growths in the mynock tunnel
	10	Destroy three small gem clusters with proton torpedoes

LOR SAN TEKKA'S RETURN

Got It?	#	Notes
	1	Hit four nightwatchers when they appear
	2	Uncovered by SN-1F4
	3	Charge the power jack on the wrecked ship
	4	Cut through a hatch with a lightsaber
	5	Astromech access inside the scavenger base
	6	Dive pool inside scavenger base
	7	Behind silver LEGO bricks on the roof
	8	Destroy four silver LEGO gears
	9	Hit the target in the middle of a large fan
	10	On a narrow ledge past the windy gap

RATHTAR HUNTING

Got It?	#	Notes
	1	Rip away the rocks at the start point with dark side Force powers
	2	On a ledge, behind a door opened with a grapple handle
	3	Shoot ten golden flowers above the pool
	4	Through an access gate near the first rathtar encounter
	5	Multi-Build cupcakes to position handles
	6	In a dive pool above the first rathtar encounter
	7	Use the Force to open a flower's petals
	8	Inside gold LEGO stactites
	9	Destroy five blue flowers shaped like bulbs
	10	Pull down a container from a high ledge with a grapple handle

CRIMSON CORSAIR

Got It?	#	Notes
	1	Open the cargo hatch with a grapple handle
	2	Target gold LEGO bricks to plug the geyser with the rock attached to the cliff face
	3	Hit three crystal lizards
	4	Shake free from the thruster pod with the Force
	5	Assemble a drill from Multi-Build bricks
	6	At the end of a narrow beam
	7	First Order terminal vending machine
	8	Use dark side Force powers to pull the cover off a giant fan
	9	Open a storage container on the upper walkway
	10	Pull down a floating lift with the Force

TROUBLE OVER TAUL

Got It?	#	Notes
	1	Inside a storage closet with silver LEGO doors
	2	Destroy four astromech droids
	3	Shoot meteors in the room above a Resistance Terminal
	4	Melt the ice in the room above a Resistance Terminal
	5	Pulled from wiring with dark side Force powers in the room below a Resistance terminal
	6	Shake loose from a vending machine, using the Force
	7	Open a door with a protocol access terminal
	8	Shoot the gold LEGO object while in the spinning hallway
	9	Behind a cracked block
	10	Use the Force to pull down the Minikit from the wrecked ceiling

OTTEGAN ASSAULT

Got It?	#	Notes
	1	Shoot down three unshielded transports
	2	In the inner rim
	3	Timed run over the floating islands
	4	Use the Force on Captain Phasma's TIE fighter
	5	Open a door with a Resistance terminal
	6	Dive pool near first defensive wall
	7	Shoot down three flying driods
	8	Silver LEGO bricks on wrecked ship
	9	Multi-Build a fishing pole
	10	Behind toxic gas near the Ottegan Commander

RED BRICKS

Icon	Got It?	Name	Level Obtained	Notes
		Stud Magnet	The Battle of Endor	After rescuing Wicket
		Infinite Torpedoes	Poe to the Rescue	Destroy everything in Kylo Ren's hidden room
		Studs x10	Lor San Tekka's Return	Score three points with a boxing robot
		Fast Interact	Rathtar Hunting	Go through the hidden door after the flower lift
		Imperial Inaccuracy	Crimson Corsair	Assemble Multi-Build bricks to the right of an energy field
		Combat Bar Rengen	Trouble Over Taul	Descend ladder revealed by Resistance Terminal, Immunity (Cold) required
		Fast Build	Chapter I: Assault on Jakku	Atop a merchant's cart after blasting a stick-figure in two locations
		Quick Access	Chapter II: Escape from the Finalizer	Build a bridge with Multi-Build bricks
		Studs x8	Chapter III: Niima Outpost	Destroy a silver LEGO container near the downed Kylo Ren's Command Shuttle.

Icon	Got It?	Name	Level Obtained	Notes
		Studs x2	Chapter IV: The Eravana	Open a locker with a grapple handle
		Studs x6	Chapter V: Takodana Castle	Behind a cracked block in the courtyard
		Destroy on Contact	Chapter VI: Attack on Takodana	Appears above a fallen tower after shooting down TIE Fighters
		Super Slap	Chapter VII: The Resistance	Get into the conveyor belt room through an access hatch
		Studs x4	Chapter VIII: Starkiller Sabotage	Build a snowman to reach an alcove
		Regenerate Hearts	Chapter IX: Destroy Starkiller Base	Defeat 15 stormtroopers summoned by a First Order terminal
		Collect Guide Studs	Chapter X: The Finale	Push a snowball across a clearing with the Force
		Super Disco Blasters	Ottegan Assault	Behind a cracked block near the start point
		The Funk Awakens	Epilogue: Luke's Island	Through an access hatch behind rocks cleared with dark side Force powers

VEHICLES

New vehicles are made available after you complete a Story Mode chapter for the first time. You also unlock a Microfighter after collecting all ten minikits in each chapter.

VEHICLES FOR USE IN HUBS

Icon	Got It?	Vehicle	Obtained
		Endor Speeder Bike	The Battle of Endor
		Rey's Speeder	Chapter I: Assault on Jakku
		Resistance Freight Transporter	Chapter VII: The Resistance
		Snow Speeder Bike	Chapter VIII: Starkiller Sabotage
		Junker Speeder Bike	Lor San Tekka's Return
		Rusty Speeder Bike	Lor San Tekka's Return
		Radon-Ulzer Podracer	Rathtar Hunting
		Voltec Wasp Podracer	Crimson Corsair
		Vulptereen 412 Podracer	Trouble Over Taul
		Rey's Speeder (Microfighter)	Chapter I: Assault on Jakku
		Poe's Blue X-wing (Microfighter)	Chapter I: Assault on Jakku
		First Order Transporter (Microfighter)	Chapter I: Assault on Jakku (Minikit)
		Special Forces TIE fighter (Microfighter)	Chapter II: Escape from the Finalizer
		The Finalizer (Microfighter)	Chapter II: Escape from the Finalizer (Minikit)

VEHICLES FOR USE IN HUBS

Icon	Got It?	Vehicle	Obtained
		Millennium Falcon (Microfighter)	Chapter III: Niima Outpost
		Quadjumper (Microfighter)	Chapter III: Niima Outpost (Minikit)
		The Eravana (Microfighter)	Chapter IV: The Eravana
		Guavian Marauder (Microfighter)	Chapter IV: The Eravana
		Imperial TIE bomber (Microfighter)	Chapter IV: The Eravana (Minikit)
		Takodana Cruiser (Microfighter)	Chapter V: Maz's Castle
		Takodana Skipper (Microfighter)	Chapter V: Maz's Castle
		Rebel Alliance Y-wing (Microfighter)	Chapter V: Maz's Castle (Minikit)
		Poe Dameron's X-wing (Microfighter)	Chapter VI: Battle of Takodana
		Kylo Ren's Command Shuttle (Microfighter)	Chapter VI: Battle of Takodana (Minikit)
		Resistance Transport (Microfighter)	Chapter VII: The Resistance
		Rebel Alliance B-wing (Microfighter)	Chapter VII: The Resistance (Minikit)
		First Order Snowspeeder (Microfighter)	Chapter VIII: Starkiller Sabotage
		Resistance X-wing (Microfighter)	Chapter IX: Destroy Starkiller Base

VEHICLES FOR USE IN HUBS (Continued)

Icon	Got It?	Vehicle	Obtained
		Imperial TIE interceptor (Microfighter)	Chapter IX: Destroy Starkiller Base (Minikit)
		First Order TIE fighter	Chapter X: The Finale
		Starkiller (Microfighter)	Chapter X: The Finale (Minikit)
		Luke's Landspeeder (Microfighter)	Epilogue: Luke's Island
		Rebel Alliance A-wing (Microfighter)	Epilogue: Luke's Island (Minikit)
		Death Star II (Microfighter)	Starkiller Destruction
		Imperial AT-AT (Microfighter)	Trouble Over Taul (Minikit)
		Millennium Falcon (Classic) (Microfighter)	The Battle of Endor
		Rebel Alliance X-wing (Microfighter)	The Battle of Endor
		Imperial AT-ST (Microfighter)	The Battle of Endor (Minikit)
		Ackbar's Starfighter (Microfighter)	Poe to the Rescue
		Rebel Alliance Snowspeeder (Microfighter)	Poe to the Rescue (Minikit)
		Jakku Scavenger (Microfighter)	Lor San Tekka's Return
		Rebel Transport (Microfighter)	Lor San Tekka's Return (Minikit)
		Prana Ship (Microfighter)	Rathtar Hunting
		Rathtar Wrangler (Microfighter)	Rathtar Hunting (Minikit)
		Meson Martinet (Microfighter)	Crimson Corsair
		Imperial Advanced TIE (Microfighter)	Crimson Corsair (Minikit)
		Sterdic Star (Microfighter)	Trouble Over Taul
		Imperial Shuttle (Microfighter)	Trouble Over Taul (Minikit)
		Ottegan Defense Fighter (Microfighter)	Ottegan Assault
		Imperial TIE fighter (Microfighter)	Ottegan Assault (Minikit)

VEHICLES USABLE IN FREE PLAY (FLIGHT MISSIONS)

icon	Got It?	Vehicle	Obtained
		Millennium Falcon (Classic)	The Battle of Endor
		Rebel Alliance X-wing	The Battle of Endor
		Resistance X-wing (Poe)	Chapter I: Assault on Jakku
		Special Forces TIE fighter	Chapter II: Escape from the Finalizer
		Millennium Falcon	Chapter III: Niima Outpost
		Han's Freighter (Eravana)	Chapter IV: The Eravana
		Guavian Marauder	Chapter IV: The Eravana

VEHICLES USABLE IN FREE PLAY (FLIGHT MISSIONS) (Continued)

icon	Got It?	Vehicle	Obtained
		Takodana Cruiser	Chapter V: Maz's Castle
		Takodana Skipper	Chapter V: Maz's Castle
		Poe Dameron's X-wing	Chapter VI: Battle of Takodana
		Resistance Transport	Chapter VII: The Resistance
		Resistance X-wing (Blue Squadron)	Chapter IX: Destroy Starkiller Base
		First Order TIE fighter	Chapter X: The Finale (Minikit)
		Death Star II	Starkiller Destruction
		Ackbar's Starfighter	Poe to the Rescue
		Jakku Scavenger	Lor San Tekka's Return
		Prana Predator	Rathtar Hunting
		Meson Martinet	Crimson Corsair
		Sterdic Star	Trouble Over Taul
		Ottegan Defense Ship	Ottegan Assault
		First Order Transporter	Chapter I: Assault on Jakku (Minikit)
		The Finalizer	Chapter II: Escape from the Finalizer (Minikit)
		Quadjumper	Chapter III: Niima Outpost (Minikit)
		Imperial TIE bomber	Chapter IV: The Eravana (Minikit)
		Rebel Alliance Y-wing	Chapter V: Maz's Castle (Minikit)
		Kylo Ren's Command Shuttle	Chapter VI: Battle of Takodana (Minikit)
		Rebel Alliance B-wing	Chapter VII: The Resistance (Minikit)
		Imperial TIE interceptor	Chapter IX: Destroy Starkiller Base (Minikit)
		Starkiller Base	Chapter X: The Finale (Minikit)
		Rebel Alliance A-wing	Epilogue: Luke's Island (Minikit)
		Rebel Alliance Snowspeeder	Poe to the Rescue (Minikit)
		Rebel Transport	Lor San Tekka's Return (Minikit)
		Rathtar Wrangler	Rathtar Hunting (Minikit)
		Imperial Advanced TIE fighter	Crimson Corsair (Minikit)
		Imperial Shuttle	Trouble Over Taul (Minikit)
		Imperial TIE fighter	Ottegan Assault (Minikit)

Hub Collectibles

CARBONITE

Collect carbonite to unlock the characters listed here. Carbonite appears only in hubs. Use the reference number to find the carbonite on the map in the Hubs section of this guide.

Got It?	Character	Hub (Ref #)	Ability Needed
	A-Wing Pilot	D'Qar (4)	Grapple Gun (x2)
	Admiral Ackbar (Classic)	D'Qar (2)	Agile/Jetpack, Aquatic
	Anakin Skywalker	Starkiller Base (9)	Force Powers, Aquatic
	Anakin Skywalker (Podracer)	Jakku (6)	None
	Bith	Jakku (7)	Astromech, BB-8
	Bobba Fett	Jakku (8)	None
	Count Dooku	Starkiller Base (3)	Grapple Gun, BB-8
	Darth Maul	Starkiller Base (2)	Agile
	Death Star Trooper	Starkiller Base (6)	None
	Emperor Palpatine	Jakku (3)	Aquatic
	Gray Squadron Pilot	D'Qar (1)	Lightsaber, Immunity (Cold)
	Greedo	Jakku (2)	Grapple Gun, Force Powers
	Han Solo (Classic)	Millennium Falcon	BB-8
	Han Solo (Stormtrooper)	Starkiller Base (5)	None
	Imperial Royal Guard	Starkiller Base (1)	Cracked LEGO
	Jawa	Jakku (5)	Grapple Gun (x2), Gold LEGO, Immunity (Toxic)
	Luke Skywalker (Episode IV)	Jakku (10)	None
	Luke Skywalker (Stormtrooper)	Starkiller Base (4)	Dark Side Force Powers, Charge Up

Got It?	Character	Hub (Ref #)	Ability Needed
	Obi Wan Kenobi	Takodana (2)	Aquatic
	Obi Wan Kenobi (Classic)	Jakku (4)	Agile, Lightsaber, Immunity (Toxic)
	Padmé Amidala	Jakku (1)	Gold LEGO
	Princess Leia (Classic)	D'Qar (3)	Astromech, Force Powers
	Princess Leia (Ewok Village)	Takodana (6)	None
	Queen Amidala	Takodana (5)	Lightsaber
	Qui Gon Jin	Takodana (1)	Cracked LEGO
	Rebel Commando	Takodana (3)	First Order
	Rebel Fleet Trooper	D'Qar (5)	Charge Up, Sharpshooter
	Scout Trooper	Starkiller Base (8)	Jetpack, Gold LEGO
	Snowtrooper (Classic)	Starkiller Base (10)	Cracked LEGO
	Stormtrooper (Classic)	Takodana (7)	Grapple Gun (x2)
	Teebo	Takodana (8)	Grapple Gun, Force Powers
	TIE Interceptor Pilot	Starkiller Base (7)	Thaw LEGO
	Tusken Raider	Jakku (9)	Force Powers
	Yoda	Takodana (4)	Staff, Agile
	Zev Senesca	D'Qar (6)	Silver LEGO

GOLD BRICKS

The following tables list the Gold Bricks discovered while exploring hubs. Gold Bricks from completing quests are not included here. Use the number in the "Map #" column to locate the Gold Bricks on the maps in the Hubs section of this guide.

D'QAR

Got It?	Map #	Skills Needed	Got It?	Map #	Skills Needed	Got It?	Map #	Skills Needed
	1	Sharpshooter		10	None		19	Force Powers
	2	Charge Up		11	Force Powers		20	Quadnoculars, Silver LEGO
	3	Gold LEGO, Aquatic		12	None		21	Charge Up
	4	None		13	None		22	BB-8
	5	BB-8		14	Protocol Droid		23	BB-8
	6	BB-8		15	Resistance		24	Grapple Gun
	7	Thaw LEGO		16	Force Powers		25	Gold LEGO
	8	Cracked LEGO		17	Silver LEGO				
	9	None		18	BB-8				

JAKKU

Got It?	Map #	Skills Needed	Got It?	Map #	Skills Needed	Got It?	Map #	Skills Needed
	1	Force Powers, Aquatic		6	Force Powers		11	Force Powers, Charge Up
	2	Silver LEGO		7	Charge Up		12	Dark Side Force Powers
	3	Force Powers		8	None		13	Grapple Gun
	4	Grapple Gun		9	Cracked LEGO				
	5	Quadnoculars, Lightsaber, First Order		10	Jetpack				

TAKODANA

Got It?	Map #	Skills Needed	Got It?	Map #	Skills Needed	Got It?	Map #	Skills Needed
	1	Force Powers		7	None		13	Cracked LEGO
	2	None		8	None		14	Gold LEGO
	3	Staff, Agile		9	BB-8		15	BB-8
	4	Command (Resistance), Grapple Gun		10	Force Powers		16	BB-8
	5	Gold LEGO		11	Force Powers				
	6	BB-8, Grapple Gun, Force Manipluation		12	Grapple Gun				

Gold Bricks continued on next page.

GOLD BRICKS (CONTINUED)

MILLENNIUM FALCON

Got It?	Map #	Skills Needed	Got It?	Map #	Skills Needed	Got It?	Map #	Skills Needed
	1	Immunity (Toxic), Resistance		3	None		5	Force Powers
	2	Immunity (Cold)		4	Dark Side Force Powers			

STARKILLER BASE

Got It?	Map #	Skills Needed	Got It?	Map #	Skills Needed	Got It?	Map #	Skills Needed
	1	Quadnoculars, Agile		6	Dark Side Force Powers		11	Thaw LEGO
	2	Thaw LEGO, Aquatic		7	None		12	Agile
	3	Grapple Gun (x2)		8	Thaw LEGO		13	None
	4	Small Access		9	Quadnoculars, Lightsaber		14	None
	5	Astromech		10	Grapple Gun		15	BB-8

ACHIEVEMENTS & TROPHIES

Got It?	Name	PlayStation 3/4 Trophy	Achvmnt. Points	Requirement
	I'll Come Back For You!	Bronze	20	Complete TFA Chapter 1—Assault on Jakku
	Classified? Me Too.	Bronze	20	Complete TFA Chapter 2—Escape from the Finalizer
	The Garbage Will Do	Bronze	20	Complete TFA Chapter 3—Niima Outpost
	…What Was The Second Time?	Bronze	20	Complete TFA Chapter 4—The Eravana
	Eyes Of A Man Who Wants To Run	Bronze	20	Complete TFA Chapter 5—Maz's Castle
	Don't Let These Dogs Scare You	Bronze	20	Complete TFA Chapter 6—Battle of Takodana
	You Wouldn't Like It	Bronze	20	Complete TFA Chapter 7—The Resistance
	Is There A Garbage Chute?	Bronze	20	Complete TFA Chapter 8—Starkiller Sabotage
	A Bag Full Of Explosives	Bronze	20	Complete TFA Chapter 9—Destroy Starkiller Base
	It Belongs To Me!	Bronze	20	Complete TFA Chapter 10—The Finale
	Speechless	Bronze	20	Complete Luke's Island
	A Long Time Ago….	Bronze	20	Complete The Battle of Endor
	Never Tell Me The Odds	Bronze	20	Complete Poe to the Rescue
	Traveled Too Far. Seen Too Much.	Bronze	20	Complete Lor San Tekka's Return
	Used To Have A Bigger Crew	Bronze	20	Complete Rathtar Hunting
	The Crimson Corsair	Bronze	20	Complete The Crimson Corsair
	Hello! Were You Looking for Me?	Bronze	20	Complete Trouble Over Taul
	It's A Trap!	Bronze	20	Complete Ottegan Assault
	The Force, It's Calling To You.	Bronze	20	Obtain "True Jedi" in any level
	Just A Scavenger	Bronze	20	Collect all Minikits in any level
	Unlearn What You Have Learned	Bronze	20	Re-build a Multi-build object
	They're Shooting At Both Of Us!	Bronze	20	Complete a Blaster Battle
	Bow To The First Order!	Bronze	20	Complete all First Order missions
	A Big Deal In The Resistance	Bronze	20	Complete all Resistance Missions
	Cryptosurgeon	Bronze	10	Create a custom character

Got It?	Name	PlayStation 3/4 Trophy	Achvmnt. Points	Requirement
	We Need More Troops!	Bronze	10	Defeat 50 stormtroopers
	Don't Get Cocky!	Bronze	10	Defeat 100 TIE fighters
	I Like That Wookiee…	Bronze	10	Complete a Free Play level playing as Maz Kanata and Chewbacca
	Hey! That's Miiiiiiine!	Bronze	10	Play as Unkar Plutt on the Millennium Falcon
	Quick on the Draw	Bronze	10	In a blaster battle, have Han Solo defeat a character who is preparing an attack
	Not The Droid You're Looking For	Bronze	10	Use the wrong type of droid on an access panel
	Traitor!	Bronze	10	Defeat Finn using FN-2199
	Family Reunion	Bronze	5	Have Kylo Ren and Han Solo in the same party
	Show Me, Grandfather	Bronze	10	Defeat Kylo Ren playing as Darth Vader
	STOP…..Kylo Time	Bronze	10	As Kylo Ren, Force Freeze another character
	Little Short For A Stormtrooper	Bronze	10	Use a hat dispenser to put a stormtrooper helmet on a small Minifigure
	Anything Else?	Bronze	10	Destroy all computer terminals in Starkiller Shield Room as Kylo Ren
	Chewie, We're Home	Bronze	10	Play as Young Hano Solo (Classic) and Chewbacca on the Millennium Falcon
	Stormtrooper Syndrome	Bronze	10	Miss your target ten times in a blaster battle
	I'm Getting Pretty Good At This!	Bronze	30	Complete a Blaster Battle without dying
	He's No Good To Me Dead	Silver	30	Complete all Bounty Hunts
	Less Than 12 Parsecs	Silver	30	Complete all Races
	60 Portions!	Silver	30	Complete all Scavenger Missions
	Red Leader	Silver	30	Purchase all Red Bricks
	The New Jedi Will Rise	Silver	30	Collect "True Jedi" on all levels
	I Can Fly Anything	Silver	40	Collect all Minikits in the game
	There Has Been An Awakening…	Gold	40	Complete The Force Awakens
	It's True. All of it…	Gold	40	Complete New STAR WARS Adventures Levels
	Force Is Strong With This One	Gold	70	Achieve 100% Completion
	The Force Awakens	Platinum		Unlock all Trophies

CHARACTERS

LEGO Star Wars: The Force Awakens takes you to several different planets in a galaxy far, far away. As you can imagine, there are a lot of different characters. The characters for use in the Story Mode levels are available as you play through the game; however, many more characters are unlocked as you find Character Tokens or complete challenges.

Once a character is unlocked, you do not automatically get to use it. Many characters must be purchased. Before you purchase a character, look at the abilities they possess. Initially, you want to pick characters that have abilities your current characters do not possess. Cultivating a collection of characters with diverse abilities will prove useful when replaying levels in Free Play.

Use the following table to discover information for every character in the game. You can even keep track of your progress by placing check marks in the "Got It?" column of the characters you've collected.

CHARACTERS

Icon	Got It?	Character	Cost	How Unlocked?	Abilities
		Adan Mose	50,000	Complete All Collectibles in Prologue: Rathtar Hunting—Rathtar Caverns	Silver LEGO, Toxic
		Admiral Ackbar (Classic)	0	Character in Carbonite—Jakku hub	Command, Swim, Resistance
		Admiral Ackbar (Episode VII)	0	Complete Prologue: Poe to the Rescue—Trash Compactor	Command, Swim, Resistance, Staff
		Admiral Statura	50,000	Complete Chapter 8: Destroy the Starkiller—Assault of Starkiller	Goggles, Resistance
		Anakin Skywalker (Episode I)	0	Character in Carbonite—Jakku hub	Small Access
		Anakin Skywalker (Episode III)	0	Character in Carbonite—Takodana hub	Agility, Lightsaber, Dark Force, Force Lightning
		Arvel Crynyd	0	Character in Carbonite—Takodana hub	Grapple, Resistance
		Athgar Heece	100,000	Complete True Jedi challenge in Chapter 1: Assault on Jakku—First Order Assault	Jetpack, Silver LEGO
		Bala-Tik	10,000	Complete All Collectibles challenge in Chapter 4: The Eravana—Freighter Chase	Grapple, Silver LEGO
		Bazine Netal	50,000	Complete True Jedi challenge in Chapter 5: Maz's Castle—Castle Hall	Agility, First Order
		BB-8	0	Complete Chapter 1: Assault on Jakku—Village Retreat	Electric Charge, Rotary Control Switch, Cold, Toxic, Small Access, Astromech
		Bith	25,000	Complete Royal Force challenge in Prologue: The Battle of Endor—Death Star Interior	None
		Blass Tyran	50,000	Complete Chapter 5: Maz's Castle—Castle Hall	Goggles, Silver LEGO
		Boba Fett	0	Character in Carbonite—Resistance Base hub	Grapple, Goggles, Silver LEGO, Jetpack
		Bollie Prindel	50,000	Complete Chapter 5: Maz's Castle—Castle Basement	Resistance
		C-3PO (Episode VII)	100,000	Complete All Collectibles challenge in Chapter 6: Attack on Takodana—Takodana Skies	Protocol Droid, Cold, Toxic

CHARACTERS

Icon	Got It?	Character	Cost	How Unlocked?	Abilities
		C-3PO (Classic)	100,000	Complete All Collectibles challenge in Prologue: The Battle of Endor—Death Star Escape	Protocol Droid, Cold, Toxic
		Captain Phasma	0	Complete Prologue: Ottegan Assault—Ottegan Pursuit	Command, Grapple, Goggles, Gold LEGO, First Order
		Captain Sidon Ithano	100,000	Complete Quick Fire Shot challenge in Chapter 5: Maz's Castle—Castle Hall	Agility, Goggles, Grapple, Toxic
		Chancellor Palpatine	0	Character in Carbonite—Jakku hub	Lightsaber, Force, Dark Force, Force Lightning
		Chewbacca	0	Complete Chapter 4: The Eravana—Freighter Battle	Strong, Silver LEGO
		Chewbacca (Twon Ketee)	0	Complete Prologue: Rathtar Hunting—Rathtar Caverns	Strong, Silver LEGO, Toxic
		Chewbacca (Wounded)	0	Complete Chapter 5: Maz's Castle—Castle Approach	Strong, Silver LEGO
		Chief Petty Officer Unamo	100,000	Complete Dameron Unchained challenge in Chapter 2: Escape from the Finalizer—Finalizer Hangar 1	Goggles, First Order
		Constable Zuvio	100,000	Complete Soap Boxing challenge in Chapter 3: Niima Outpost—Niima Outpost	Staff
		Count Dooku	0	Character in Carbonite—Starkiller hub	Lightsaber, Force, Dark Force, Force Lightning
		Cratinus	50,000	Complete All Collectibles challenge in Chapter 6: Attack on Takodana—Castle Corridors	Small Access
		Crokind Shand	50,000	Complete True Jedi challenge in Chapter 4: The Eravana—Freighter Battle	Silver LEGO
		Croll Jenkins	50,000	Complete Pacifist challenge in Prologue: Rathtar Hunting—Rathtar Caverns	Grapple, Toxic
		Croz Danoc	50,000	Complete All Collectibles challenge in Prologue: Rathtar Hunting— Loading Area	Silver LEGO, Toxic
		Crusher Roodown	250,000	Complete Golden Sands challenge in Chapter 3: Niima Outpost—Jakku Graveyard Flight	Strong
		Darth Vader	0	Complete Prologue: The Battle of Endor—Death Star Interior	Lightsaber, Force, Dark Force, Force Choke, Toxic
		Dasha Promenti	50,000	Complete Loggerheads challenge in Chapter 9: The Finale—Starkiller Forest	Agility, Goggles
		Davan Marak	50,000	Complete Luggabeast Master challenge in Chapter 3: Niima Outpost—Niima Outpost	Strong, Silver LEGO
		Death Star Trooper	0	Character in Carbonite—Starkiller hub	None
		Dr. Kalonia	50,000	Complete All Collectibles challenge in Chapter 8: Destroy the Starkiller—Rey's Escape	Goggles, Resistance
		EGL-21 "Amps"	25,000	Complete All Collectibles challenge in Chapter 3: Niima Outpost—Niima Outpost	Cold, Toxic,
		Ello Asty	50,000	Complete All Collectibles challenge in Chapter 9: The Finale—Oscillator Bombing Run	Agility, Grapple, Resistance
		Emperor Palpatine	1,000,000	Complete Like Lightning challenge in Prologue: The Battle of Endor—Death Star Interior	Force, Dark Force, Force Lightning
		Finn	0	Complete Chapter 3: Niima Outpost—Niima Outpost	Grapple, First Order, Toxic
		Finn (Junction Box)	50,000	Complete True Jedi challenge in Chapter 8: Destroy the Starkiller—Oscillator Interior	Grapple, First Order, Toxic, Lightsaber
		Finn (Starkiller)	0	Complete Chapter 9: The Finale—Starkiller Forest	Grapple, First Order, Toxic, Lightsaber
		Finn (Takodana)	0	Complete Chapter 6: Attack on Takodana—Castle Hall	Grapple, First Order, Toxic, Lightsaber

CHARACTERS

Icon	Got It?	Character	Cost	How Unlocked?	Abilities
		First Order Engineer	50,000	Complete TIEd Down challenge in Chapter 2: Escape from the Finalizer—Finalizer Hangar 2	Goggles, First Order
		Officer Sumistu	100,000	Complete All Collectibles challenge in Chapter 2: Escape from the Finalizer—Finalizer Hangar 2	Goggles, First Order
		Lieutenant Mitaka	50,000	Complete Keep Your Head On! challenge in Chapter 2: Escape from the Finalizer—Finalizer Hangar 2	Goggles, First Order
		Fitness General Hux	100,000	Complete All Collectibles challenge in Prologue: Poe to the Rescue—Trash Compactor	Goggles, Grapple, First Order, Command
		Flametrooper (Episode VII)	50,0000	Complete Cover Commander challenge in Chapter 1: Assault on Jakku—First Order Assault	First Order, Melt Ice, Gold LEGO
		FN-1824	0	Complete Chapter 8: Destroy the Starkiller—Rey's Escape	Goggles, First Order
		FN-2187	0	Complete Chapter 2: Escape from the Finalizer—Finalizer Hangar 1	Grapple, First Order
		FN-2187 (Helmetless)	25,000	Complete Chapter 2: Escape from the Finalizer—Star Destroyer Exterior	Grapple, First Order
		FN-2199	250,000	Complete All Collectibles challenge in Chapter 6: Attack on Takodana—Castle Escape	First Order, Cracked LEGO
		GA-97	25,000	Complete Just a Helping Hand challenge in Chapter 5: Maz's Castle—Castle Hall	Protocol Droid, Cold, Toxic
		Gaff Kaylek	50,000	Complete I Have the High Ground! challenge in Prologue: Rathtar Hunting— Loading Area	Grapple, Toxic
		General Hux	100,000	Complete Power to the People challenge in Chapter 7: Starkiller Sabotage—Starkiller Crash Site	Goggles, Command, First Order
		General Leia	100,000	Complete True Jedi challenge in Chapter 6: Attack on Takodana—Takodana Skies	Grapple, Command, Resistance
		General Leia (ALT)	100,000	Complete Bush Whacker challenge in Epilogue: Luke's Island	Grapple, Command, Resistance
		GNK-143 (Gonk Droid)	10,000	Complete The Brave Little Droid challenge in Chapter 1: Assault on Jakku—Jakku Graveyard	Cold, Toxic, Electric Charge
		Goss Toowers	50,000	Complete Tower Control challenge in Chapter 6: Attack on Takodana—Takodana Skies	Resistance
		Gray Squadron Pilot	0	Character in Carbonite—Resistance Base hub	Grapple
		Greedo	0	Character in Carbonite—Takodana hub	Grapple
		Grummgar	250,000	Complete Full Stream challenge in Chapter 5: Maz's Castle—Castle Approach	Strong, Cracked LEGO
		GTAW-74 "Geetaw"	100,000	Complete Chapter 3: Niima Outpost—Niima Bombardment	Cold, Toxic
		Guavian Death Ganger	50,000	Complete Wookiee Cookie challenge in Chapter 4: The Eravana—Freighter Chase	Grapple, Silver LEGO
		Guavian Gunner	250,000	Complete No Match for a Good Blaster challenge in Chapter 4: The Eravana—Freighter Chase	Gold LEGO
		Gym Stormtrooper	50,000	Complete Sayonara Dianoga challenge in Prologue: Poe to the Rescue—Trash Compactor	Grapple, First Order
		Han Solo	0	Complete Chapter 4: The Eravana—Freighter Battle	Grapple, Goggles
		Han Solo (Classic)	0	Character in Carbonite—Starkiller hub	Goggles, Grapple
		Han Solo (Endor)	0	Complete Prologue: The Battle of Endor—Endor Shield Generator	Goggles, Grapple
		Han Solo (Starkiller)	0	Complete Chapter 7: Starkiller Sabotage—Starkiller Crash Site	Goggles, Grapple

CHARACTERS

Icon	Got It?	Character	Cost	How Unlocked?	Abilities
		Han Solo (Stormtrooper)	0	Character in Carbonite—Jakku hub	Grapple
		Han Solo (Twon Ketee)	0	Complete Prologue: Rathtar Hunting—Rathtar Caverns	Goggles, Grapple, Toxic
		Heavy Trooper (Episode VII)	100,000	Complete True Jedi challenge on Poe to the Rescue—Asteroid Escape	Gold LEGO, First Order
		Hobin Carsamba	50,000	Complete True Jedi challenge in Chapter 3: Niima Outpost—Jakku Graveyard Flight	Goggles, Toxic
		Hoogenz	25,000	Complete True Jedi challenge in Chapter 3: Niima Outpost—Niima Outpost	Grapple, Toxic
		Hot Tub Stormtrooper (Episode VII)	50,000	Complete Load of Rubbish challenge in Prologue: Poe to the Rescue—Trash Compactor	Grapple, First Order
		Hot Tub Stormtrooper Alt	50,000	Complete All Collectibles challenge in Prologue: Poe to the Rescue—Asteroid Escape	Grapple, First Order
		HURID-327	250,000	Complete Classic Misdirection challenge in Chapter 5: Maz's Castle—Castle Approach	Strong, Cracked LEGO, Cold, Toxic
		Ilco Munica	50,000	Complete No DESERTing challenge in Chapter 1: Assault on Jakku—Village Retreat	Strong, Staff
		Imperial AT-ST Pilot	50,000	Complete Chicken Stomp challenge in Prologue: The Battle of Endor—Endor Shield Generator	Goggles
		Infrablue Zedbeddy Coggins	50,000	Complete True Jedi challenge in Chapter 5: Maz's Castle—Castle Basement	Small Access
		Jawa	0	Character in Carbonite—Takodana hub	Small Access
		Jessika Testor Pava	100,000	Complete True Jedi challenge in Chapter 8: Destroy the Starkiller—Assault of Starkiller	Agility, Grapple, Resistance
		JJ Abrams	100,000	Complete All Collectibles challenge in Epilogue: Luke's Island	Grapple, Goggles, Command, Resistance, First Order
		K-3PO	100,000	Complete Tunnel Trouble challenge in Prologue: Poe to the Rescue—Asteroid Escape	Cold, Toxic, Protocol Droid
		Kanjiklub Gang Member	50,000	Complete True Jedi challenge in Chapter 4: The Eravana—Freighter Chase	Grapple
		Kanjiklubber	50,000	Complete True Jedi challenge in Chapter 4: The Eravana—Freighter Shutdown	Goggles
		Kathleen Kennedy	100,000	Complete True Jedi challenge in Epilogue: Luke's Island	Grapple, Command, Resistance, First Order, Silver LEGO
		Kaydel Ko Connix	50,000	Complete All Collectibles challenge in Prologue: Ottegan Assault—Ottegan Pursuit	Goggles, Resistance
		Korr Sella	100,000	Complete All Collectibles challenge in Chapter 7: Starkiller Sabotage—Starkiller Crash Site	Resistance
		Kylo Ren	500,000	Complete Finn-ess challenge in Chapter 9: The Finale—Starkiller Forest	First Order, Lightsaber, Force, Dark Force, Force Freeze
		Kylo Ren (Hooded)	500,000	Complete All Collectibles challenge in Chapter 1: Assault on Jakku—First Order Assault	First Order, Lightsaber, Force, Dark Force, Force Freeze
		Kylo Ren (Masked)	0	Complete Prologue: Ottegan Assault—Ottegan Pursuit	First Order, Lightsaber, Force, Dark Force, Force Freeze
		Lando Calrissian (General)	0	Complete Prologue: The Battle of Endor—Death Star Escape	Grapple, Command
		Lieutenant Bastian	100,000	Complete Turret Termination challenge in Chapter 9: The Finale—Oscillator Bombing Run	Grapple, Resistance, Toxic
		Logray	50,000	Complete All Collectibles challenge in Prologue: The Battle of Endor—Endor Shield Generator	Small Access, Command
		Lor San Tekka	100,000	Complete All Collectibles challenge in Chapter 1: Assault on Jakku—Village Retreat	Goggles, Grapple, Staff

CHARACTERS

Icon	Got It?	Character	Cost	How Unlocked?	Abilities
		Luke Skywalker (Episode IV)	0	Character in Carbonite—Jakku hub	Lightsaber, Force, Jedi Mind Trick, Grapple
		Luke Skywalker (Episode VI)	0	Complete Prologue: The Battle of Endor—Death Star Interior	Agility, Lightsaber, Force, Jedi Mind Trick
		Luke Skywalker (Stormtrooper)	0	Character in Carbonite—Starkiller hub	None
		M9-G8	50,000	Complete Rey Run challenge in Chapter 8: Destroy the Starkiller—Rey's Escape	Cold, Toxic, Astromech
		Major Brance	50,000	Complete Missile Intercept challenge in Chapter 8: Destroy the Starkiller—Assault of Starkiller	Goggles, Resistance
		Major Ematt	50,000	Complete I've Got a Bad Feeling About This challenge in Chapter 8: Destroy the Starkiller—Rey's Escape	Goggles, Resistance
		Maz Kanata	0	Complete Chapter 6: Attack on Takodana—Castle Hall	Goggles, Small Access
		Mi'no Teest	50,000	Complete Chapter 5: Maz's Castle—Castle Hall	Grapple
		Monn Tatth	25,000	Complete All Collectibles challenge in Chapter 3: Niima Outpost—Jakku Graveyard Flight	Grapple, Goggles
		MSE-3-M813M	25,000	Complete Smash Hits challenge in Chapter 7: Starkiller Sabotage—Shield Room Approach	Cold, Toxic, Small Acess
		Neeb Kizzle	25,000	Complete Don't Spill a Drop challenge in Chapter 1: Assault on Jakku—First Order Assault	None
		Nien Nunb	50,000	Complete Quad Lasers challenge in Prologue: The Battle of Endor—Death Star Escape	Resistance
		Nien Nunb (X-Wing)	50,000	Complete Lap of Honor challenge in Chapter 9: The Finale—Oscillator Bombing Run	Resistance
		Obi Wan Kenobi (Episode III)	0	Character in Carbonite—Takodana hub	Lightsaber, Force, Jedi Mind Trick, Agility
		Obi Wan Kenobi (Episode IV)	0	Character in Carbonite—Starkiller hub	Lightsaber, Force, Jedi Mind Trick
		O-MR1	100,000	Complete Crystal Caves challenge in Prologue: Poe to the Rescue—Asteroid Escape	Protocol Droid, First Order, Cold, Toxic
		Oni Jass	100,000	Complete True Jedi challenge in Prologue: Rathtar Hunting— Loading Area	Silver LEGO, Toxic
		Ophi Egra	25,000	Complete A load of old Bloggins challenge in Chapter 1: Assault on Jakku—Village Retreat	None
		Oskus Stoorat	50,000	Complete Let's Call it a TIE challenge in Chapter 6: Attack on Takodana—Castle Escape	Grapple
		Ottegan Acolyte	25,000	Complete Otte-gone challenge in Prologue: Ottegan Assault—Ottegan Pursuit	Grapple
		Ottegan Warrior	50,000	Complete All Collectibles challenge in Prologue: Ottegan Assault—Ottegan Surface	Staff
		Ozeer Tenzer	50,000	Complete Seasoned Professional challenge Prologue: Rathtar Hunting— Loading Area	Grapple, Toxic
		Padmé Amidala	0	Character in Carbonite—Starkiller hub	Grapple
		Pamich Nerro Goode	50,000	Complete Will you help me? challenge in Prologue: Ottegan Assault—Ottegan Surface	Goggles, Resistance
		Petty Officer Thanisson	50,000	Complete Wampa Stompa challenge in Chapter 7: Starkiller Sabotage—Starkiller Crash Site	Goggles, First Order
		Poe Dameron	0	Complete Chapter 1: Assault on Jakku—Village Retreat	Grapple, Goggles, Resistance
		Poe Dameron (D'Qar)	100,000	Complete Snow BB-8 challenge in Chapter 9: The Finale—Starkiller Showdown	Grapple, Goggles, Resistance

CHARACTERS

Icon	Got It?	Character	Cost	How Unlocked?	Abilities
		Poe Dameron (Flight Suit)	0	Complete Chapter 6: Attack on Takodana—Takodana Skies	Grapple, Goggles, Resistance
		Poe Dameron (Helmetless)	0	Complete Chapter 8: Destroy the Starkiller—Assault of Starkiller	Grapple, Goggles, Resistance
		Poe Dameron (Prisoner)	0	Complete Chapter 2: Escape from the Finalizer—Finalizer Hangar 1	Grapple, Goggles, Resistance
		Prashee	50,000	Complete Fight Fire with Fire challenge in Chapter 6: Attack on Takodana—Castle Corridors	Small Access
		Praster Barun	50,000	Complete True Jedi challenge in Prologue: Ottegan Assault—Ottegan Surface	Agility, Command
		Praster Ommien	50,000	Complete Chapter 5: Maz's Castle—Castle Hall	None
		Princess Leia (Classic)	0	Character in Carbonite—Starkiller hub	Grapple, Command, Resistance
		Princess Leia (Endor)	0	Complete Prologue: The Battle of Endor—Endor Shield Generator	Grapple, Command, Resistance
		Princess Leia (Ewok Village)	0	Character in Carbonite—Jakku hub	Grapple, Command, Resistance
		Pru Sweevant	10,000	Complete Tidy as you Go challenge in Chapter 5: Maz's Castle—Castle Basement	Silver LEGO, Small Access
		PZ-4CO	50,000	Complete Snowballed challenge in Chapter 9: The Finale—Starkiller Showdown	Protocol Droid, Cold, Toxic
		Queen Amidala	0	Character in Carbonite—Jakku hub	None
		Quiggold	50,000	Complete All Collectibles challenge in Chapter 5: Maz's Castle—Castle Hall	Strong, Gold LEGO
		Qui-Gon Jinn	0	Character in Carbonite—Takodana hub	Agility, Lightsaber, Force, Jedi Mind Trick
		Quinar	50,000	Complete Chapter 3: Niima Outpost—Jakku Graveyard Flight	Strength, Cold
		R2-D2 (Episode VII)	50,000	Complete Epilogue: Luke's Island	Astromech, Cold, Toxic
		R2-KT	100,000	Complete True Jedi challenge in Chapter 9: The Finale—Oscillator Bombing Run	Astromech, Cold, Toxic
		R2-Q5	100,000	Complete Minor Inconvenience challenge in Prologue: Ottegan Assault—Ottegan Pursuit	Cold, Toxic, Astromech
		R-3PO	50,000	Complete Dest-droid challenge in Chapter 2: Escape from the Finalizer—Finalizer Hangar 1	Protocol Droid, Cold, Toxic
		R5-D8	50,000	Complete Falling with Style challenge in Chapter 2: Escape from the Finalizer—Star Destroyer Exterior	Cold, Toxic, Astromech
		R5-J2	50,000	Complete All Collectibles challenge in Chapter 2: Escape from the Finalizer—Finalizer Hangar 1	Cold, Toxic, Astromech
		Razoo Qin-Fee	250,000	Complete The Tentacle Menace challenge in Chapter 4: The Eravana—Freighter Shutdown	Silver LEGO
		Rebel Commando	0	Character in Carbonite—Takodana hub	Grapple
		Rebel Scout Trooper	0	Character in Carbonite—Starkiller hub	Goggles
		Resistance General	25,000	Complete All Collectibles challenge in Chapter 8: Destroy the Starkiller—Assault of Starkiller	Goggles, Resistance
		Rey	0	Complete Chapter 3: Niima Outpost—Niima Outpost	Agility, Goggles, Staff
		Rey (Junction Box)	50,000	Complete All Collectibles challenge in Chapter 8: Destroy the Starkiller—Oscillator Interior	Agility, Goggles, Staff

CHARACTERS

Icon	Got It?	Character	Cost	How Unlocked?	Abilities
		Rey (Resistance)	0	Complete Epilogue: Luke's Island	Agility, Goggles, Resistance, Lightsaber, Staff
		Rey (Scavenger)	0	Complete Chapter 1: Assault on Jakku—Jakku Graveyard	Agility, Goggles, Staff
		Rey (Starkiller)	0	Complete Chapter 9: The Finale—Starkiller Showdown	Agility, Goggles, Lightsaber, Staff
		Rey (Takodana)	0	Complete Chapter 5: Maz's Castle—Castle Approach	Agility, Goggles
		Rey (Young)	100,000	Complete Floor is Lava! challenge in Chapter 5: Maz's Castle—Castle Basement	Small Access
		Royal Guard	0	Character in Carbonite—Jakku hub	Staff
		Sache Skareet	25,000	Complete TIE Die challenge in Chapter 6: Attack on Takodana—Takodana Skies	Grapple, Resistance
		Sarco Plank	50,000	Complete True Jedi challenge in Chapter 3: Niima Outpost—Niima Bombardment	Silver LEGO, Toxic
		Scout Trooper	0	Character in Carbonite—Takodana hub	Goggles
		Sifter	25,000	Complete Chapter 3: Niima Outpost—Niima Bombardment	Cold, Toxic, Small Access
		Snap Wexley	0	Complete Chapter 6: Attack on Takodana—Takodana Skies	Grapple, Resistance
		Snowtrooper (Episode VII)	100,000	Complete True Jedi challenge in Chapter 7: Starkiller Sabotage—Starkiller Crash Site	Cold, First Order, Grapple
		Snowtrooper (Classic)	0	Character in Carbonite—Starkiller hub	Cold
		Snowtrooper Officer (Episode VII)	10,000	Complete Mouse Hunt challenge in Chapter 7: Starkiller Sabotage—Phasma	Silver LEGO, Cold, First Order, Command
		Special Forces TIE Fighter Pilot (Episode VII)	10,000	Complete Blow TIE! challenge in Chapter 2: Escape from the Finalizer—Finalizer Exterior	Grapple, First Order
		Stormtrooper Captain (Episode VII)	10,000	Complete Evasive Manoeuvres challenge in Chapter 7: Starkiller Sabotage—Phasma	Silver LEGO, First Order
		Stormtrooper (Classic)	100,000	Complete Fuel Cells challenge in Prologue: The Battle of Endor—Endor Shield Generator	Grapple
		Stormtrooper (Episode VII)		Complete Chapter 8: Destroy the Starkiller—Rey's Escape	Grapple, First Order
		Stormtrooper Combat Engineer	100,000	Complete Post Processing challenge in Chapter 8: Destroy the Starkiller—Oscillator Interior	First Order
		FN-2112	100,000	Complete Post Processing challenge in Chapter 8: Destroy the Starkiller—Oscillator Interior	Command, Silver LEGO, First Order
		Sudswater Dillifay Glon	100,000	Complete Chapter 5: Maz's Castle—Castle Approach	Small Access
		Taryish Juhden	10000	Complete Chapter 3: Niima Outpost—Niima Bombardment	Grapple, Staff
		Tasu Leech	50,000	Complete BB-Ball challenge in Chapter 4: The Eravana—Freighter Shutdown	Grapple
		Taybin Ralorsa	50,000	Complete True Jedi challenge in Chapter 5: Maz's Castle—Castle Approach	None
		Technician Mandetat	50,000	Complete Thermal Heating challenge in Chapter 7: Starkiller Sabotage—Shield Room Approach	Goggles, First Order
		Teebo	0	Character in Carbonite—Jakku hub	Small Access, Command
		Teedo	50,000	Complete A Proper Scavenger challenge in Chapter 1: Assault on Jakku—Jakku Graveyard	Small Access, Staff

CHARACTERS

Icon	Got It?	Character	Cost	How Unlocked?	Abilities
		TIE Fighter Pilot (Episode VII)	100,000	Complete Probation challenge in Chapter 3: Niima Outpost—Jakku Graveyard Flight	Grapple, First Order
		TIE Interceptor Pilot	0	Character in Carbonite—Takodana hub	Goggles
		Trentus Savay	50,000	Complete Blind Rage challenge in Prologue: Ottegan Assault—Ottegan Surface	Grapple, Resistance
		Trinto Duaba	50,000	Complete Chapter 5: Maz's Castle—Castle Basement	Staff
		Tusken Raider	0	Character in Carbonite—Jakku hub	Staff
		Ubert "Sticks" Quaril	50,000	Complete I'm Rubber, You're Glue challenge in Chapter 6: Attack on Takodana—Attack on Takodana	None
		Unkar Goon	50,000	Complete Group Shot challenge in Chapter 3: Niima Outpost—Niima Bombardment	Strong
		Unkar Plutt	100,000	Complete All Collectibles challenge in Chapter 3: Niima Outpost—Niima Bombardment	Strong
		Unkar Thug	50,000	Complete Flawless Coverage challenge in Chapter 3: Niima Outpost—Niima Bombardment	Strong
		Varmik	50,000	Complete All Collectibles challenge in Chapter 5: Maz's Castle—Castle Approach	Agility, Silver LEGO, Strong
		Varond Jelik (Twon Ketee)	0	Complete Prologue: Rathtar Hunting—Rathtar Caverns	Agility, Toxic, Staff
		Volzang Li-Thrull	50,0000	Complete All Collectibles challenge in Chapter 4: The Eravana—Freighter Shutdown	Gold LEGO, Melt Ice
		Wampa	0	Character in Carbonite—Takodana hub	Strong, Cracked LEGO, Cold
		Wedge Antilles	0	Complete Prologue: The Battle of Endor—Death Star Escape	Grapple
		Wi'ba Tuyll	50,000	Complete Cook up a Storm challenge in Chapter 6: Attack on Takodana—Castle Escape	Silver LEGO
		Wicket	0	Complete Prologue: The Battle of Endor—Endor Shield Generator	Command, Small Access
		Wollivan	50,000	Complete All Collectibles challenge in Chapter 5: Maz's Castle—Castle Basement	Small Access
		Yoda	0	Character in Carbonite—Starkiller hub	Lightsaber, Force, Jedi Mind Trick, Small Access
		Yolo Ziff	100,000	Complete Rapid Oscillator challenge in Chapter 8: Destroy the Starkiller—Assault of Starkiller	Grapple, Resistance
		Zev Senesca	50,000	Complete Fast Reactor challenge in Prologue: The Battle of Endor—Death Star Escape	Grapple, Cold
		Zylas	50,000	Complete We Need to Get Out of Here! challenge in Prologue: Rathtar Hunting—Rathtar Caverns	Strength, Toxic

CHAPTER 1:
ASSAULT ON JAKKU
Village Retreat

CHARACTERS

	Poe Dameron		BB-8

UNLOCKS

	Lor San Tekka	Complete All Collectibles challenge.
	Ilco Munica	Complete No DESERTing challenge.
	Ophi Egra	Complete A Load of Old Bloggins challenge.

GOLD BRICK CHALLENGES

Name	Mode	Notes
Level Complete	Any	Complete the level.
True Jedi	Any	Collect 18,000 studs.
All Collectibles	Freeplay	Find all the Minikits.
No DESERTing	Any	Smash 3 pots hiding villagers within.
A Load of Old Bloggins	Any	Return all 3 bloggins to their pen.

COLLECTIBLES

Type	Mode	Notes
Minikit	Any	Return all 3 bloggins to their pen.
Minikit	Free Play	Use the Force to lower this Minikit to the ground.

RESISTANCE BASE HUB

When the game begins, you control Poe Dameron and BB-8. The admiral wants to talk to you, so follow the trail of green studs to the command bunker. The door is locked, so use the Resistance terminal to the door's side. Two rows of symbols appear. When the top and bottom of a column match, press the button that appears below to lock it in. Once you've made three matches, the door unlocks. Enter the command bunker.

Inside, Poe receives his orders to go to Jakku and collect some vital intelligence. Exit the bunker and follow the trail of studs back to Poe's X-wing. The steps leading to the landing platform have been destroyed. Move to the pile of bricks and prepare to assemble them. Select the steps and then build away. Finally, get to the X-wing and set a course for Jakku.

JAKKU HUB

Once you arrive on Jakku, follow a trail of studs to a large container. Use the Resistance console and match the symbols to open the container. Assemble the bricks that fall out into a level select terminal, and then use it to begin the first level—Village Retreat.

FIND THE FIRST WEAPONS CACHE

The First Order is on its way to Jakku. The villagers need some way to defend themselves. There are three weapons caches hidden throughout the village. You must find them all. The first is in a hut on the village's left side. Break up some bricks and then reassemble them into a charge panel. Switch to BB-8 and move to the panel. Press the button that appears on the screen to shoot a power cable, and then move the stick left and right to keep the arrow centered. This powers up the panel and some steps appear.

Take control of Poe again. Walk up the steps into the hut and smash everything. Then assemble the pile of bricks into a droid. Once completed, the droid walks out of the hut and then opens up and deploys several blasters for the villagers to use.

MINIKIT

You will need a Force user in order to get this Minikit. Since you don't have one during Story Mode, you will have to come back in Free Play. The Minikit is located on the far left side of the village near where the first cache is located. Move the Force user to the left of the hut and then press the button that appears to move the Minikit down from the rock wall so you can get it.

COMPLETE CHALLENGES FIRST

For this level and all others, it's important to complete the challenges early on, or at least before completing the objectives for the level. Once the last objective is complete, the level ends no matter whether you have attempted the challenges or not. For this level, be sure to get the challenges done before going after the third weapons cache.

CHALLENGE:
NO DESERTING

Three of the villagers are afraid of the First Order and hide in pots. Two are located near the top of the level near the huts, and the third is near the bottom. Smash the pots to get them out to fight. This not only earns you a Gold Brick, but it also unlocks Ilco Munica.

FIND THE SECOND WEAPONS CACHE

The second weapons cache is hidden in the center of the village. Move to the circular area near a tower. Smash an orange and white crate and then assemble the pieces into a rotary control switch switch. Take control of BB-8 and move to the switch. Press the button that appears on-screen, and then follow the prompts to move the control stick.

Switch back to Poe, and move to the Resistance console which appears on the tower's left side. Match the symbols in order to open the second cache of weapons. Only one more to go.

CHALLENGE:
A LOAD OF OLD BLOGGINS

Completing this challenge provides several rewards. Not only do you get a Gold Brick and unlock Ophi Egra, but you also get a Minikit. How can you get these? Locate three bloggins in the village. They are small creatures. Jump onto them and ride them into the corral on the village's right side and then hop off. Once all three are in the corral, the challenge is completed.

FIND THE THIRD WEAPONS CACHE

The villager who knows how to open the last weapons cache is locked in a hut on the village's right side. You need to help him get out. As Poe, fire a grappling hook at the orange target to pull down a crate so it breaks into pieces. Assemble those bricks into a rotary control switch on the right. Take control of BB-8 and use the launcher to propel the droid onto a platform suspended from a crane.

Switch to Poe and break the rotary control switch. Then reassemble it into a crank at the base of the crane. Turn the crank to rotate the crane and move BB-8 to the left. Switch to BB-8 and roll off the platform and to the astromech terminal on the left. To solve the puzzle that appears on the terminal, rotate the outer piece so the inner piece fits. Complete this task to unlock the door to the hut. Once it's open, the villager runs out and deploys the last weapons cache.

UNLOCK FORCE USERS

You do not have any Force users at the start of the game. However, as soon as you can, return to the Resistance Base hub. There, you can access the first of four Level Select terminals. By playing through the Battle of Endor levels, you unlock Luke Skywalker (Episode VI) and Darth Vader. Both of these characters are Force users. They both come in handy to get collectibles during Free Play.

First Order Assault

CHARACTERS

	Poe Dameron		BB-8

UNLOCKS

	Athgar Heece	Complete True Jedi challenge.
	Kylo Ren (Hooded)	Complete All Collectibles challenge.
	Neeb Kizzle	Complete Don't Spill a Drop challenge.
	Flametrooper (Episode VII)	Complete Cover Commander challenge.

GOLD BRICK CHALLENGES

Name	Mode	Notes
Level Complete	Any	Complete the level.
True Jedi	Any	Collect 25,000 studs.
All Collectables	Freeplay	Find all the Minikits.
Don't Spill a Drop	Any	Complete the Multi-Build puzzle at the end of the level without making any mistakes.
Cover Commander	Any	Complete the cover section without being defeated.

COLLECTIBLES

Type	Mode	Notes
Minikit	Any	Use goggles and grapple on the X-wing at the start.
Minikit	Free Play	Use a dark side Force user to destroy a panel.

DESTROY THE FIRST ORDER LANDING CRAFT

While trying to escape from Jakku, Poe's X-wing is damaged. Both he and BB-8 are caught in the assault on the village. You need to fight your way through the village. However, some enemies and a landing craft block your way. Start by fighting the stormtroopers. Poe's blaster can hit them from a distance.

Switch to BB-8 and move near the charge terminal. Use the droid to power it up and cause the terminal to break. Take control of Poe again and then assemble the pile of bricks into a laser turret. Take aim at the target on the turret and shoot at it with Poe's blaster to activate it. The turret blows up the landing craft that was blocking your path.

MINIKIT

Before leaving the first area, use Poe's goggles to scan the X-wing. This reveals an orange brick. Shoot Poe's grapple gun at it and pull on the engine to reveal a Minikit.

STORMTROOPER SHOOTOUT

Advance to the left through the gap in the flames. As you do, another landing craft delivers more stormtroopers to the village. Poe takes cover behind a barrier. Press the Fire button to pop up from behind cover and shoot. After clearing out the first wave, another landing craft drops off the next wave.

The stormtroopers assemble a turret. Watch out for it because it can cause a lot of damage. Instead of shooting at the turret directly, shoot at the red fuel cell to the turret's right. When the red fuel cell blows up, it takes the turret with it. Press the Jump button to duck behind cover, then move to the barrier to the right. Use Poe's goggles to locate a target on the landing craft hovering overhead. Then shoot the stormtrooper and the target on the landing craft to send it flying away.

CHALLENGE:
COVER COMMANDER

When Poe gets into the shootout with the stormtroopers and takes cover, you need to be careful. Stay alive through this shootout to earn a Gold Brick and unlock the Flametrooper character.

ADVANCE THROUGH THE VILLAGE

Your path to the left is once again blocked by flames. Shoot at a target to the water tower's right with Poe's blaster. Assemble the bricks that fall into either one of the two rotary control switch structures. Then use BB-8 on the rotary control switch to knock down the water tower and put out the flames. Continue to the left and fight off some more stormtroopers.

Another landing craft blocks your way. Use Poe's grapple ability to pull off the landing craft's top part and assemble the bricks into an astromech terminal. Switch to BB-8 and solve the puzzle to activate the landing craft's engines and send it flying away.

As you move to the left, a flametrooper and two other stormtroopers block your way. However, they are protected by a shield. Break up a red and white crate near the shield, then assemble the pieces into one of two things: a giant popcorn container or a droid. No matter which you choose, the enemies will be defeated.

MINIKIT

This Minikit is hidden behind a panel which requires a dark side Force user. Unlock a character such as Darth Vader or Kylo Ren to get this Minikit during Free Play. Move near the panel located to the left of the water tower you destroyed and use the Force.

EXTINGUISH THE LAST FLAMES

As you get to the village's far left side, you see one last wall of flames separating you from the villagers under attack. Assemble the pile of bricks into a rotary control switch in the center of the area near the water tank. Take control of BB-8 and use the rotary control switch to move the water container to the left.

Switch to Poe and break up the rotary control switch; then reassemble the bricks to the left to make a water pump. Jump on the pump to fill the container with water. Once full, break the pump and assemble the rotary control switch again. Move

the water container to the right. Break the rotary control switch again and assemble the pieces onto the small tower to the right. Shoot at the target which appears with Poe's blaster to activate the water sprinkler and put out the flames. Finally, move through the opening in the fence toward the villagers to complete the level.

CHALLENGE:
DON'T SPILL A DROP

In order to complete this challenge, assemble the Multi-Build structures in the correct order (details provided in the "Extinguish the Last Flames" section of this chapter). Completing this challenge earns a Gold Brick and unlocks Neeb Kizzle.

Jakku Graveyard

CHARACTERS

	Rey (Scavenger)		BB-8

UNLOCKS

	GNK-143 (Gonk Droid)	Complete The Brave Little Droid challenge.
	Teedo	Complete A Proper Scavenger challenge.

GOLD BRICK CHALLENGES

Name	Mode	Notes
Level Complete	Any	Complete the level.
True Jedi	Any	Collect 35,000 studs.
All Collectibles	Freeplay	Find all the Minikits.
The Brave Little Droid	Any	Defeat 5 Teedos with BB-8.
A Proper Scavenger	Any	Destroy every object within the Destroyer as Rey.

COLLECTIBLES

Type	Mode	Notes
Minikit	Any	Climb up some rails inside the Star Destroyer.
Red Brick (Stud Multiplier x2)	Free Play	Destroy the gold container.

RESCUE BB-8 AND GET INSIDE THE STAR DESTROYER

BB-8 fled from the village and into the Jakku desert, which contains a graveyard of ships from a decades old battle between the Empire and the Rebellion. However, BB-8 is captured by some Teedos scouring the graveyard for scrap. Rey needs to help the little droid.At the start, you need to deal with a Teedo riding a luggabeast.Break up some of the junk to the beast's right and then assemble it into one oftwo objects. Either one will work. Defeat all of the Teedos. Then use Rey's goggles on the panel at the back of the area to find a crack. It takes something strong to break a cracked block, so climb onto the luggabeast and ride it over to the cracked panel. Charge the crack to break it open.

CHALLENGE:
THE BRAVE LITTLE DROID

Instead of using Rey to defeat the Teedos, use BB-8. He can zap them. Defeat a total of five Teedos with BB-8 and you earn a Gold Brick, as well as unlock GNK-143. There are four Teedos outside of the Star Destroyer and some more inside.

Behind the crack is a charge panel. Use BB-8 to power it up. This breaks open the shield generator dome of the Star Destroyer. Defeat the Teedo that drops out. Then assemble the pieces on the ground into a grab rail. As Rey, jump to the rail and climb onto the platform. Move to the right and use her ability to wall run across the gap to the right. Then jump across a series of small pads.

RED BRICK
(STUD MULTIPLIER X2)

Come back to this level in Free Play mode when you have a character who can destroy gold LEGO bricks. After opening the shield generator dome, climb into it and then break open the gold container to get a Red Brick. After you purchase and activate this Red Brick, the number of studs you collect will be doubled. Acquire this Red Brick as soon as possible.

After getting across the pads, jump to a flusher switch and grab onto it. As you pull it down with your weight, a charge panel deploys from the side of the wreck. Switch to BB-8 and power it up to open the hatch so you can enter the wrecked Star Destroyer.

INSIDE THE STAR DESTROYER

Take control of Rey and enter the Star Destroyer. Move to the right until you get to a gap. Jump across another series of pads to get to the other side. When you get to the other side, break up some objects and then assemble the pieces into a rotary control switch.

CHALLENGE:
A PROPER SCAVENGER

While inside the Star Destroyer, there are 24 objects which can be destroyed. If you use Rey to destroy all 24, you complete this challenge, earn a Gold Brick, and unlock Teedo as a character. Part of this area requires BB-8, so be careful not to use him to destroy the objects or you will not complete this challenge.

MINIKIT

After crossing over the small pads, move all the way to the right to find some rails. Jump up to them and crawl to the right. Jump across to a couple handholds to get this Minikit.

Target a socket on the wall and throw Rey's staff into it. Now jump to the staff and twirl around it. Jump to another pole and then to the platform on the left. Do a wall run to the left to get to another platform. Pull yourself up onto the platform, then push a crate of junk along a path to the left and off the edge. Drop down and assemble the pieces into a rotary control switch.

Switch to BB-8 and use the rotary control switch to launch the droid to a higher walkway. Roll to the left to pick up a blue stud, then roll to the right until you see a small hatch. Move BB-8 through the hatch and into a control room. Inside, use the astromech panel and solve the puzzle to extend a series of handholds. Move back through the small hatch.

Take control or Rey and climb the handholds to get up to where BB-8 is located. Move to the left along the walkway to get to the wall jump. Jump back and forth between these two walls to get to the top, and then head to the right. Slide under a gap and then do a wall run to get to a climbing wall. Get to the top and continue to the right. Then drop down to a lower area.

Rey is once again separated from BB-8. Smash all the objects in this area, and then assemble the pieces into a staff switch along the back wall. Use Rey's staff to turn the switch and operate a crane to pick up a wrecked TIE fighter and make a ramp out of it. Now BB-8 can return to Rey's side.

Break up the staff switch, and then assemble a rotary control switch at the bottom of the area near the door. Use BB-8 on this rotary control switch to open the door so you can exit the Star Destroyer and complete the level.

GET A BLUE STUD

Before opening the door to exit the Star Destroyer, build a rotary control switch to the left with the pieces in the final area. This can launch BB-8 up to the pipe over the door. Roll around to get the blue stud.

JAKKU HUB

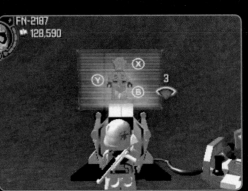

Poe Dameron has been captured by the First Order in the village on Jakku. Follow the trail of green studs toward a landing craft.

Once you get there, you take control of a stormtrooper. Use the First Order terminal. Press the buttons that appear on the screen to move pieces until you create a red First Order character. You can now use the level select terminal to continue to the next chapter.

CHAPTER 2:
ESCAPE FROM THE FINALIZER

Finalizer Hangar 1

GET TO THE HANGAR

Poe Dameron was captured by the First Order. However, a stormtrooper designated FN-2187 has decided to help him escape. FN-2187 has decided that the First Order is not for him. Start off by walking Poe past the First Order crew. Poe is handcuffed as part of the ruse. Lead Poe down the stairs past the enemies.

Once you get to the bottom of the stairs, Poe is free. The path to the next area is blocked, so push on a container to the right and slide it along a checkered path. Then push that same container up towards the top of the screen. As you start to push the larger container to the right, FN-2187 will have to help out since it is too large for one character to move by himself. Push it until it falls down and creates a bridge across a gap.

Cross the container and break up an object near a small access hatch. Assemble the pieces into a lift platform and ride it to the top.

CHARACTERS

	Poe Dameron (Prisoner)		FN-2187

UNLOCKS

	R5-J2	Complete All Collectables challenge
	Chief Petty Officer Unamo	Complete Dameron Unchained challenge
	R-3PO (Protocol Droid)	Complete Des-droid challenge

GOLD BRICK CHALLENGES

Name	Mode	Notes
Level Complete	Any	Complete the level.
True Jedi	Any	Collect 15,000 studs.
All Collectables	Freeplay	Find all the Minikits.
Dameron Unchained	Any	Return to defeat the First Order crew near the start
Des-droid	Any	Walk the protocol droid to its doom!

COLLECTIBLES

Type	Mode	Notes
Minikit	Free Play	Use a strong character to pull on orange handles.
Minikit	Free Play	Use a small character to go through a small access hatch.

MINIKIT

This Minikit can only be acquired during Free Play. Before riding the lift to the hangar level, use a small character such as BB-8 to go through the access hatch. The hatch leads to the Minikit.

CREATE A DISTRACTION

Once Poe and FN-2187 have reached the hangar, they need to get over to a TIE fighter. However, they will need a distraction. The nearby speeder can do just that—with the help of a protocol droid to activate the speeder. There just happens to be a red droid on a platform to the right. You just have to get the droid to the speeder. Move to the right and use Poe's goggles by the checkered pad. Grapple a container out of the wall and then push it to the right to create the first half of a bridge.

Walk onto the container bridge and then jump across to the other side. Grapple another container out of the wall. Be sure to stand back so it doesn't fall on you. Then slide the container to the left so the protocol droid, which can't jump, can walk across.

CHALLENGE:
DES-DROID

Before using the protocol droid to activate the speeder, walk it off the edge to destroy it. Not only do you earn a Gold Brick, but you also unlock R-3PO.

Switch to the protocol droid and walk it across the bridge of containers. Continue to the protocol droid terminal to the speeder's left and activate it. You must solve a puzzle at this terminal. Watch the order in which four symbols appear. Then press the symbol buttons in the same order to solve it. This powers up the speeder and sends it crashing into the hangar. It looks like the distraction brought attention *to* you rather than away from you.

DEPLOY A TIE FIGHTER

Now that the speeder is out of your way, move into the hangar area and fight the stormtroopers. Once they are cleared out, assemble the pieces in this area into a lift pad on the right. Send one character up the lift and onto a walkway. Follow it to the left just in front of the windows. Jump and grab onto a red bar to pull down a panel and expose some circuitry.

CHALLENGE:
DAMERON UNCHAINED

After you've fought some stormtroopers, return to the start and defeat all of the enemies in this area. This earns a Gold Brick and also unlocks Chief Petty Officer Unamo. Look around for a blue stud below the door that you enter the level through.

MINIKIT

When in Free Play mode, move to the left of the build pile on the hangar floor. At the end of the walkway, find the container. Use a strong character such as Chewbacca to pull on the orange handles and acquire the Minikit inside.

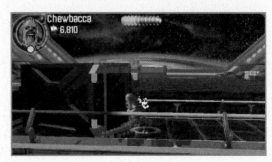

Now destroy the lift and reassemble the pieces into a grapple turret. Activate it to pull on the circuitry and break open the wall of the control tower. Then break up the turret and reassemble the pieces into the lift once again.

Take the lift to the higher walkway and continue into the control tower. Defeat all of the enemies inside. As FN-2187, use the First Order terminal. Press the buttons as they appear on the screen to complete a character with all red pieces. Once you've done this, a TIE fighter is released and placed on the hangar floor to complete the level.

Finalizer Hangar 2

CHARACTERS

	Poe Dameron (Prisoner)		FN-2187

UNLOCKS

	First Order Officer	Complete All Collectibles challenge.
	First Order Engineer	Complete TIEd Down challenge.
	Lieutenant Mitaka	Complete Keep Your Head On! Challenge.

GOLD BRICK CHALLENGES

Name	Mode	Notes
Level Complete	Any	Complete the level.
True Jedi	Any	Collect 18,000 studs.
All Collectibles	Free Play	Find all the Minikits.
TIEd Down	Any	Defeat 15 stormtroopers while in the TIE fighter.
Keep Your Head On!	Any	Get through cover without getting hit.

COLLECTIBLES

Type	Mode	Notes
Minikit	Any	Destroy all the Gold containers with the TIE fighter.
Red Brick (Perfect Deflect)	Free Play	Use the Force to move a panel.

GET TO THE TIE FIGHTER

Poe and FN-2187 have a TIE fighter in sight. However, stormtroopers are blocking their way. Take cover and begin shooting at them. Use Poe's googles on a large container to find a grapple point which you can pull on to get it out of the way.

CHALLENGE:
KEEP YOUR HEAD ON!

To complete this challenge, earn a Gold Brick, and unlock Lieutenant Mitaka, you must get through the cover section of this level without taking any damage. Remember to press the Jump button to duck if you start getting shot at.

During the second wave, you must defeat nine stormtroopers. Since most of them are firing at Poe, take control of FN-2187 and open fire. Then move forward to the next row of cover.

RED BRICK
(PERFECT DEFLECT)

During Free Play, after moving to the second wave of the cover section, switch to FN-2187 so you are near some blue sparkles. Then switch to a Force user, such as Darth Vader, and use the Force to lift a panel to get the Red Brick.

ESCAPE FROM THE HANGAR

You are now in the TIE fighter, hovering inside the hangar. You must clear out the hangar and then escape. Begin by firing at the control tower windows.

A large turret appears and opens fire. There is no way to destroy it from where you are located. Shoot at the red target on the level's right side. This allows you to get close to the turret. Now you can use Poe's googles to locate orange hooks on the turret. Use Poe to grapple and pull on one of the grapple points. Then switch to FN-2187 and grapple the hook on the other side. As you pull on it, you destroy the turret. The way is now open for you to get to the TIE fighter.

CHALLENGE:
TIED DOWN

While inside the TIE fighter, defeat 15 stormtroopers. This unlocks the First Order Engineer and also earns you a Gold Brick.

Once the control tower is in ruins, the TIE fighter turns toward the hangar exit. However, before you leave, you need to destroy eight of the TIE fighters so there are fewer to pursue you. Four are along the walls to the left and the others are on the right side. Once all are eliminated, Poe flies the TIE fighter out of the hangar.

MINIKIT

Three gold containers are on the floor of the hangar. They take several shots to destroy. Eliminate all three of them to get the Minikit.

Star Destroyer Exterior

DESTROY EIGHT TURRETS

Poe and FN-2187 have made it to a TIE fighter and flown out of the Star Destroyer. However, if they want to have a chance of reaching Jakku, they must knock out the turrets on the Finalizer. All of these turrets are located on the sides of the Star Destroyer at mid-level. Destroy them

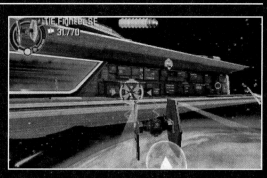

with your TIE fighter's cannons. There are also other TIE fighters that attack. Shoot them, and then collect the torpedoes they drop. You can then fire the torpedoes at other TIE fighters or use them to destroy turrets.

CHARACTERS

	SF TIE fighter

UNLOCKS

	Special Forces TIE Fighter Pilot (Episode VII)	Complete Blow TIE! Challenge.
	R5-D8	Complete Falling with Style challenge.

GOLD BRICK CHALLENGES

Name	Mode	Notes
Level Complete	Any	Complete the level.
True Jedi	Any	Collect 40,000 studs.
All Collectibles	Freeplay	Find all the Minikits.
Blow TIE!	Any	Destroy 15 TIE fighters in the arena section.
Falling with Style	Any	Make it through the flight route toward Jakku without being destroyed.

COLLECTIBLES

Type	Mode	Notes
Minikit	Any	Shoot a TIE fighter in the interior at the front of the Star Destroyer.
Minikit	Free Play	Destroy 10 turrets.

MINIKIT

At the level's start, fly toward the Star Destroyer's interior part at the front. Shoot a TIE fighter in this area to get the first Minikit.

DESTROY THE LARGE TURRETS

Once the turrets on the side are eliminated, two large turrets deploy on the Star Destroyer's top side near the stern. These are more difficult to blow up. You need to use torpedoes. Rearm your torpedoes by shooting down some TIE fighters.

Then destroy both of the large turrets with the torpedoes.

CHALLENGE:
BLOW TIE!

Before destroying all eight turrets, take some time to shoot down 15 TIE fighters. This earns a Gold Brick and unlocks the Special Forces TIE fighter Pilot (Episode VII).

There are ten small turrets on top of the Finalizer. Destroy them all before you blow up the two large turrets to earn this Minikit.

Now fly to the stern of the Finalizer and take out a huge turret with several pillars. Move the TIE fighter left and right to aim at the pillars. Shoot until the gold cores are exposed, and then keep firing to destroy them.

ESCAPE FROM THE FINALIZER

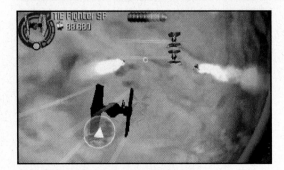

It's now time to make a break for Jakku. As you head towards the planet, the Star Destroy fires several missiles. Dodge them as they get close by moving around. Also shoot down the enemy TIE fighters that try to attack you. Fly through the circles of studs as you head towards Jakku. This helps keep you on course and also provides the studs you need to complete the True Jedi challenge.

FALLING WITH STYLE

While flying toward Jakku, avoid being destroyed by the TIE fighters or missiles. Completing this challenge unlocks the droid R5-D8 and earns another Gold Brick.

JAKKU HUB

After Poe and FN-2187 (now renamed Finn by Poe) crash land on Jakku, you return to the Jakku Hub. This time you have Rey and BB-8. Hop onto the nearby speeder bike and follow the trail of green studs. Fight off some Teedos along the way.

When you get to the gate to the Niima Outpost, it is blocked by a shield. Assemble the pieces into an astromech terminal on the left. Use BB-8 to solve the puzzle. Switch back to Rey and break the terminal. Reassemble it into a bounce pad on the right. Then throw her staff at the socket in the middle of the gate. Jump on the bounce pad to reach the pole on the right. Twirl around to the staff, and then on to another pole on the left.

After twirling on the poles, two targets appear. Walk away from the gate until Rey's staff returns to her. Then go back and throw the staff at the targets to lower the shield. Finally, follow the trail of green studs into the outpost and to the level select terminal so you can begin the next chapter.

CHAPTER 3:
NIIMA OUTPOST
Niima Outpost

GET THROUGH THE OUTPOST

First Order stormtroopers have arrived at Niima Outpost. After meeting up with Finn, Rey and BB-8 need to find a way to escape. Start by eliminating the stormtroopers to the right of where the characters begin. Then use Rey to slide under the gap in the large wall which blocks your progress.

CHARACTERS

	Rey		Finn
	BB-8		

UNLOCKS

	Hoogenz	Complete True Jedi challenge.
	EGL-21 "Amps"	Complete All Collectibles challenge.
	Constable Zuvio	Complete Soap Boxing challenge.
	Davan Marak	Complete Luggabeast Master challenge.

GOLD BRICK CHALLENGES

Name	Mode	Notes
Level Complete	Any	Complete the level.
True Jedi	Any	Collect 30,000 studs.
All Collectables	Freeplay	Find all the Minikits.
Luggabeast Master	Any	Defeat 3 stormtroopers with a captured luggabeast.
Soap Boxing	Any	Smash 4 scrap washing machines.

COLLECTIBLES

Type	Mode	Notes
Minikit	Free Play	Use a dark side Force user to break a red and black object.
Red Brick (Stud Multiplier x4)	Free Play	Destroy a cracked LEGO crate and then the gold crate inside.

CHALLENGE:
SOAP BOXING

Four scrap washing machines are scattered throughout this level. Destroy all of them to earn a Gold Brick and unlock Constable Zuvio. The first washing machine is located near where you begin. The second washing machine is opposite the spo where Rey must twirl on the poles. The third machine is after the rotary control switch which launched BB-8, and the final one is near the level's end in front of the fence with the luggabeast.

After defeating the stormtroopers on the other side of the wall, break up some crates. Assemble the Multi-Build to the left to make a turret which blasts the wall down so the rest of your party can catch up. Break the turret and then reassemble the pieces into a grapple hook on a nearby spaceship. Switch to Finn and use his grapple gun to hook and then pull on the side of the spaceship to reveal a First Order terminal. Have Finn solve the puzzle to make a red First Order character to move the ship out of your way.

Continue to the right and engage more stormtroopers. Use Finn's blaster to shoot at them from long range and to defeat the enemies up on a walkway. Once they are dispatched, take control of Rey and use her googles to find a small access hatch. Switch to BB-8 and go through the hatch.

BB-8 emerges on an upper level to the right. Use the droid to defeat some stormtroopers, and then power up a charge panel. This causes two poles to emerge from the sand. Switch to Rey and throw her staff at a socket near the poles. Jump and grab onto the staff, then twirl around to jump to the other poles and get to where BB-8 is waiting. Smash some crates and build the pieces into a ladder for Finn to climb.

Take control of Finn and climb the ladder. Use him to pull on the grapple hook to start a conveyor belt. A target appears over the belt, so shoot at it with Finn's blaster. A cylinder drops down and explodes; rebuild the pieces into a rotary control switch. Switch to BB-8 and use the rotary control switch to spring over an AT-AT leg and get to the other side.

MINIKIT

A red and black object is to the right of the conveyor belt. Use a dark side Force user, such as Darth Vader, to break it open and get the Minikit.

Move BB-8 into the AT-AT wreck and use the astromech terminal. Solve the puzzle to lift the large leg and allow Finn and Rey to catch up. Switch to Rey and, after defeating some stormtroopers, break a crate on the right and assemble the pieces into a wall run. Have Rey run across to the other side. Break up some more objects near the end of the run and build them into a staff switch. Use Rey's staff to turn the switch and rotate the walker's head so the group can get back together again. Fight off some stormtroopers to the right and then break up more crates. Use the pieces to create a rotary control switch. Switch to BB-8 and use him on the rotary control

switch to lower the gate to a corral. Take control of Rey or Finn and hop onto the back of the luggabeast. Ride it to the right and break through the large blocks with the cracks on them.

CHALLENGE:
LUGGABEAST MASTER

After breaking though the first cracked blocks, use the luggabeast to defeat three stormtroopers. This unlocks Davan Marak and earns a Gold Brick.

RED BRICK
(STUD MULTIPLIER X4)

Once in the corral with the stormtroopers, use the luggabeast to break a crate with a crack on it. Then use a character who can destroy gold LEGOs to break the gold crate to get to the Red Brick inside.

Continue to the back of the corral and use the luggabeast to break through another barrier of cracked blocks. Ride it through the opening to complete the level.

Niima Bombardment

CHARACTERS

	Rey		Finn
	BB-8		

UNLOCKS

	Taryish Juhden	Complete the level.
	Sarco Plank	Complete True Jedi challenge.
	Unkar Plutt	Complete All Collectibles challenge.
	Unkar Goon	Complete Group Shot challenge.
	Unkar Thug	Complete Flawless Coverage challenge.

GOLD BRICK CHALLENGES

Name	Mode	Notes
Level Complete	Any	Complete the level.
True Jedi	Any	Collect 25,000 studs.
All Collectibles	Free Play	Find all the Minikits.
Group Shot	Any	Defeat 3 stormtroopers with the turret or bomb Multi-Build.
Flawless Coverage	Any	Complete the spaceport cover section without being defeated.

COLLECTIBLES

Type	Mode	Notes
Minikit	Free Play	Destroy a silver container.
Minikit	Free Play	Move through flames.

ADVANCE THROUGH THE CONTROL TOWER

Han Solo and Chewbacca are trying to get away from the gang members as well as the rathtars. As Han Solo, move down and to the right. Use his goggles to find a silver door on one of the containers. Then switch to Chewbacca and throw a thermal detonator at the door to blow it up and clear the passageway. This leads to a cover section where you have to shoot at gangers. In the first part of this section, shoot at the pad and the console to cause an explosion that defeats the enemy behind the shield.

CHALLENGE:
GROUP SHOT

When constructing the Multi-Build, ensure there are at least three stormtroopers in the area. Once the bomb or turret defeats them, you earn a Gold Brick and unlock the Unkar Goon.

MINIKIT

After using the Multi-Build to defeat the stormtroopers and remove the landing craft, you can access a back area. Use a character with the ability to destroy silver objects, such as Chewbacca, to break open the silver container and get the Minikit.

Your way to the right is blocked, another Multi-Build is near the gray wall. Assemble it into a staff switch to the left. Then use Rey's staff on the switch to rotate the crane so a grapple hook is in position. Finn can use this to reach the top of the control tower.

Now break up the staff switch and rebuild the pieces into a rotary control switch. Use BB-8 on the rotary control switch to open a panel and reveal a climbing wall. Rey can use this to reach the top. Use both Rey and Finn to push a crate along a checkered pad until a target appears on the climbing wall. Take control of Finn and shoot at the target with his blaster to blow up the gray wall so you can continue.

CONTINUE TO THE SPACEPORT

Make your way up the stairs and onto a platform. Shoot a target on the right side, and then pick up the wheel that drops to the floor. Carry it to the socket on the left and turn it to open a gate that leads to the space port.

Switch to Rey and assemble the piece into a staff switch. Use Rey's staff to turn the switch and rotate the turret. Take control of BB-8 and power up the charge pad on the turret. The turret fires at a TIE fighter and causes it to leave behind a pile of bricks to the gate's left.

As you advance into the spaceport, First Order landing craft drop off more stormtroopers. Defeat a few and then a second landing craft lands. Shoot 12 more stormtroopers and a TIE fighter will fly in and blow up some containers revealing a small access hatch.

Assemble the pieces into a rotary control switch and put BB-8 to work rolling on it. This opens the gate so your group can reach the Millennium Falcon and get away from Niima Outpost.

CHALLENGE:
FLAWLESS COVERAGE

While fighting against the stormtroopers in the cover section of the level, avoid being defeated. Use cover as necessary. By doing this, you not only earn a Gold Brick but also unlock the Unkar Thug.

MINIKIT

The second Minikit is in the flames to the left of the spaceport gate. You will need a character who can walk through flames, such as the Flametrooper, to reach the Minikit.

Switch to BB-8 and roll through the small access hatch to get around to the side of the landing craft. Power up the charge pad on the craft and send it flying away.

GET TO THE MILLENNIUM FALCON

Your ride off the planet is behind another gate. To begin your effort in opening the gate, shoot at the target near some flames to open a door and deploy a small droid. Take control of Sifter and move the droid over a couple piles of sand to reveal some bricks.

Jakku Graveyard Flight

GRAVEYARD OF GIANTS

Rey is flying the Millennium Falcon for the first time and is under attack by lots of TIE fighters. As you fly trough this first area, dodge the wreckage and shoot at the TIE fighters. Watch the red reticule that appears over your ship.

This means a TIE fighter is targeting you from behind, so keep moving and dodging to avoid taking damage.

CHARACTERS

	Millennium Falcon (Episode VII)

UNLOCKS

	Quinar	Complete the level.
	Hobin Carsamba	Complete True Jedi challenge.
	Monn Tatth	Complete All Collectibles challenge.
	TIE fighter Pilot (Episode VII)	Complete Probation challenge.
	"Crusher" Roodown	Complete Golden Sands challenge.

GOLD BRICK CHALLENGES

Name	Mode	Notes
Level Complete	Any	Complete the level.
True Jedi	Any	Collect 22,000 studs.
All Collectibles	Any	Find all the Minikits.
Probation	Any	Destroy 5 probe droids.
Golden Sands	Any	Destroy 3 gold LEGO arches.

COLLECTIBLES

Type	Mode	Notes
Minikit	Any	Destroy 4 gold ships on the ground in the arena section.
Minikit	Any	Destroy a TIE fighter flying around the edge of the arena.

CHALLENGE:
PROBATION

While flying around, watch for five probe droids. Shoot at and blow them up to unlock the TIE fighter Pilot (Episode VII) and also earn a Gold Brick.

CHALLENGE:
GOLDEN SANDS

Another way to get a Gold Brick is to shoot the three gold arches in this area. It's tough to get this challenge while also going after the probe droids, so you may want to try playing this level another time to get both challenges. Completing this challenge also unlocks "Crusher" Roodown.

DESTROY EIGHT TIE FIGHTERS

As you get through the valley, a dogfight begins against lots of TIE fighters. Shoot down eight of them without getting destroyed in the process.

MINIKIT

In this arena area, there are four pieces of wreckage on the ground. Destroy all four to get the first Minikit.

MINIKIT

Fly around the edges of the arena. One of the TIE fighters in this area has a Minikit. Shoot it down to get the Minikit.

FLY THROUGH THE STAR DESTROYER

In order to get away from the TIE fighters, Rey decides to fly through the wreckage of a Star Destroyer. Dodge the debris while also avoiding being shot by the TIE fighter behind you.

CHAPTER 4:
THE ERAVANA
Freighter Battle

CHARACTERS

	Rey		Finn

UNLOCKS

	Crokind Shand	Complete True Jedi challenge.

GOLD BRICK CHALLENGES

Name	Mode	Notes
Level Complete	Any	Complete the level.
True Jedi	Any	Collect 30,000 studs.
All Collectibles	Free Play	Find all the Minikits.
Wrath-tar	Any	Avoid the rathtar tentacles.
Once a Stormtrooper, Always a Stormtrooper	Any	Defeat 10 gang members as Finn.

COLLECTIBLES

Type	Mode	Notes
Minikit	Free Play	Cut through a door with a lightsaber and then complete a minigame.
Red Brick (Stud Magnet)	Free Play	Get through a silver door and the cold at the end of the level.

TAKODANA HUB

After escaping from Jakku, the Millennium Falcon's power converter becomes damaged. You need to repair the ship. Take control of BB-8 and use the astromech terminal to solve a puzzle and open a door. The room on the other side is filled with poisonous gas. Switch to Finn and use his grapple gun to get the respirator on the far wall. Now Finn can enter the room and turn the wheel for the vent controls to get the gas out of the room.

Switch to Rey and enter the room. Insert her staff into the staff switch and then push it around to fix the power converter. This opens a door which allows you to access the level select terminal. Follow the trail of green studs to the terminal and start the next level.

GET TO THE CORRIDOR ON THE RIGHT

The Millennium Falcon is caught in a tractor beam and pulled into a large freighter. Han Solo and Chewbacca want their ship back. However, two different groups board the freighter, and neither are very happy with Han Solo.

As Rey tries to isolate the two gangs, she inadvertently releases the rathtars from their cages.

Move your characters forward and then to the left. Poison gas blocks your way. Take control of Finn; he can use his respirator to get through the gas. Once on the other side, use the control valve to shut off the flow of gas and the passageway will clear up.

Switch to Rey and catch up with Finn. Then use the wall run to move back to the right. When you get to a platform, move to the right side and throw her staff at a socket in the wall. Then jump over and twirl around the staff and around three poles to get to the platform on the far side. Smash some crates and then assemble the pieces into a staff switch. Use Rey to turn the switch and rotate a walkway into place so Finn can catch up.

CHALLENGE:
WRATH-TAR

After Rey rotates the platform, you take control of Finn on the other side. Don't just go running down the passageway. There are three grates along the wall. To complete this challenge, you must get past all three without taking damage from the rathtar tentacles. Approach each grate carefully and wait for the tentacles to come out. When the tentacles retreat back into the wall, move past the grate.

MINIKIT

There is a saber cut on the wall behind the staff socket. Use a character with a lightsaber and cut through the door. Inside, a rathtar has taken the Minikit. Watch the grates rattle. When they stop, attack the last grate that rattled and the rathtar will throw the Minikit out for you to collect.

FOLLOW THE PASSAGE TO THE RIGHT

Defeat any enemies and then use Finn's grapple gun on the grapple point to pull down a crate.

CHALLENGE:
ONCE A STORMTROOPER, ALWAYS A STORMTROOPER

There are lots of gang members in the passageways. To earn the Gold Brick, be sure to use Finn to defeat ten of these enemies.

Move into the room to the right of the malfunctioning doorway. Turn a crank to rotate a cylinder until a red circle and the goggle symbols appear. Take control of Rey and use her goggles to find a target. Either throw her staff at it or use Finn's blaster to shoot it. This deactivates the electricity blocking your way to the right. Be ready to fight some more gang members.

Continue along the passage to the right, being careful to avoid taking damage from rathtar tentacles that come out of the grates along the wall. Eventually, you fall down to a lower level when the walkway collapses.

GET TO THE EXIT

Down in the lower level, take control of Rey and slide under the gap in the wall. Smash some crates to reveal pieces to a Multi-Build. Assemble the pieces into a grapple hook on the left wall. Then switch to Finn and use his grapple gun to get up and over the wall. Break the hook so you can then rebuild the pieces into a platform on the right. Pull the platform out with Finn's grapple gun. Climb onto the platform and then jump to the handholds near the top of the wall so you can get over.

RED BRICK
(STUD MAGNET)

Before exiting the level, use Chewbacca or another character to destroy the large silver door to the exit's right. The Red Brick is inside the room; however, it is very cold in there. Switch to a character who can withstand the cold, such as BB-8, and grab the Red Brick to add it to your collection.

The large door you need to access is locked. It takes two people to unlock and open it. As Rey, throw your staff at the socket to the door's right. Then jump and hang from it. Switch to Finn and then jump and grab onto the Flusher switch to the door's left. Once the door opens, move to the ladder and climb it to complete the level.

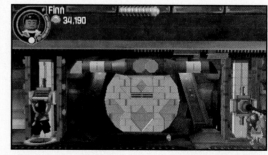

Freighter Chase

ADVANCE THROUGH THE CORRIDORS

Han Solo and Chewbacca are trying to get away from the gang members as well as the rathtars. As Han Solo, move down and to the right. Use his goggles to find a silver door on one of the containers. Then switch to Chewbacca and throw a thermal detonator at the door to blow it up and clear the passageway. This leads to a cover section where you have to shoot at gangers.

CHALLENGE:
NO MATCH FOR A GOOD BLASTER

During the cover section, be sure to use Han Solo. Shoot two of the gangers while not taking any damage to earn this Gold Brick and also unlock the Guavian Gunner. You want this character since it can destroy gold objects; many collectibles are hidden in gold objects.

After the cover section, Han and Chewbacca advance and take cover again. However, you can't hit the gangers who are hiding behind cover of their own. Take control of Chewbacca and throw thermal detonators at the two silver objects holding down the grate in the floor. Once they detonate, the rathtar underneath the grate will take care of the enemies for you.

FIND THE POWER CELLS

Han, Chewbacca, and BB-8 find themselves locked in a room. The controls for the door contains one power cell. However, three other power cells are missing. You need to find them and put them back into the controls. The first one is on the floor in the middle of the room. Pick it up and carry it over to the controls. The second is inside the silver container; use Chewbacca's thermal detonators to access it, and then carry it over to the controls.

Break up several crates in the room and then assemble the pieces into a rotary control switch. Use BB-8 on the rotary control switch to activate a trash compactor and push the last power cell out of a hatch. Pick it up and place it in the controls to open the door. Then exit the room.

CHARACTERS

	Han Solo		Chewbacca
	BB-8		Finn
	Rey		

UNLOCKS

	Kanjiklub Gang Member	Complete True Jedi challenge.
	Bala Tik	Complete All Collectibles challenge.
	Guavian Death Ganger	Complete Wookiee Cookie challenge.
	Guavian Gunner	Complete No Match for a Good Blaster challenge.

GOLD BRICK CHALLENGES

Name	Mode	Notes
Level Complete	Any	Complete the level.
True Jedi	Any	Collect 27,000 studs.
All Collectables	Free Play	Find all the Minikits.
Wookiee Cookie	Free Play	Find Chewbacca's 3 cookie stashes.
No Match for a Good Blaster	Any	Defeat 2 gangers with Han's blaster, without taking any damage.

COLLECTIBLES

Type	Mode	Notes
Minikit	Any	Collect this one while being chased by a rathtar.
Minikit	Free Play	Use a character with the Force to get this Minikit.

MINIKIT

In the power cell room, use a character with the Force to open the crate on the room's left side. This reveals the Minikit.

The level now shifts to Rey and Finn. They have to run away from a rathtar. Keep moving and dodge the objects that stand in your way to get away from the dangerous creature.

CHALLENGE:
WOOKIEE COOKIE

Chewbacca has hidden three stashes of cookies around the freighter. You must find them to collect this Gold Brick and unlock the Guavian Death Ganger. The first stash is at the start. Break up containers on the right side of the room to find a pile of ice. Then select a character that can melt ice, such as the Flametrooper, and get the first stash.

The second stash is in the power cell room. Use a character who can destroy gold objects to break the gold container and get another stash.

The final cookies are in the last area where you must rescue Finn. Blow up the silver container to get the last stash and complete this challenge.

MINIKIT

While running away from the rathtar, a Minikit will appear on the right side. As soon as you see it, jump up and hit it to add it to your collection.

Finn and Rey slide underneath a door. However, the rathtar grabs Finn with its tentacles. Rey must save him by shutting the large door. Assemble the Multi-Build into a switch on the right side of the room. Then pull on the switch to send power through the cables. Break up the switch and then rebuild it into a staff switch in the middle of the room. Rey must use her staff to turn the switch and rotate the cables into position above the door so they make a connection.

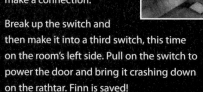

Break up the switch and then make it into a third switch, this time on the room's left side. Pull on the switch to power the door and bring it crashing down on the rathtar. Finn is saved!

Freighter Shutdown

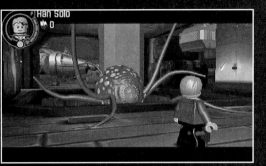

CHARACTERS

	Han Solo		BB-8
	Finn		Rey

UNLOCKS

	Kanjiklubber	Complete True Jedi challenge.
	Volzang Li-Thrull	Complete All Collectibles challenge.
	Razoo Qin-Fee	Complete The Tentacle Menace challenge.
	Tasu Leech	Complete BB-Ball challenge.

GOLD BRICK CHALLENGES

Name	Mode	Notes
Level Complete	Any	Complete the level.
True Jedi	Any	Collect 16,000 studs.
All Collectables	Free Play	Find all the Minikits.
The Tentacle Menace	Free Play	Scare off 3 rathtar tentacles.
BB-Ball	Any	Score a basket with BB-8.

COLLECTIBLES

Type	Mode	Notes
Minikit	Free Play	Destroy a gold panel and then use a First Order terminal.
Minikit	Free Play	Use the Force to move a ladder and then to destroy a container.

GET THE CONTAINER ON THE LEFT

The characters have almost made it to the Millennium Falcon. However, a rathtar blocks the way. Take control of either Han or Finn and move to the right. Fire your grapple gun at the double grapple point and pull a crate down to the ground where it breaks. Assemble the Multi-Build into a climbing wall on the side of a container

Switch to Rey and climb up the wall. Throw her staff into a socket on the wall and then jump over to it. Twirl around the staff and then jump across to some poles to finally reach the platform on the left. Assemble some bricks into a switch and then activate it to lower a platform above the poles. Watch out for holes in the walls. Rathtar tentacles come out of them and attack you.

CHALLENGE:

CHALLENGE: THE TENTACLE MENACE

Rathtar tentacles reach for you from three different locations. Hit the tentacles to scare them away and earn a Gold Brick and unlock Razoo Qin-Fee. The first location is on the upper platform at the far-left side where Rey builds a switch. The second is above the climbing wall. The third is on the level's right side. After using the Force to move a ladder and getting up on a container, double-jump to the left onto a platform.

Break up the climbing wall and reassemble it into a rotary control switch on the left. Take control of BB-8 and use the rotary control switch to launch him to the platform. Activate an astromech terminal and solve the puzzle to move a large container over by the rathtar.

CHALLENGE:

BB-BALL

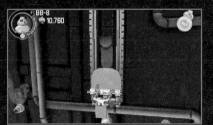

After BB-8 activates the astromech terminal, drop down and use the rotary control switch again to launch him through a hoop. This unlocks Tasu Leech and adds a Gold Brick to your collection.

Now move to the right and shoot the target on the container with Han's or Finn's blaster. This causes some bricks to drop out. Assemble them into a base structure which you will add to later.

MINIKIT

A gold panel is on a container to the rathtar's left. Destroy it using a character with that ability. Then use Finn to access a First Order terminal. Complete the puzzle to get the Minikit.

GET THE CONTAINER ON THE RIGHT

Now head to the level's right side. Take control of Finn and walk through the toxic spill using his respirator. Once on the other side, shoot his grapple gun at the hook and pull down a container.

You must now assemble the pieces of a Multi-Build into three switches and activate them in the correct order. Look at the red, orange, and blue wires along the wall. You need to light up the panels above them. So build a switch in front of each and then step on it to activate it. The correct order is left, right, and then center. Once complete, a large container on the right opens.

Locate some pieces inside the container and assemble them into a droid that will clean up the toxic spill. It then annoys the rathtar and ends up in pieces. Assemble the pieces into a rotary control switch and lift. Move a character onto the lift and then switch to BB-8. Use the rotary control switch to raise the lift. Press a switch at the top to deploy another container.

MINIKIT

This Minikit is on the level's right side. Use a character with the Force to move a ladder down. Then climb onto the top of the container. Use the Force again to break open a small crate and get the Minikit.

CLEAR A PATH TO THE MILLENNIUM FALCON

The rathtar breaks up the container. Assemble the pieces into a turret on top of the base. Have a character take control of the turret and begin shooting at the rathtar. Once it is dazed, shoot at the support behind it. Continue doing this until the support is completely destroyed and drops on top of the rathtar. Now your group can reach the Millennium Falcon and make their escape.

TAKODANA HUB

After leaving the large freighter, Han Solo flies the Millennium Falcon to Takodana and lands on this planet. Once on the ground, move toward the level select terminal. As you approach, a creature removes the power cell and carries it into a tree. Use Rey's goggles to find silver bricks along a wall. Switch to Chewbacca and blow up the silver bricks with a thermal detonator. Then have Chewbacca pull on some strength handles.

Use Finn's grapple gun to pull on a hook up in the tree to get some more bricks. Then assemble all of these pieces into a catapult. Grapple the hook on the catapult to pull it back and fire a rock at the creature in the tree. After it drops the power cell, pick it up and place it into the slot near the level select terminal. Once the cell is replaced, you can use the terminal to begin Chapter 5.

CHAPTER 5:
MAZ'S CASTLE
Castle Approach

GET TO THE CASTLE

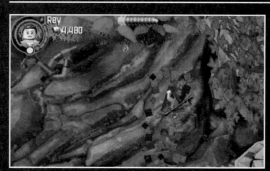

Now that the party has landed on Takodana, it is time to head to Maz's castle to find a way to get BB-8 to the Resistance. Take control of Rey and get up the climb wall along the back cliff. At the top, jump across to the left and then swing around a series of poles to get to solid ground.

Move to the left and use Rey's goggles near a tree to locate a pair of grapple hooks. Switch to Finn or Han and then use their grapple guns to pull on the hooks together and knock the tree down. Assemble the pieces into a jump pad and jump to the platform where Rey is waiting. There is another Grapple Hook up there. Grapple it to open a fallen log, and then move through the inside to get across a stream.

CHARACTERS

	Rey (Takodana)		Finn
	Han Solo		BB-8

UNLOCKS

	Sudswater Dillifay Glon	Complete the level.
	Taybin Ralorsa	Complete True Jedi challenge.
	Varmik	Complete All Collectibles challenge.
	HURID-327	Complete Classic Misdirection challenge.
	Grummgar	Complete Full Stream challenge.

GOLD BRICK CHALLENGES

Name	Mode	Notes
Level Complete	Any	Complete the level.
True Jedi	Any	Collect 21,000 studs.
All Collectibles	Free Play	Find all the Minikits.
Classic Misdirection	Any	Point all the signs away from the castle.
Full Stream	Any	Wake Grummgar up in a single attempt.

COLLECTIBLES

Type	Mode	Notes
Minikit	Free Play	Use a protocol droid.
Minikit	Free Play	Use a small access hatch to get to a balcony.

CHALLENGE:
CLASSIC MISDIRECTION

A sign showing the way to Maz's castle is to the left of the tree where Rey uses her goggles. Hit the sign to turn it around so it points in the wrong direction. There are two more signs along the way to the castle. Be sure to hit and spin them around as well to earn a Gold Brick and unlock HURID-327.

Once through the log, switch to BB-8 and go through the small access hatch to get to the other side of another stream. Once there, power up a charge panel on a crashed starship. This causes it to ignite an engine and then blow up. A vine is left behind. Switch to the other characters and jump across to the vine and then on to the area where BB-8 is located.

Follow the path to the left to a Wall kick along the back cliff. Take control of Rey and jump your way to the top of the wall. Move to the left and then push a container along a checkered path and off the side of the cliff. Switch to Finn or Han and then assemble the pieces into a ramp that will help you get to the top of the cliff. Keep moving to the left to get to Maz's Castle.

MINIKIT

A Minikit is inside a cage just outside of the entrance to Maz's castle. You will need to use a protocol droid, such as R-3PO, during Free Play to access the protocol terminal and solve the puzzle. You must watch four symbols appear in a specific order and then repeat the order to win.

GET GRUMMGAR TO MOVE

As you enter the castle's courtyard, a large sleeping creature by the name of Grummgar blocks the entrance. You must find a way to wake him without losing an arm in the process. Use Rey or Han's goggles to find a Grapple Hook on the lamp on the courtyard's right side.

Grapple the hook to pull it down. This provides the pieces for a Multi-Build.

MINIKIT

This Minikit is on a balcony on the courtyard's right side. You can only get it during Free Play. Use BB-8 to go through the small access hatch. Then switch to another character and jump across to the balcony where the Minikit is located.

CHALLENGE:
FULL STREAM

You must follow several steps to wake up Grummgar. To complete this challenge and earn a Gold Brick, construct the Multi-Builds in the correct order (follow the directions listed in the final two paragraphs of this section). As an additional reward, you also unlock Grummgar.

Start off by assembling the pieces to the left into a claw-like machine. Use BB-8 to power up the charge panel and activate the machine. The machine will remove a tree, revealing a climb wall. Take control of Rey and climb it. At the top, jump across to the balcony on the right. Hit the flower pots to break them up.

Drop back to the ground and assemble the pieces into a pipe that diverts the water from the downspout to a pump. Now break apart the claw machine and reassemble it into a water cannon near the hoses. Once again, power up a charge panel with BB-8 to activate the cannon. Spray Grummgar with water to wake him up. He then walks through the door into the castle. Follow him in to complete the level.

Castle Hall

FINN'S TASK

The group walks into Maz's place. To complete the level, three of the characters must complete their individual tasks. Start off with Finn. Walk to the left from the entrance and talk to Captain Sidon Ithano. He wants to see how good you are with a blaster.

Finn must shoot ten bottles in a shooting gallery minigame. Don't worry about shooting anything else. Only the bottles count toward completing this task.

CHARACTERS

	Rey (Takodana)		Finn
	Han Solo		BB-8
	Chewbacca		

UNLOCKS

	Praster Ommlen	Complete the level.
	Bazine Netal	Complete True Jedi challenge.
	Quiggold	Complete All Collectibles challenge.
	GA-97	Complete the Just a Helping Hand challenge.
	Captain Sidon Ithano	Complete Quick Fire Shot challenge.

GOLD BRICK CHALLENGES

Name	Mode	Notes
Level Complete	Any	Complete the level.
True Jedi	Any	Collect 28,000 studs.
All Collectibles	Free Play	Find all the Minikits.
Just a Helping Hand	Free Play	Help all the patrons of the bar.
Quick Fire Shot	Any	Shoot all 10 bottles in the shooting gallery in less than 15 seconds.

COLLECTIBLES

Type	Mode	Notes
Minikit	Free Play	Use a lightsaber to cut down a lamp near the entrance.
Minikit	Free Play	Destroy 3 gold lamps.

CHALLENGE:
QUICK FIRE SHOT

To earn a Gold Brick and unlock Captain Sidon Ithano, you must shoot ten bottles in under 15 seconds. Don't be distracted by the target or other objects. Focus on shooting just the bottles and you will successfully complete this challenge.

CHEWBACCA'S TASK

After Finn completes the shooting gallery, Chewbacca walks into the room. Take control of him. Grummgar, the big creature that was blocking the doorway in the previous level, is sitting at a table. Break up some containers near his table and then assemble them into a hammer-like object.

To the right of the door are some strength handles. Pull on them to begin putting a series of gears into motion. This causes the hammer to break a cover over a silver object on the wall. Now throw a thermal detonator at the silver object to blow it up. After it falls on Grummgar, he becomes upset and challenges Chewbacca to an arm wrestling match. The second task is completed.

MINIKIT

This Minikit is on top of a pillar next to the door. You need a character with a lightsaber for this. Stand at the blue icon on the floor and slice through the pillar to cut it down so you can reach the Minikit.

CHALLENGE:

CHALLENGE: JUST A HELPING HAND

GA-97 can be unlocked when you complete this challenge. Use a character with the Force ability to help people in the castle. For the first one, use the Force to fix a scooter on the floor to the door's right. Now move to the drink bar on the room's right side and use the Force to pick up mugs from the floor and set them on a counter.

HAN SOLO'S TASK

Two tasks completed; one more to go. Head to the room's far-right side and break up a beverage cart into a Multi-Build. Assemble the pieces into a staff switch to the right and use Rey and her staff to turn it. This lifts a door and reveals a small access hatch.

Switch to BB-8 and go through the hatch. The droid emerges behind the beverage counter. Use BB-8 on the astromech terminal to solve a puzzle that gets the beverage machine working.

Now that customers have something to drink, they need a place to sit. Switch to Han and break up the staff switch. Then reassemble it into some chairs and a table to the left. This completes the level.

MINIKIT

To get the second Minikit, you need a character with a rapid fire weapon such as Phasma or the Guavian Gunner that can destroy gold objects. Shoot at the three gold lamps hanging from the ceiling. Once the third lamp is destroyed, the Minikit will fall to the floor.

Castle Basement

ADVANCE THROUGH THE BASEMENT

Rey and BB-8 advance into the castle's basement while the other characters are busy upstairs. Move through this corridor and defeat any womp rats that try to attack you.

CHARACTERS

	Rey (Takodana)		BB-8

UNLOCKS

	Bollie Prindel	Complete the level.
	Infrablue Zedbeddy Coggins	Complete True Jedi challenge.
	Wollivan	Complete All Collectibles challenge.
	Pru Sweevant	Complete Tidy as you Go challenge.
	Rey (Young)	Complete Floor is Lava! Challenge.

GOLD BRICK CHALLENGES

Name	Mode	Notes
Level Complete	Any	Complete the level.
True Jedi	Any	Collect 45,000 studs.
All Collectibles	Free Play	Find all the Minikits.
Tidy as You Go	Any	Destroy all of the objects in the first corridor.
Floor is Lava!	Any	Collect the upper gear without touching the ground once you've started.

COLLECTIBLES

Type	Mode	Notes
Minikit	Free Play	Destroy the silver object in the final room.
Red Brick	Free Play	Use the Force to open a wall in the final room.

CHALLENGE:

TIDY AS YOU GO

While walking down the corridor, destroy the 17 objects located on either side. This earns a Gold Brick and unlocks Pru Sweevant.

When you get to the corridor's end, move to the left and break the wall into pieces. Assemble the pieces into a rotary control switch. Then use BB-8 on the rotary control switch to raise a gate just enough so Rey can slide under it.

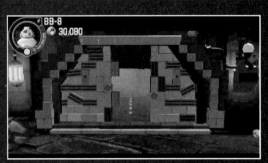

After Rey slides to the other side, break up containers to get pieces for a Multi-Build. Construct a crank on the right side near the gate, and then turn the crank to raise the gate so BB-8 can get under it. Fight off some more womp rats, then break up the crank and reassemble it as an astromech terminal. Use BB-8 to solve the puzzle and open a door that allows you to move further into the basement.

CONTINUE TO THE CHAMBER

Move through the doorway and continue toward some large statues. Defeat the goons that try to stop you along the way. Break up objects near the statue and assemble the pieces into a staff switch. As Rey, use your staff to turn the switch and cause the statues to rotate and reveal a charge panel. Use BB-8 to power it up and open another door.

Continue along the corridor, defeating womp rats as you go. Then turn to the left and move into a large chamber.

RED BRICK
(STUD MULTIPLIER X6)

Before taking the left turn to the large chamber, use a dark side character with the Force, such as Darth Vader, to open a gate blocking off an alcove. Then switch to a character that can destroy the gold container to get the Red Brick.

SOLVE THE CHAMBER PUZZLE

As you enter the large chamber, the door closes behind you. Move into the center of the room and break the lamp and the container. Assemble the lamp pieces into a staff switch on the left, and then have Rey turn it to open a small door. Defeat the womp rats that come out, and then pick up a gear and carry it to the back wall. Place it on the left side where an arrow indicates.

Now assemble the other pieces in the center into a rotary control switch, and use BB-8 to activate it. This causes some pillars on the room's right side to rise and form bar hops. Switch to Rey and jump onto these bar hops to reach a platform

on the right. Jump to the left and twirl around a few poles to get to another platform on the room's left side.

CHALLENGE:
FLOOR IS LAVA!

Once Rey starts jumping up the pillars, you must treat the floor like it is lava. If you touch it, you won't die; however, you won't complete this challenge. Stay on the platforms until you complete the task. This unlocks Rey (Young) and earns a Gold Brick.

Switch back to BB-8 and use the rotary control switch again to move a climbing wall out from an alcove. This allows Rey to climb the wall and jump up to a pole. Jump to the left to a couple hand holds and then to a ledge. Pull yourself up and then walk along the ledge to get to another platform. Break a lamp there, assemble the pieces into a staff switch, then turn it to open a door to an alcove below.

Drop to the ground floor and pick up the gear inside the alcove. Carry it to the back wall and place it in position on the right side. Then break up the staff switch on the floor and reassemble it into a pole in the middle of the gears. Jump to the pole and twirl around it to open a door in the center of the back wall. Go through the doorway to complete the level.

MINIKIT

This Minikit is located in the large chamber. Use a character that can destroy silver objects to blow up the silver door on the right side. Then go in and grab the Minikit.

TAKODANA HUB

Rey and BB-8 need to escape through the woods. Break up a circular object in the center of this area, and then build the pieces into a gear structure on a wall. Jump and grab onto a pole to open a door. Switch to BB-8 and roll through the open door and onto a lift.

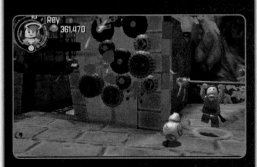

Take control of Rey again and jump up some handholds to the lift's left. Locate a staff switch and turn it to bring BB-8 up to the higher area. Follow the pathway to a rotary control switch which BB-8 can use to open a gate. Advance through the gate and follow a trail of green studs all the way to a level select terminal. Use the terminal to begin the next chapter.

CHAPTER 6:
ATTACK ON TAKODANA
Castle Corridors

CHARACTERS

	Finn (Takodana)		Chewbacca (Wounded)
	Han Solo		Maz Kanata

UNLOCKS

	Cratinus	Complete All Collectibles challenge.
	Prashee	Complete Fight Fire with Fire challenge.
	Ubert "Sticks" Quaril	Complete I'm Rubber, You're Glue challenge.

GOLD BRICK CHALLENGES

Name	Mode	Notes
Level Complete	Any	Complete the level.
True Jedi	Any	Collect 20,000 studs.
All Collectibles	Free Play	Find all the Minikits.
Fight Fire with Fire	Free Play	Destroy 5 objects as the Flametrooper with the flamethrower weapon.
I'm Rubber, You're Glue	Free Play	Defeat a stormtrooper by deflecting his bolts back at him.

COLLECTIBLES

Type	Mode	Notes
Minikit	Any	Use goggles to find a saber wall and then climb it.
Minikit	Free Play	Use the Force to get this Minikit down from the top of a pillar.

PUT OUT THE FLAMES

The First Order troops have attacked and set fire to the castle. For your group to escape, they must put out some flames which are keeping them trapped.

Defeat the stormtroopers in the area. Then, using Finn's lightsaber, cut down a pillar on the room's left side. Assemble the pieces into a pair of grapple hooks, and then use Finn and Han Solo to grapple them and pull. This breaks away the wall and a water pipe puts out the nearest flames.

CHALLENGE:
FIGHT FIRE WITH FIRE

For this challenge, you need the Flametrooper character. Use a flamethrower to destroy five objects in the castle. This earns a Gold Brick and unlocks Prashee.

DEFEAT THE FLAMETROOPERS IN THE SHIELDS

There are two flametroopers guarding the castle's exit. Unfortunately, the flametroopers are each protected by their own shields, so you can't just attack them normally. Before you can deal with them, you must first defeat eight stormtroopers that attack.

Along the back wall, use Han Solo's goggles to locate a wall kick. Select Finn and press the Jump button to jump back and forth between the sides of the wall. When you reach the top, grab the Minikit.

CHALLENGE:
I'M RUBBER, YOU'RE GLUE

Even though Finn has a lightsaber, he is not trained in the ways of the Force. However, characters such as Luke Skywalker and Darth Vader can deflect laser blasts back at the enemy. Hold down the Attack button when an enemy fires and there is a chance that the blast will deflect back. Defeat a stormtrooper with this tactic to earn a Gold Brick and unlock Jbert "Sticks" Quaril.

After the stormtroopers have been defeated, use Finn's lightsaber to cut through a wall to the right. This lets you enter a room with a small access hatch. Switch to Maz Kanata and go through the hatch. This takes her to an upper room. Push a pile of bricks along a checkered path so it crashes down to the floor below.

The bricks on the floor are a Multi-Build. Assemble the pieces into a cake that explodes and it takes care of the shield-protected flametrooper on the left.

Now build a bomb out of the pieces to the right and defeat the second flametrooper.

This Minikit is on top of a pillar in an alcove to the flametroopers' right. Use a character with the Force to move the Minikit down to where you can reach it

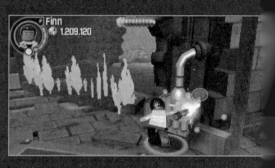

Finally, use Finn's lightsaber to cut through some water pipes near the exit. This puts out the last flames. Your group can now escape from the castle.

Castle Escape

TAKE COVER

You've made it out of the castle and now find yourself in the middle of a battle with the First Order. TIE fighters are strafing your position and stormtroopers are shooting at you. Quickly move to the barricade on the right as Finn or Han Solo. Target the grapple hook and grapple it to pull yourself to a higher platform overlooking the battlefield.

CHALLENGE:
LET'S CALL IT A TIE

To complete this challenge, earn a Gold Brick, and unlock Oskus Stooratt, you must avoid taking any damage from the TIE fighters. Watch for the large red icons to appear behind the barricades. This informs you of an incoming attack. Quickly move to another barricade before the damage hits. You don't have much of a warning, so move quickly!

From the higher platform, you have a great angle for attacking the enemy. Shoot at the red and black explosive container so you can defeat several enemies with a single explosion. Then pick off the remaining stormtroopers.

Once the first wave is defeated, your group moves to the next section of barricades. This time you face a turret inside a shield as well as stormtroopers. You are not going to be able to shoot your way through this one. Take control of Han Solo and move to the right. Use his goggles to find a silver part of a statue on the right. Quickly switch to Chewbacca and throw a thermal detonator at the silver base to cause the statue to topple and crush the turret. Second wave cleared.

Two landing craft arrive and drop off more stormtroopers. Not only do they shoot at you, but they also throw thermal detonators. If one lands near you, quickly move to cover behind another barricade before it detonates. There are two explosive containers near the enemy lines, so target those to get more bang from your shots.

CHARACTERS

	Finn (Takodana)		Chewbacca (Wounded)
	Han Solo		

UNLOCKS

	Riot Control Stormtrooper / FN-2199	Complete All Collectibles challenge.
	Wi'ba Tuyll	Complete Cook Up a Storm challenge.
	Oskus Stooratt	Complete Let's Call it a TIE challenge.

GOLD BRICK CHALLENGES

Name	Mode	Notes
Level Complete	Any	Complete the level.
True Jedi	Any	Collect 20,000 studs.
All Collectibles	Free Play	Find the Minikit and Red Brick.
Let's Call it a TIE	Any	Don't take any damage from the TIE fighters.
Cook up a Storm	Any	Use each of the Multi-Build models to defeat FN-2199.

COLLECTIBLES

Type	Mode	Notes
Minikit	Free Play	Look in a puddle in the courtyard.
Red Brick (Destroy on Contact)	Free Play	Use a dark side Force user during the cover section on a wall.

RED BRICK
(DESTROY ON CONTACT)

Some red and black bricks are on a building behind the stormtroopers' position. Use a dark side character with the Force, such as Kylo Ren or Darth Vader, to break apart those bricks to get this Red Brick.

The final stage of the cover section has you shooting at enemies as they emerge from the landing craft. Keep shooting at them until the landing craft fly away. Then two explosive containers near a wall will become visible. Shoot them both to blast a hole in the wall so you can advance to the next area.

DEFEAT FN-2199

As your group enters a courtyard, stormtroopers arrive and try to box you in. There is no cover here, so move in and attack. Your first objective is to defeat 12 stormtroopers. The key is to keep moving so you don't take damage.

MINIKIT

This Minikit is hidden in a puddle on the courtyard's left side. Use a character that can swim, like Admiral Ackbar, to retrieve this Minikit.

After defeating 12 stormtroopers, a riot control stormtrooper drops in from a landing craft. This is FN-2199, Finn's former squad mate. This is a tough enemy to beat. Stay away from him since you can't hurt him with normal attacks. When a red icon appears under you, run. FN-2199 is coming at you with a jump attack.

Keep dodging until one of FN-2199's slam attacks breaks up some bricks into a Multi-Build. You now have your choice of three different objects to build. It does not matter which you choose; they will all stun FN-2199 temporarily and allow you to move in and inflict some damage.

CHALLENGE:
COOK UP A STORM

When fighting FN-2199, be sure to use each of the three different Multi-Build objects to stun him. This variety earns you a Gold Brick and unlocks Wi'ba Tuyll.

Once FN-2199 recovers, get out of the way. Wait for him to break up the object so you can build another. You need to do this stun-and-attack sequence three times to reach the final fight. Finn takes on his former friend using the lightsaber. Press the buttons that appear on-screen to finally win.

Takodana Skies

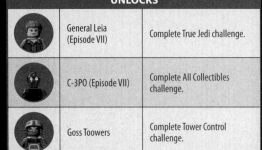

THE APPROACH

The Resistance has arrived on Takodana. As Poe Dameron, you are taking the lead in your X-wing starfighter. Your squadron is making a low approach down a river valley to avoid detection until you arrive at the castle. Fly through rings of studs and add them to your collection. There are no enemies during this phase.

CHARACTERS

	Poe Dameron (Flight Suit)		Snap Wexley

UNLOCKS

	General Leia (Episode VII)	Complete True Jedi challenge.
	C-3PO (Episode VII)	Complete All Collectibles challenge.
	Goss Toowers	Complete Tower Control challenge.
	Sache Skareet	Complete TIE Die challenge.

GOLD BRICK CHALLENGES

Name	Mode	Notes
Level Complete	Any	Complete the level.
True Jedi	Any	Collect 100,000 studs.
All Collectibles	Free Play	Find all the Minikits.
Tower Control	Any	Destroy the 5 towers during the approach to the battlefield.
TIE Die	Any	Save the transporter without it taking damage.

COLLECTIBLES

Type	Mode	Notes
Minikit	Any	Destroy the jammer tower on the castle.
Minikit	Any	Destroy the 3 transport ships before they land.

CHALLENGE:
TOWER CONTROL

While making the approach, there are five towers located along the sides of the river. Destroy all of them to earn a Gold Brick and unlock Goss Toowers. The first is near the start on the right side. Then they alternate sides for each subsequent tower.

SHOOT DOWN 12 TIE FIGHTERS

Once you arrive at the castle, the level turns into a large dogfight. Your job is to shoot down a dozen TIE fighters. Use the small x-shaped reticle to help aim your shots.

DESTROY THE 3 TRANSPORT SHIPS

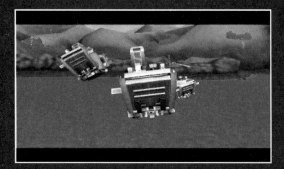

The First Order are sending more stormtroopers to the castle. You need to prevent these reinforcements from arriving. Look for the thicker arrow-shaped reticles on the screen to help you locate the transport ships. Then focus on destroying them instead of the TIE fighters. If you take too long trying to destroy the transport ships, they will land and become

Shoot down all three transport ships before they can land to collect this Minikit.

PROTECT THE GENERAL'S TRANSPORT

General Leia has arrived on the scene. Her transport is a bit early and there are still TIE fighters in the area. Use the thicker arrow-shaped reticle to find this ship in the sky and then fly in close. Shoot down any TIE fighters that get near it and prevent it from being destroyed. Continue flying as an escort until the level is completed.

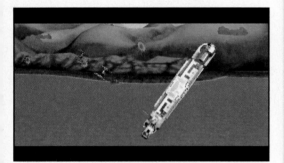

CHALLENGE:
TIE DIE

To complete this challenge, you must ensure that the General's transport does not take any damage. This is a tough one. You need to focus on all the TIE fighters near the transport and shoot them down. You will be rewarded with a Gold Brick as well as unlock Sache Skareet.

This Minikit is hidden in the jammer at the castle. You must destroy the silver structure to get it. Wait until the General's transport arrives, along with some TIE fighters with torpedoes. Shoot down these TIE fighters and collect the torpedoes. Then fire torpedoes at the silver structure to destroy the jammer and get the Minikit.

RESISTANCE BASE HUB

After leaving Takodana, you've arrived at the Resistance Base. Han Solo will be leading a team to Starkiller Base, and you need to help him prepare by getting ammo, supplies, and Wookiee cookies. Follow the trail of green studs to the Supplies Bunker. Once inside the bunker, locate a small access hatch near a gate. Send BB-8 through the hatch and use a rotary control switch on the inside to open the gate. Then switch to a character with a lightsaber and cut through a smaller gate to get the ammo.

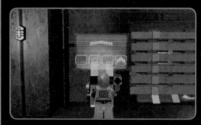

Next, climb a ladder and push a container on the left along a checkered path until it falls to the floor and breaks. Build the pieces into a lift and use it to get C-3PO up to the higher walkway. Use the protocol droid terminal and solve the memory puzzle to open the gate to the right and get the supplies.

All that remains are the Wookiee cookies. Talk to Nien Nunb by the terminal and large locked door. Since he does not speak Basic, you need to use someone who can translate, such as C-3PO. Nien wants ice cream in order to help you.

Climb the ladder. Move to the right along the walkway, and use Leia to shoot at the grapple point on the ceiling and swing across to a walkway on the bunker's opposite side. Use the Resistance terminal near a door and solve the puzzle by matching symbols to open the door. Once inside, push a block of ice out of the small room and drop it on the floor. Jump down and pick up the ice cream and take it to Nien Nunb. He will open the locked door so you can get the cookies. Finally, return to the Millennium Falcon to continue to the next chapter.

CHARACTERS

	Han Solo (Starkiller)		Finn (Takodana)
	Chewbacca		

UNLOCKS

	Snowtrooper (Episode VII)	Complete True Jedi challenge.
	Korr Sella	Complete All Collectibles challenge.
	General Hux	Complete Power to the People challenge.
	Petty Officer Thanisson	Complete Wampa Stompa challenge.

GOLD BRICK CHALLENGES

Name	Mode	Notes
Level Complete	Any	Complete the level.
True Jedi	Any	Collect 40,000 studs.
All Collectibles	Free Play	Find the Minikit and red brick.
Power to the People	Any	Complete the Power Bridge puzzle without losing power.
Wampa Stompa	Free Play	Defeat the wampa.

COLLECTIBLES

Type	Mode	Notes
Minikit	Any	Build a snowman and then jump up it to get to a higher area.
Red Brick (Mega Melee)	Free Play	Defeat the wampa.

STARKILLER BASE HUB

Han Solo has crash landed the Millennium Falcon on Starkiller Base. Now you need to open the emergency locker. Follow the trail of green studs to the locker. Switch to Chewbacca and throw a thermal detonator at the silver containers. When they blow up, assemble the pieces into a terminal; then use it to connect power to the locker.

Take control of Han and use his goggles to find a couple Grapple hooks. Grapple them and pull. Assemble the pieces that fall to the ground into another terminal and use it to connect the other power supply to the locker. Finally build a level select terminal with the bricks from the locker and use it to continue to the next level.

GET AWAY FROM THE CRASH SITE

Just as your characters get out of the Millennium Falcon, they are attacked by probe droids. Shoot them to clear away any resistance. Then grapple the hook on the radar dish and pull it down. Assemble the pieces into the first part of a turret.

Switch to Finn and use his lightsaber to cut through a boulder on the area's right side to get some more bricks. Finish assembling the turret, then jump onto the pad on the turret to fire it and melt some ice. Now take control of Chewbacca and throw a thermal detonator at the silver rock to create an exit from the crash site.

ADVANCE TO THE BASE

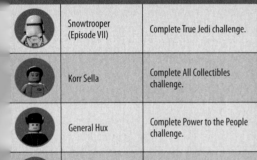

Shimmy along a ledge as you continue to the right. Use Han and Finn to grapple a pair of hooks and pull down some bricks. Assemble them into a ladder. Switch to Chewbacca and climb the ladder. At the top, pull on some strength handles to break away rocks and reveal a series of

Move to the right and break up a large container. With this Multi-Build, assemble a turret. It will destroy another turret and defeat several of the enemies in the area. Then assemble the pieces of the turret that was destroyed into a large magnet that will pull on some metal near a large door.

MINIKIT

After the turret does its job, break it up and reassemble it into a snowman next to a cliff on the left. Jump onto the snowman. Then jump to some handholds. Use them to get to a platform on the right where the Minikit is located.

Defeat the enemies that arrive on the scene. Then use Han or Finn to fire their blasters at the targets above the large door. Once the door opens, use Finn to get to the top of the wall kick. Go to the right at the top and break up some objects so you can use the pieces to build a grappling cannon. As it fires and deploys a cable, jump up and zip-line down the cable to get over the laser barrier.

Defeat the stormtroopers near the fence. Then use Finn's lightsaber to cut through the fence's power supply to bring it down and let Han and Chewbacca through.

CHALLENGE:
WAMPA STOMPA

There is a small access hatch in the cliff side to the right of the laser fence. Use BB-8 to get through it and into the wampa's cave. Switch to another character and defeat the wampa to earn a Gold Brick and unlock Petty Officer Thanisson.

RED BRICK
(MEGA MELEE)

After you defeat the wampa, this Red Brick appears in the cave. Be sure to pick it up before you leave the cave.

OPEN THE LARGE DOOR

Take control of Chewbacca and move to the right. Throw a thermal detonator at the silver weather station to blow it up into a pile of pieces for a Multi-Build.

Assemble a switch to the door's left. Then activate the switch. As soon as you see a small blue circle of power begin moving through the cable, break the switch. Now quickly reassemble it into a junction box above the door. You need to do this before the power gets there so it will continue to its destination at a terminal. Finally, use Finn to activate the First Order terminal and complete the puzzle to open the door. Enter the lift platform to complete the level.

CHALLENGE:
POWER TO THE PEOPLE

To complete this challenge, you must get the power to the terminal on the first try without making any mistakes. If you succeed, you get a Gold Brick and unlock General Hux.

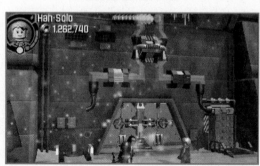

Shield Room Approach

PUT OUT THE FLAMES

MINIKIT

A Minikit is at the start. Use the Flametrooper to melt the ice. Then switch to a character who can swim, such as Admiral Ackbar. Go through the water to get to an upper platform where a couple snowtroopers are making a snowman. Defeat them and break the snowman to get the Minikit.

Take control of Finn at the start and move to the right. Continue along a pathway until you come across some toxic gas. Finn can use his respirator to get through it. Then drop down to a lower area.

CHALLENGE:
SMASH HITS

There are five radar transmitters in this level. The first is right at the start. Destroy them all to get a Gold Brick and unlock MSE-3-M813M.

At the bottom of the icy slide, defeat a couple enemies and then break up the objects to get a Valve handle. Pick it up and put it in a socket near some controls. Turn the valve handle to shut off the toxic gas so the other characters can get past it. Then climb the pole to the left of the controls to reach the higher area.

Continue to the right, but do not cross the red lines on the walkway. If you do, a large turret will fire on you. Instead, head down some stairs and destroy the control panel on the back wall to reveal some strength handles. Switch to Chewbacca and pull on them to get a pile of bricks. Assemble them into a mini snowspeeder which takes off and deals with

CHARACTERS

	Han Solo (Starkiller)		Finn (Takodana)
	Chewbacca		

UNLOCKS

	MSE-3-M813M	Complete Smash Hits challenge.
	Technician Mandetat	Complete Thermal Heating challenge.

GOLD BRICK CHALLENGES

Name	Mode	Notes
Level Complete	Any	Complete the level.
True Jedi	Any	Collect 40,000 studs.
All Collectibles	Free Play	Find all the Minikits.
Smash Hits	Any	Smash 5 First Order Radar Transmitters.
Thermal Heating	Any	Take out 3 stormtroopers with a thermal detonator.

COLLECTIBLES

Type	Mode	Notes
Minikit	Free Play	Melt ice and then swim to a higher platform to destroy a snowman.
Minikit	Free Play	Use the Force on a panel near the end of the level.

Take control of Han Solo and head up the stairs. Continue to the right and use his grapple gun to shoot at a grapple hook and swing across a gap. Next use his goggles to locate a target on a water pipe. Shoot it to release water that will freeze and create a ledge. Chewbacca can now shimmy across to catch up.

GET INTO THE SHIELD ROOM

Your crew is now outside the shield room entrance. They need to get through the door. Han and Finn must use their grapple guns to pull on a pair of grapple hooks to reveal a silver door. Switch to Chewbacca and toss a thermal detonator at the door to break it open.

CHALLENGE:
THERMAL HEATING

After blowing up the silver door, three snowtroopers attack. Use Chewbacca's thermal detonators to defeat all three. Just hold down the Attack button and place the target over each. Release to throw the bomb at them. You must get all of them with the explosives to earn this Gold Brick and unlock Technician Mandetat.

Defeat the enemies on the other side of the silver door. Then take control of Finn and use the First Order terminal on the left side. This releases a damaged probe droid which crashes and forms a pile of bricks in the center of the room.

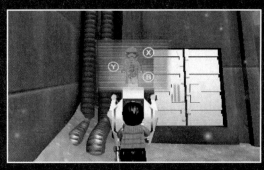

MINIKIT

After Finn uses the First Order terminal, use a character with the Force to open the panel next to the terminal to get the Minikit.

The bricks are a Multi-Build. Assemble them into a jump pad on the left. Then jump and grab onto a handle. Hang there and switch to another character. Break up the jump pad and then assemble it again on the right side. Jump on the pad and grab onto the handle. After the hatch opens, climb the ladder to complete the level.

Phasma

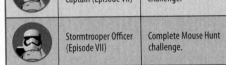

OPEN THE BLAST DOOR

Captain Phasma and her troops have withdrawn into the shield room and closed a blast door behind them. You need to open that door. Start off by using Han and Finn to grapple the two hooks and pull down some bricks.

Assemble the bricks into some strength handles. Switch to Chewbacca and pull on the handles to rip open the door. Now your team can get into the shield room.

CHARACTERS

	Han Solo (Starkiller)		Finn (Takodana)
	Chewbacca		

UNLOCKS

	Stormtrooper Captain (Episode VII)	Complete Evasive Manoeuvres challenge.
	Stormtrooper Officer (Episode VII)	Complete Mouse Hunt challenge.

GOLD BRICK CHALLENGES

Name	Mode	Notes
Level Complete	Any	Complete the level.
True Jedi	Any	Collect 20,000 studs.
All Collectibles	Free Play	Find all the Minikits.
Evasive Manoeuvres	Any	Successfully avoid 5 of Phasma's missile attacks.
Mouse Hunt	Any	Exterminate 3 Mouse Droids.

COLLECTIBLES

Type	Mode	Notes
Minikit	Any	Destroy 3 surveillance cameras.
Minikit	Free Play	Use the Force to lower this Minikit.

MINIKIT

After pulling down the bricks behind the grapple hooks, use a character with the Force to bring down a Minikit that is located at the top of the room.

MINIKIT

There are three surveillance cameras in this level. Shoot all three to earn a Minikit. The first is in the room at the start, on the wall to the left side. The other two are in the shield room. One is on the left wall and the other on the right.

DEFEAT CAPTAIN PHASMA

As you enter the shield room, you take cover behind some barricades. Begin by defeating the stormtroopers attacking you. Watch out for thermal detonators thrown by the Phasma. Move to another barricade quickly to avoid taking damage.

Once you clear the first wave of enemies, a silver panel appears under Captain Phasma, who is hiding behind a shield. Select Chewbacca and throw a thermal detonator at the silver panel to blow it up.

MOUSE HUNT

While fighting in the shield room, several mouse droids will roll across the floor. Destroy three of them to get a Gold Brick and unlock the Stormtrooper Officer. Don't worry if you miss one. There are several that move through this room.

Another wave of stormtroopers arrives and attacks with blasters while Captain Phasma throws thermal detonators. Keep moving and defeat the stormtroopers. Then when another silver panel appears, throw an explosive of your own at it.

Captain Phasma now takes control of a turret. Not only does it fire lasers, but also rockets that can cause a lot of damage. Don't waste time shooting at the turret. Instead, take cover and shoot at the stormtroopers.

EVASIVE MANOEUVRES

A beeping is audible when Phasma is about to launch a missile. When you hear the sound, take cover. If there is a blue targeting icon near you, quickly move to cover behind another barricade to avoid being hit. Dodge five of her rocket attacks to earn a Gold Brick and unlock the Stormtrooper Captain.

After several rocket attacks, the turret has to cool down for a few seconds. Two targets appear over the cooling ports on the bottom of the guns. Take aim and shoot one of the targets. You can only hit one per round. Survive another set of attacks and then, when the turret is cooling again, hit the second target to finally destroy the turret.

Captain Phasma is blown out of her seat in the turret and down to the floor of the shield room. Chewbacca moves forward and grabs her. Press the buttons that appear on the screen to defeat her. This forces her to lower the shields so the Resistance attack on Starkiller Base can begin.

STARKILLER BASE HUB

Before you can begin the next chapter, you must reach the level select terminal. Start off by leading your characters along the trail of green studs to the detention center. However, the officer there has a few errands for you to run before he will admit you. You must acquire some items. The first, Galaxy Guzzler, is to the left in a large container. Use the Flametrooper to melt the ice holding the door shut. Then switch to the Snowtrooper to blast the objects inside until you find the beverage. Pick it up to complete your first task.

The hologame controller, your next item, is located on some shelves to the left of the Galaxy Guzzler. Use the Flametrooper to melt the gold legs of the shelf so that it collapses. Then break the crates on top to get the controller. Two items down. One more to go.

The final item, a devious torture device known as a feather, is located in a strong container. Use the icons on the screen to locate it. You can't break open the container with your weapons. You need something stronger. Push the container along a checkered path to the end. Then go over to a parked snowspeeder and use the controls to fire its blasters at the container. Retrieve the feather and then return to the officer. He will open the door to the detention center and the level select terminal is now available for you to use.

CHAPTER 8:
DESTROY THE STARKILLER
Assault of Starkiller

INGRESS TO THE OSCILLATOR

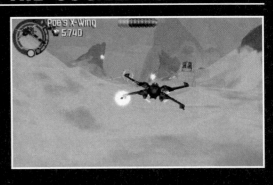

Since Han Solo and his team have lowered the shields around Starkiller, Poe Dameron and his squadron of X-wings have exited hyperspace and are making their run toward their main target. Watch out for turret towers and TIE fighters as you make your run.

CHARACTERS

	Poe Dameron (Helmetless)

UNLOCKS

	Admiral Statura	Complete the level.
	Jessika Testor Pava	Complete True Jedi challenge.
	Resistance General	Complete All Collectibles challenge.
	Major Brance	Complete Missile Intercept challenge.
	Yolo Ziff	Complete Rapid Oscillator challenge.

GOLD BRICK CHALLENGES

Name	Mode	Notes
Level Complete	Any	Complete the level.
True Jedi	Any	Collect 20,000 studs.
All Collectables	Any	Find all the Minikits.
Missile Intercept	Any	Shoot 5 missiles out of the air.
Rapid Oscillator	Any	Hit all the Oscillator weak points in 2 minutes.

COLLECTIBLES

Type	Mode	Notes
Minikit	Any	Destroy the middle of 3 falling rocks.
Minikit	Any	Destroy an object near the oscillator.

CHALLENGE:
MISSILE INTERCEPT

Near the level's start, missiles appear from the sides and head toward the other X-wings. You can see the smoke trails they leave behind. Shoot down five of these missiles before they hit their targets to earn a Gold Brick and unlock Major Brance. This is tough and you have to be quick to hit those missiles in time.

MINIKIT

Listen to Poe's warnings. When he yells out "Evasive Maneuvers!" get ready for some rocks to fall in front of you. There are a total of three rocks that fall. Be sure to shoot and destroy the second rock to fall. There is a Minikit inside. (It happens so fast that you may not know if you got it until the end of the level.)

DESTROY THE OSCILLATOR VENTS

Once you reach the oscillator, you have a big fight on your hands. Your objective is to destroy six of the vents on the oscillator. There are turrets and lots of TIE fighters defending this area. The vents are shielded, so you need to use torpedoes. To get those torpedoes, shoot down the Special Forces TIE fighters.

Once you have some torpedoes, go after the vents. They are located at the edges of the oscillator structure. One torpedo will do the job for each vent.

RAPID OSCILLATOR

The quicker you can destroy the six vents, the better. If you are able to do this in under two minutes, you earn a Gold Brick and unlock Yolo Ziff. Make sure to focus on getting the torpedoes from the Special Forces TIE fighters and then targeting the vents.

There are turrets around the exterior of the oscillator. You can destroy them with your X-wing's lasers. By destroying them as they appear, you limit the firepower being shot at you.

MINIKIT

A single TIE fighter is flying around the perimeter of the oscillator structure. It is towing a crate behind it. Shoot the crate to add the Minikit to your collection.

Rey's Escape

CHARACTERS

	Rey (Starkiller)		FN-1824

UNLOCKS

	Dr. Kalonia	Complete All Collectibles challenge.
	M9-G8	Complete Rey Run challenge.
	Major Ematt	Complete I've Got a Bad Feeling About This challenge.

GOLD BRICK CHALLENGES

Name	Mode	Notes
Level Complete	Any	Complete the level.
True Jedi	Any	Collect 45,000 studs.
All Collectables	Free Play	Find the Minikit and Red Brick.
Rey Run	Any	Escape within 7 minutes.
I've Got a Bad Feeling About This	Free Play	What's behind the doors?

COLLECTIBLES

Type	Mode	Notes
Minikit	Free Play	Use the Force to move a pipe to get to this Minikit.
Red Brick (Stud Multiplier x 8)	Any	Pick it up near the end of the level.

ESCAPE FROM THE DETENTION CENTER

Rey has used her newfound abilities to escape. Using a Jedi mind trick, she has convinced a stormtrooper, FN-1824, to help her get to safety. Start off by moving to the right. Throw Rey's staff at the socket in the wall and jump over to it. Twirl around and jump to a platform. Move through a corridor and out to another platform. From there, jump to a series of handholds to get to a hang rail. Shimmy across it to the left, and then jump to the platform as the stormtroopers patrolling it leave.

CHALLENGE:
REY RUN

This is a tough challenge. You must complete the level within seven minutes. If you can do this, you earn a Gold Brick and unlock M9-G8. When going for this challenge, don't worry about getting studs or collectibles. Just go for speed.

Move to the left and use the staff switch to lower a bar to FN-1824. Once he grabs on, rotate the switch the opposite direction to bring him up. Switch to the stormtrooper and use his grapple gun to pull on a hook and lower a climbing wall. Take control of Rey again and use the climbing wall to get to the next platform.

Defeat some stormtroopers and then break some crates to reveal bricks for a Multi-Build. Build a Grapple hook on the edge of the platform so FN-1824 can use it to get up to that level. Now break the hook structure and rebuild it as a ladder to the next higher platform. Climb the ladder and then use the grapple gun again to pull on another hook to reveal a target.

MINIKIT

On the platform where you shoot a target, use a character with the Force to move a pillar on the left side. This creates a bridge over to a walkway on the left, where you can pick up this Minikit.

As FN-1824, shoot a grapple at the hook and swing across the gap. Use the First Order terminal to extend a bridge for Rey to get across. Switch to Rey and run across the bridge. Ascend the climbing wall, move to the right, and break some crates. Then assemble the pieces into a checkered path. Now push the large plug on the left into the socket on the right to open a door below.

Take control of FN-1824 and move through the open doorway and then all the way down and to the right. Grapple to a small area using a Grapple hook and then break up some containers. Assemble the Multi-Build into a switch on the right. This raises one pylon above and lowers another. Switch to Rey and use a wall run to get to a higher floor. Move under the raised pylon and stop by the second pylon. Switch back to FN-1824 and break the switch. Reassemble it on the left to raise the right pylon so Rey can continue to the right. Finally, Rey can use a switch to open doors on the right so both characters can continue.

Use the large air vent to lift you up to a higher platform on the right. Defeat some stormtroopers and then break up some containers. Put together the pieces to make an elevator that carries you to a higher level. As Rey, use a wall run to the left and then shimmy across a bar. When you get to a platform, jump onto a dangling wire and climb up. From there, jump across to a pole and twirl around it. Jump over to more poles and finally get to a platform with a First Order terminal. Shoot at the target to the right of the terminal to deploy a probe droid with a hook.

FORCE REWARDS

While replaying this level during Free Play, look for sparkles near vents. Use the Force to open these vents and collect the studs which come pouring out. There are a few of these vents throughout the level.

Switch to FN-1824. Fire the grapple gun at a Grapple hook and swing across to a higher platform on the right. Defeat the stormtroopers and then shoot at a target located above the platform to lower a ladder. Climb the ladder and then grapple over to the left using the probe droid hook. Finally use the First Order terminal to deploy some poles from the wall.

CHALLENGE:
I'VE GOT A BAD FEELING ABOUT THIS

At the spot where FN-1824 shoots the target to lower the ladder, move to the right to find a large door. Use a character with the Force during Free Play to open the door. Then defeat all of the enemies who come out of the door to earn a Gold Brick and unlock Major Ematt.

RED BRICK
(STUD MULTIPLIER X8)

This Red Brick is on a strut that extends out from the wall just to the First Order terminal's left. Jump along the strut to get the Red Brick and add it to your collection.

Switch to Rey and jump over to the first pole. Twirl around it and then jump across to the other poles to reach a climbing wall. Climb to the top to complete the level.

Oscillator Interior

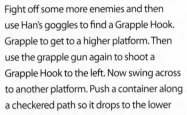

CHARACTERS

	Han Solo (Starkiller)		Chewbacca

UNLOCKS

	Finn (Junction Box)	Complete True Jedi challenge.
	Rey (Junction Box)	Complete All Collectibles challenge.
	FN-2112	Complete No Need for Alarm challenge.
	Stormtrooper Combat Engineer	Complete Post Processing challenge.

GOLD BRICK CHALLENGES

Name	Mode	Notes
Level Complete	Any	Complete the level.
True Jedi	Any	Collect 30,000 studs.
All Collectibles	Free Play	Find all the Minikits.
No Need for Alarm	Any	Destroy the sentry droid to prevent more stormtroopers from being alerted.
Post Processing	Any	Smash the 5 posts.

COLLECTIBLES

Type	Mode	Notes
Minikit	Any	Use a Multi-Build to get this Minikit.
Minikit	Free Play	Go through a small access hatch.

PLANT THE FIRST CHARGE

Han and Chewbacca need to plant four explosive charges within the interior of the oscillator to create a breach for Poe and his squadron of X-wings. At the start, move to the right and defeat some stormtroopers. Once they are defeated, shoot at a couple targets on either side of a shield to lower it so you can continue.

Fight off some more enemies and then use Han's goggles to find a Grapple Hook. Grapple to get to a higher platform. Then use the grapple gun again to shoot a Grapple Hook to the left. Now swing across to another platform. Push a container along a checkered path so it drops to the lower walkway. Switch to Chewbacca and blow up the silver container with a thermal detonator. Finally, assemble the pieces into an explosive charge. One down, three more to go.

PLANT THE SECOND CHARGE

Move to the left and defeat the stormtroopers on this side of the walkway. Then use Han Solo's grapple gun to pull on a hook and break away a section of the wall. Assemble the pieces into an explosive charge.

STORMTROOPERS ON A BREAK

During Free Play, destroy some containers to the left of the second charge and build a Launch pad. Select BB-8 and use the Launch pad to launch the droid to a higher platform where three off-duty stormtroopers are enjoying themselves. There are no collectibles here; however, this is a fun place to visit.

PLANT THE THIRD CHARGE

Move to the right and then descend the stairs to the ground floor. Go to the left and defeat any enemies you find. Switch to Chewbacca and pull on some strength handles along the back wall. This breaks away some pieces for a Multi-Build. Assemble the build to the right to lower a small droid down a section. Break the build and then reassemble it on the left to get the droid all the way out of the storage cell.

Take control of the sentry droid and move it to a square socket by the stairs. Activate the socket with the droid to reveal some bricks which can be assembled into the third charge.

CHALLENGE:
POST PROCESSING

There are five posts located along the railing on the ground floor. Destroy all of these posts to get a Gold Brick and unlock the Stormtrooper Combat Engineer.

MINIKIT

There is a small access hatch to the right of where you plant the third charge. Use BB-8 or another small character to move through the hatch and enter an area under the stairs where this Minikit is located.

PLANT THE FOURTH CHARGE

Head to the right of the stairs and attack the stormtroopers in this area. Clear them out and then deal with the sentry droid in this area.

CHALLENGE:
NO NEED FOR ALARM

Destroy the sentry droid to the right of the stairs as quickly as you can. Not only will this prevent it from calling more stormtroopers to the area, but you also get a Gold Brick and unlock FN-2112.

Break up some containers at the far right side of this area to find a small wheel. Then carry it to the back wall toward the center of this area and place it in a socket. Don't use it yet. In the middle of this area are some pieces surrounded by studs. They are a Multi-Build which you can use to build some strength handles to the left. Pull on the handles with Chewbacca and then switch to Han and turn the wheel to expose a hook. Grapple the hook and assemble the pieces into the last charge to complete the level.

MINIKIT

Before building the last charge, use the Multi-Build that made the handles to instead build a panel to the right. This opens a door to a small area where the second Minikit is located. Be sure to grab it.

STARKILLER BASE HUB

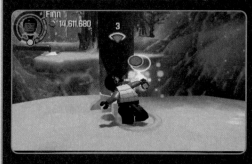

Finn and Rey must escape from Starkiller. Follow the trail of green studs through the snow. Defeat any enemies you come across. When you come to a large tree, use Finn's lightsaber to cut it down. Switch to Rey and walk across the fallen tree to get across a deep chasm.

Throw her staff into a socket on the tree. Then jump onto the staff and twirl around it and a few more poles to get across another chasm. After a TIE fighter crashes, use Rey's goggles to find a hook on the TIE fighter's solar panel.

Take control of Finn and walk across a narrow fallen tree. Use his grapple gun on the hook and pull the solar panel so that it forms a bridge across the chasm. Jump over to the panel and then across to where Rey is waiting. Continue to a large, fallen tree and cut through it with the lightsaber to reveal a level select terminal. Use the terminal to begin the next chapter.

CHAPTER 9:
THE FINALE
Oscillator Bombing Run

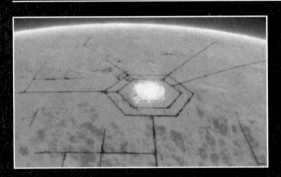

CHARACTERS

	Poe Dameron's X-wing		Resistance X-wing

UNLOCKS

	R2-KT	Complete True Jedi challenge.
	Ello Asty	Complete All Collectibles challenge.
	Lieutenant Bastian	Complete Turret Termination challenge.
	Nien Nunb (X-wing)	Complete Lap of Honor challenge.

GOLD BRICK CHALLENGES

Name	Mode	Notes
Level Complete	Any	Complete the level.
True Jedi	Any	Collect 36,000 studs.
All Collectibles	Any	Find all the Minikits.
Turret Termination	Any	Destroy 5 trench turrets.
Lap of Honor	Any	Destroy each oscillator panel in one lap.

COLLECTIBLES

Type	Mode	Notes
Minikit	Any	Destroy the blue container in the tunnel.
Minikit	Any	Destroy the gold pipes in the trench.

SHOOT DOWN 15 TIE FIGHTERS

The ground team has detonated the explosives and created a breach in the oscillator structure. It is time for Poe and his squadron of X-wings to head to the surface and finish the job. However, before they can do that, they need to take out the TIE fighters flying cover for the oscillator. Once you shoot down 15 TIE fighters, you fly to the surface.

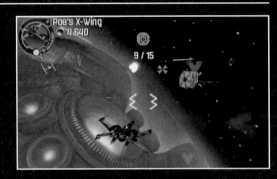

APPROACH THE BREACH

Before you can get to the breach, you must follow a trench. In addition to avoiding objects, you also need to watch out for fire from enemy TIE fighters and turrets. Stay in the trench until you take an interior passage.

MINIKIT

While flying through the trench, look for gold pipes that block part of your path. Shoot and destroy them to get a Minikit.

CHALLENGE:
TURRET TERMINATION

While flying through the trench, there are turrets along the sides that shoot at you. Target the green lights on the turrets and fire back at them. Destroy five turrets to complete this challenge and earn a Gold Brick as well as unlock Lieutenant Bastian.

When you reach the end of the first trench, you then fly into a tunnel. Watch out for structures inside and shoot at the TIE fighters that follow you in. Keep moving to avoid fire from behind until you get to the end.

MINIKIT

While flying through the tunnel, look for a TIE fighter with a blue container behind it. It appears in the areas with the blue hexagonal openings where the tunnel splits up. Shoot the blue container to get the Minikit.

As you exit the tunnel, you enter another trench. Continue shooting turrets and TIE fighters as you avoid taking damage. Keep going until you reach the end of the trench and fly through the breach.

DESTROY THE OSCILLATOR PANELS

Once you fly through the breach, you are inside the oscillator structure. There are three colored oscillator panels—red, blue, and yellow. As you fly around the interior of the area, shoot the panels as they come into view. You will keep flying around until you destroy all three to complete the level.

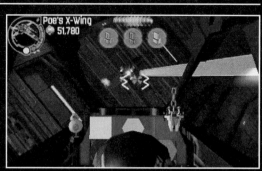

CHALLENGE:
LAP OF HONOR

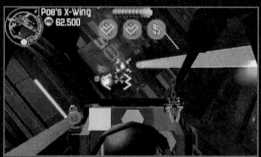

This is a tough challenge. However, doing so earns a Gold Brick and unlocks Nien Nunb. To complete this challenge, you must destroy all three oscillator panels in one lap. That means you only get one chance to destroy each one. Aim to the right so you can begin shooting as soon as you see the first panel, and then move the reticle to the left to follow it. Then move the reticle to the right and repeat the tactic with the next two. You may have to play this level a few times to get the timing down. Try using the brakes to slow down your fighter to make it easier to destroy each panel on the first pass.

Starkiller Forest

CHARACTERS

	Finn (Starkiller)		Rey (Starkiller)

UNLOCKS

	Dasha Promenti	Complete Loggerheads challenge.
	Kylo Ren	Complete Finn-ess challenge.

GOLD BRICK CHALLENGES

Name	Mode	Notes
Level Complete	Any	Complete the level.
True Jedi	Any	Collect 10,000 studs.
All Collectibles	Free Play	Find all the Minikits.
Loggerheads	Any	Get Kylo to chop down 3 trees.
Finn-ess	Any	Defeat Kylo with one life.

COLLECTIBLES

Type	Mode	Notes
Minikit	Free Play	Destroy a silver container.
Minikit	Free Play	Pull on some strength handles.

FIGHT KYLO REN

As Rey and Finn are escaping from the oscillator, they are stopped by Kylo Ren. Kylo throws Rey into a tree, leaving only Finn able to resist. Finn is no match for Kylo Ren's attacks. Therefore, for most of the battle, keep moving. Watch for when Kylo Ren makes a charge attack and quickly jump out of the way.

CHALLENGE:
LOGGERHEAD

Using objects to block Kylo Ren's attacks is a good idea. Try to put the trees between you and him. As Kylo Ren attacks, he may cut down the tree in the process. Get him to cut down all three trees in this area and you earn a Gold Brick and unlock Dasha Promenti.

While avoiding Kylo Ren, watch for button icons to appear on the screen. Press the indicated buttons to block an attack. Then button mash until you push Kylo Ren back and stun him.

While he is stunned, Kylo Ren is vulnerable. Move in and inflict as much damage as possible before he recovers. You need to do this at least twice.

CHALLENGE:
FINN-ESE

This is another tough challenge. You must defeat Kylo Ren without letting Finn be defeated by losing all of his health. Keep moving and dodging while also breaking up objects to find hearts to restore your health. Also, you need to make those opportunities to go on the attack worth it.

HELP FINN

After Finn inflicts some damage on Kylo Ren, Kylo stops Finn and holds him with the Force. Now you have to take control of Rey and help out Finn.

MINIKIT

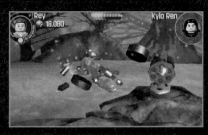

When you first switch control from Finn to Rey, there is a silver container to the left of Rey. Switch to a character who can destroy silver objects and break the container to get this Minikit.

MINIKIT

Before building the Multi-Build, move all the way to the right. Use a character with the Force ability to lift a boulder out of the way to reveal some strength handles. Switch to Chewbacca and pull on the handles to get the Minikit.

Move to the right and hit a large tree trunk to knock it down. Cross over it to get to another area. Break up several objects until you find pieces to a Multi-Build. Assemble the pieces into either object on the right or left; both will effectively stun Kylo Ren.

You now automatically take control of Finn once again. Move in and hit Kylo Ren while he is vulnerable. Then move away and avoid him again until you have another opportunity to engage Kylo.

Instead of becoming stunned, Kylo Ren counterattacks and knocks Finn to the ground. As he tries to use the Force to get the lightsaber, you switch to Rey. Repeatedly press the button that appears on-screen to get the lightsaber for yourself and complete the level.

237

Starkiller Showdown

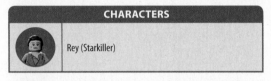

CHARACTERS

	Rey (Starkiller)

UNLOCKS

	PZ-4CO	Complete Snowballed challenge.
	Poe Dameron (D'Qar)	Complete Snow BB-8 challenge.

GOLD BRICK CHALLENGES

Name	Mode	Notes
Level Complete	Any	Complete the level.
True Jedi	Any	Collect 7,000 studs.
All Collectibles	Free Play	Find all the Minikits.
Snowballed	Any	Take out 3 snowtroopers with one attack.
Snow BB-8	Any	Build a BB-8 snowman.

COLLECTIBLES

Type	Mode	Notes
Minikit	Free Play	Melt a chunk of ice to get the Minikit inside.
Red Brick (Explosive Bolts)	Free Play	Have BB-8 enter small hatch.

DEFEAT KYLO REN

The fighting against Kylo Ren here is similar to that of the previous level. This time, you are fighting as Rey instead of Finn. Kylo Ren can't be hurt at the start, so move away and be ready to dodge his attacks. Rey's double-jump ability can help her stay out of the way of his lightsaber.

When a button icon appears on the screen, press it and then button mash to stun Kylo Ren.

This is your chance to move in and inflict some damage on him. Hit him as many times as you can before he jumps to the side to recover.

While Kylo Ren is sitting out the fight for a bit, three snowtroopers drop into the trench area and attack. Defeat them to continue the duel with Kylo Ren.

CHALLENGE: SNOWBALLED

This challenge requires you to defeat three snowtroopers with a single attack. To do this, wait until the three stormtroopers are near each other. Then jump toward the middle of them and, while in the air, press the Attack button to come down with a smash attack. For doing this, you earn a Gold Brick and unlock PZ-4CO.

Once the stormtroopers are defeated, Kylo drops back in. Continue avoiding him until you have a chance to stun and damage him. Fight off another wave of stormtroopers, then duel Kylo Ren for a third time.

This time, Kylo uses the Force to immobilize Rey. You now take control of Finn. There are three trees with Grapple Hooks on them. Select the one closest to Kylo Ren and grapple it. This knocks snow down on Kylo Ren and breaks his Force grip on Rey.

As Kylo Ren runs away, you can take control of both Finn and Rey. Jump on the rocks to get out of the trench. Then move to the right and use both characters to push a large boulder along the checkered path.

As Rey, use your lightsaber to get to the top of a wall jump. Then move toward Kylo Ren.

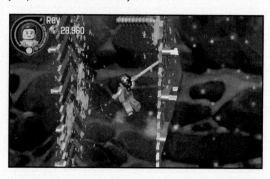

Kylo Ren is now vulnerable to your attack. Watch out for his attacks, then move in and inflict damage until you've reduced his health meter all the way. Finally, you have a button-mash contest with Kylo Ren to defeat him.

MINIKIT

A chunk of ice is to the left of the trees with the hooks on them. Use a Flametrooper to melt the ice to get the Minikit.

CHALLENGE:
SNOW BB-8

Before pushing the large boulder, use Finn to grapple the trees again to drop some more snow into the trench. Then climb down and build a snow BB-8 to get a Gold Brick and unlock Poe Dameron (D'Qar).

As the boulder rolls, Rey falls and grabs onto a rail. Shimmy to the right and then drop onto a narrow ice ledge. Move to the right and then jump across a series of handholds to get to another ledge. Continue to the right and then jump to a pole. Twirl around a few poles to reach a narrow beam. Move across it and then jump on some pads to get to a larger area to the right.

RED BRICK
(EXPLOSIVE BOLTS)

Use a character with the Force ability to move a rock from in front of a small access hatch. Then switch to BB-8 and move through the hatch to get to a chamber where the Red Brick is located.

RESISTANCE BASE HUB

Once you return to the Hub, follow the trail of green studs toward the Millennium Falcon. Once you get there, a new level select terminal will deploy. This one will take you to the Epilogue level.

EPILOGUE:
LUKE'S ISLAND

FIND LUKE

Rey and Chewbacca have arrived at the island on the planet shown on the map. Now Rey needs to get to the top of the mountain to try and find Luke Skywalker. As Rey, move to the right. Use the wall run to get to the other side of a gap. Then throw Rey's staff at a target on the cliff

side. This drops a boulder into the gap so Chewbacca can get across.

CHARACTERS

	Rey (Resistance)		Chewbacca

UNLOCKS

	R2-D2	Complete the level.
	Kathleen Kennedy	Complete True Jedi challenge.
	JJ Abrams	Complete All Collectibles challenge.
	General Leia (Alt)	Complete Bush Whacker challenge.

GOLD BRICK CHALLENGES

Name	Mode	Notes
Level Complete	Any	Complete the level.
True Jedi	Any	Collect 32,000 studs.
All Collectables	Free Play	Find both Red Bricks.
Stud Cove	Free Play	Find the secret area in the level.
Bush Whacker	Any	Destroy all 3 bush props.

COLLECTIBLES

Type	Mode	Notes
Red Brick (Dark Side)	Free Play	Swim through a water access to a small island.
Red Brick (Stud Multiplier x10)	Free Play	Destroy a gold object.

RED BRICK
(DARK SIDE)

Break up rocks and objects in the area where you begin the level to find a water access spot. Switch to a character who can use it, such as Admiral Ackbar, and swim through it to a small island where you can collect this Red Brick.

CHALLENGE:
BUSH WHACKER

Break three green bushes with red flowers in order to earn a Gold Brick and unlock General Leia.

Switch to Chewbacca. Jump across the watery gap and continue to the right. Head up the stairs and pull on some strength handles to break a container into pieces for a Multi-Build. Assemble the pieces into another strength handle to the left, and then pull on it to move some stairs for Rey to use.

Take control of Rey and head up the stairs. Throw her staff into the socket. Jump over to the staff and twirl around it. Jump to another pole and then to the ledge on the right. There is a rock on a checkered path, but you can't move it just yet. Switch back to Chewbacca and break the strength handles. Reassemble them into a weight to the right. Pull the weight to the end of the path so Rey can push the rock off the edge. Then assemble the pieces into steps so you can reach the top of the ledge.

─── CHALLENGE: ───

STUD COVE

Use BB-8 to go through a small access hatch on the ledge near the checkered path. This leads to a secret area and earns a Gold Brick.

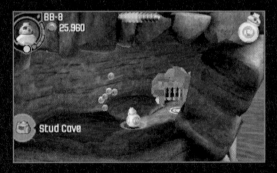

Shoot the target on the cliff side to drop some bricks. Assemble them into some strength handles. After Chewbacca pulls on them, a boulder falls and creates some steps. Climb the steps and continue to a new area. Move to the right and use Chewbacca to pull on some more strength handles. This clears away vines from around some Twirl poles. Switch to Rey and move to the left and down, so you can jump across to the first pole on the left. Twirl around and jump from pole to pole to get to a narrow ledge. Shimmy along it to the right until you can get to an area where you can jump up to the walkway.

Ascend the steps and smash a stack of stone into a pile of bricks. Assemble the pieces into a staff switch. Use the switch to move a lever that clears the pathway of boulders so Chewbacca can get through.

Take control of Chewbacca and move to the right. Pull on yet another set of strength handles to extend a platform. While Chewbacca holds on, switch to Rey and jump to the top of the platform and then on to the pathway. From here on, Rey is on her own.

Head up the stairs to the next area. Walk to the right and push a rock along a checkered path to pull down a narrow beam. Then walk across the beam to get to the other side.

RED BRICK
(STUD MULTIPLIER X10)

A small building is just to the right of the narrow beam. Destroy the gold object inside with a character like Captain Phasma.

Walk to the right and use the wall kick to jump your way to the higher area. Continue up the stairs and follow the pathway until you reach the object of your search—Luke Skywalker.

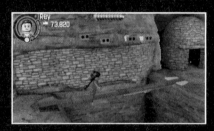

PROLOGUE:
THE BATTLE OF ENDOR
Endor Shield Generator

CHARACTERS

	Han Solo (Endor)		Princess Leia (Endor)
	Chewbacca		Wicket

UNLOCKS

	Logray	Complete All Collectibles challenge.
	Stormtrooper (Classic)	Complete Fuel Cells challenge.
	Imperial AT-ST Pilot	Complete Chicken Stomp challenge.

GOLD BRICK CHALLENGES

Name	Mode	Notes
Level Complete	Any	Complete the level.
True Jedi	Any	Collect 40,000 studs.
All Collectables	Free Play	Find all the Minikits.
Fuel Cells	Any	Take out 3 enemies with fuel cells.
Chicken Stomp	Any	Stomp on 3 stormtroopers while piloting the AT-ST.

COLLECTIBLES

Type	Mode	Notes
Minikit	Free Play	Use the Force to play some drums up in a tree.
Minikit	Free Play	Use goggles to find a container with the Minikit inside.

DESTROY THE AT-ST

Han Solo and Princess Leia are leading an attack on the shield generator on Endor's moon. They must lower the shields so the Rebel fleet can destroy the second Death Star. Begin by defeating the stormtroopers in the first area. Then, when an AT-ST arrives, destroy some objects on the right side and assemble them into strength handles. Switch to Chewbacca and pull on the handles to move a large log hanging from a tree into position.

Move to the area's left side and shoot at a target on a rope. This frees an Ewok named Wicket who can help you. Take control of Wicket and move through the small access hatch on the tree to reach the higher platform.

Once at the top, break up an object on the platform and then assemble the pieces into a ladder that drops from the tree. Switch to Chewbacca and climb the ladder. Then pull on the strength handles to move another log into position. Both logs then swing towards the AT-ST and destroy it, clearing the way for you to continue.

ADVANCE THROUGH THE FOREST

Travel down the forest path until you come across some logs. Take cover behind them and then engage the stormtroopers here. Defeat them all, then continue moving through the forest until you

CHALLENGE:
FUEL CELLS

You can earn a Gold Brick and unlock the Stormtrooper Classic by completing this challenge. Just defeat three stormtroopers by shooting fuel cells and causing them to explode. You can get at least two of them here, and then another one later at a second cover part of the level.

Take control of Wicket and interact with the three Ewoks by the log. Then move to the small access hatch and climb through it to reach the higher area. The Ewoks will follow and help Wicket push the large stack of logs. The logs roll down and destroy another AT-ST.

As Wicket, break up the wrecked walker into a Multi-Build, and then assemble the pieces into a turret to the left. The turret will blow up the log and allow the rest of your group to follow you. Then break up the turret and assemble the pieces into a lift on the right. You will need R2-D2 to use the astromech terminal and lower the lift so your characters can use it.

MINIKIT

This Minikit is up in a tree. Use the walker Multi-Build to construct a lift in the center next to a tree. Use it to reach a platform in the tree. Then switch to a character with the Force and use this ability to play some drums and get the Minikit.

Reach the next area and defeat the stormtroopers. Break up some machinery, then reassemble the pieces into a Grapploe Hook on the pole. Switch to Han Solo and shoot the grapple gun at the hook to swing onto the top of an AT-ST. Press the buttons that appear on the screen to defeat the enemy and take control of the walker.

GET TO THE SHIELD GENERATOR BUNKER

Move the AT-ST along the forest floor, defeating enemies as you go. When you arrive at a raised bridge, fire the laser cannons at the gold bricks in the nets to lower the bridge. Keep moving through the forest. Near the end of this area, you face another AT-ST. Take aim at it with your laser cannons and open fire to destroy it.

CHALLENGE:
CHICKEN STOMP

While piloting the AT-ST, pressing the Jump button will cause it to lift a leg and stomp the ground. Use this attack to defeat three stormtroopers. Not only will you earn a Gold Brick, but you also unlock the Imperial AT-ST Pilot.

Once you arrive at a log, the AT-ST can go no further. Han Solo gets out and joins his group. Continue forward to a ledge. Use Han's and Leia's grapple guns to pull on a pair of hooks to drop a part from an AT-ST and break it into pieces. Assemble the pieces into steps so you can reach the top of the ledge.

INFILTRATE THE BUNKER

Move toward the bunker and take cover behind some logs. Shoot at the stormtroopers guarding the bunker. Chewbacca can throw a thermal detonator to destroy a silver container which provides cover to the enemy.

As you are fighting, an AT-ST arrives and begins firing on you along with a turret on top of the bunker. Switch to Wicket and move through a small access hatch. When he emerges on the bunker's roof, attack the turret and break it up. Then reassemble it into a punch cannon that fires a boxing glove at the walker to destroy it.

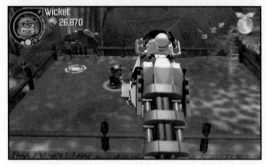

MINIKIT

During Free Play, while on the bunker's roof, switch to a character with goggles and use them to find a container. Break it open to get the Minikit.

After the AT-ST is destroyed, the remainder of the enemies outside of the bunker run away. Now you need to get inside. Switch to Han Solo. Break up objects in front of the bunker and then assemble the pieces into a hat dispenser. Use the dispenser to put an Imperial helmet on Han's head. Then use the terminal to the bunker door's left to fool the Imperials inside. Once they open the door, enter the bunker to complete the level.

Death Star Interior

ATTACK THE EMPEROR

Luke Skywalker and Darth Vader must work together to defeat the Emperor. While avoiding falling objects and the lightning attacks from the Emperor, use either character's Force ability to move the two giant arms to attack Palpatine.

CHARACTERS

	Luke Skywalker (Episode VI)		Darth Vader

UNLOCKS

	Bith	Complete Royal Force challenge.
	Emperor Palpatine	Complete Like Lightning challenge.

GOLD BRICK CHALLENGES

Name	Mode	Notes
Level Complete	Any	Complete the level.
True Jedi	Any	Collect 8,000 studs.
All Collectibles	Free Play	Find the Minikit and the Red Brick.
Royal Force	Any	Take out 3 Royal Guards with the Force.
Like Lightning	Any	Defeat the Emperor's Force-lightning, as fast as lightning.

COLLECTIBLES

Type	Mode	Notes
Minikit	Free Play	Use a rotary control switch to get up onto a catwalk.
Red Brick (Quick Access)	Free Play	Use a rotary control switch to get up onto a catwalk.

CHALLENGE:
ROYAL FORCE

The Emperor is protected by the Royal Guards. Instead of attacking them with a lightsaber, use the Force to attack and defeat three of them. Darth Vader's force pull and force choke abilities work well for this. For completing this challenge, you earn a Gold Brick as well as unlock the Bith character.

The Emperor takes control of the giant arms and throws some bricks in your direction. They are a Multi-Build. Assemble the pieces into miniature starfighters. Building to the left makes a TIE fighter. Use Darth Vader and the Force to cause the ship to attack the Emperor.

After the attack, break the TIE fighter and assemble the pieces to the right to make an X-wing. Now use Luke Skywalker and the Force to make it attack the Emperor. After the Emperor recovers, he picks up the two characters with the Force and throws them to a lower area.

DEFEAT THE EMPEROR

Palpatine protects himself with the Force so you can't attack him directly. Instead, use the bomb dispensers along the back wall. There is one on the left and one on the right. Use Luke's force ability to pick up a bomb from the left side and throw it at the Emperor; then go to the other side and use Darth Vader's force destroy ability to get the second bomb and throw it at the Emperor as well.

There are two targets above the Emperor. Throw a lightsaber at them to bring a catwalk crashing down on the Emperor. This breaks through his defenses.

RED BRICK
(QUICK ACCESS)

Before completing all the attacks against the Emperor while he is protecting himself with the Force, break up some objects in the area and build a rotary control switch. During Free Play, switch to BB-8 and use the rotary control switch to launch the droid onto some catwalks. Find the Red Brick on the right side.

MINIKIT

While on the catwalks as BB-8, go to the left side to grab the Minikit.

The Emperor is through playing games. After throwing Luke to the side, he begins attacking Darth Vader with Force lightning. Quickly press the button that appears on-screen to deflect the lightning with your lightsaber. Continue to do this until you defeat the Emperor once and for all.

CHALLENGE:
LIKE LIGHTNING

During the final duel between the Emperor and Darth Vader, be sure to win each of the button-pushing phases without a defeat. For your effort, you not only earn a Gold Brick, but you also unlock Emperor Palpatine.

Death Star Escape

FLY TO THE REACTOR

Han's team has taken the shield generator and disabled the shields protecting the Death Star. You can now make your run to destroy it. This level begins with you flying along the space station's surface and down trenches while approaching the tunnel which leads into the Death Star's center. Watch out for TIE fighters and turrets as you make your run.

CHARACTERS

	Lando Calrissian (General)		Wedge Antilles

UNLOCKS

	C-3PO	Complete All Collectibles challenge.
	Nien Nunb	Complete Quad Lasers challenge.
	Zev Senesca	Complete Fast Reactor challenge.

GOLD BRICK CHALLENGES

Name	Mode	Notes
Level Complete	Any	Complete the level.
True Jedi	Any	Collect 16,000 studs.
All Collectibles	Any	Find all the Minikits.
Quad Lasers	Any	Destroy 4 turbolaser towers.
Fast Reactor	Any	Destroy the reactor core within 60 seconds.

COLLECTIBLES

Type	Mode	Notes
Minikit	Any	Destroy a container on top of a structure in the trench.
Minikit	Any	Destroy the container towed behind a TIE fighter in the reactor area.

CHALLENGE:
QUAD LASERS

While making the run on the surface, there are several turbolaser turrets that fire on you. Destroy four of them to earn a Gold Brick and unlock Nien Nunb. The turrets appear along the trench's sides, and three appear just before you enter the tunnel.

MINIKIT

This Minikit is awarded if you can shoot a container along the trench. It appears at the top of a small structure you must fly under. Look for the triangular targeting reticle to appear in the center of your path. Shoot it before ducking under the structure to collect your reward. You must shoot fast to get this one!

After braving the trench, you now fly through a tunnel which takes you inside the Death Star. The key here is to collect studs and avoid being destroyed. A TIE fighter follows you into the tunnel. The red reticle that appears on-screen is the TIE fighter's targeting system. Don't let

it hover over your ship or you will take damage when the enemy fires. Avoid obstacles and fly all the way to the reactor.

DESTROY THE REACTOR CORE

When you get to the reactor area, there are several steps you must complete to destroy the core. First destroy the three power regulators. They are located near the top of the core. They are easier to hit if you slow down as you approach them. However, that also makes it easier for the TIE fighters to hit you, so use caution.

The two reaction generators are located at the top and bottom of the reactor core. They are reinforced, so you need torpedoes to destroy them. TIE fighters with torpedoes now enter the area. Look for the pink trails behind them. Shoot these enemies down and collect their torpedoes. Then launch the torpedoes at the reaction generators to destroy them.

Once the power regulators are destroyed, shields drop over the core. Now you must destroy all of the shield plating. Fly around and fire as fast as you can to eliminate those shields.

MINIKIT

A TIE fighter is flying around the edge of the reactor chamber. It is towing a container behind it. Shoot the container to get the Minikit stored inside.

CHALLENGE:
FAST REACTOR

This is a tough challenge. If you can complete it, you earn a Gold Brick and unlock Zev Senesca. You must destroy the reactor core within 60 seconds. The time starts as soon as you enter the chamber. It takes some practice to complete this, but Red Bricks such as Infinite Torpedoes can really help.

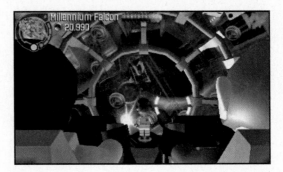

After the reactor core is destroyed, you must fly back through the tunnel to escape before the Death Star explodes. Dodge the obstacles and get out as quickly as you can to complete the level.

POE TO THE RESCUE

Trash Compactor

CHARACTERS

	Poe Dameron (Flight Suit)		Admiral Ackbar (Episode VII)
	BB-8	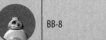	C-3PO (Episode VII)

UNLOCKS

	Fitness General Hux	Complete All Collectibles challenge.
	Gym Stormtrooper	Complete Sayonara Dianoga challenge.
	Hot Tub Stormtrooper	Complete Load of Rubbish challenge.

GOLD BRICK CHALLENGES

Name	Mode	Notes
Level Complete	Any	Complete the level.
True Jedi	Any	Collect 20,000 studs.
All Collectibles	Free Play	Find 2 Minikits and the Red Brick.
Sayonara Dianoga	Any	Build each Multi-Build variant to defeat the dianoga 4 times.
Load of Rubbish	Any	Destroy the 3 strange piles of rubbish.

COLLECTIBLES

Type	Mode	Notes
Minikit	Any	Move through toxic waste.
Minikit	Free Play	Pull on strength handles.
Red Brick (Infinite Torpedoes)	Free Play	Use the Force near the end of the level.

ACTIVATE THE PRESSURE MAINTENANCE HATCH

The First Order has kidnapped Admiral Ackbar. Poe Dameron has been sent to rescue him. After breaking out of the detention level, the characters jumped down a garbage chute to escape from Captain Phasma and the stormtroopers. Now you must get them out of the trash compactor. Begin by moving from one pile of garbage to another. However, a dianoga in the water prevents your crossing. Break up the nearby object and then assemble the pieces of the Multi-Build into either object. After your build causes the dianoga to withdraw under the water, quickly cross over to the chamber's right side.

CHALLENGE:
SAYONARA DIANOGA

This challenge requires you to use Multi-Builds four times to get the dianoga to go under the water. Each time, you must use a different build. In the first area, build one object and use it. Then break it up and build the second object. Later, when you must deal with the dianoga again, build two different objects with the Multi-Build. This earns the Gold Brick and unlocks the Gym Stormtrooper.

When you reach the chamber's right side, use Poe's grapple gun to pull on a hook to reveal a water access. Switch to Admiral Ackbar and jump into the water to find some bricks and assemble them into a rotary control switch.

CHALLENGE:
LOAD OF RUBBISH

There are three strange piles of rubbish spread throughout this level. They all have a stormtrooper helmet on top. Destroy them all to earn a Gold Brick and unlock the Hot Tub Stormtrooper.

Switch to BB-8 and use the rotary control switch to launch the droid across the chamber and onto a catwalk. Roll to the left and use the astromech terminal to activate the pressure maintenance hatch.

MINIKIT

After launching BB-8 onto the catwalk, and before going to the left, drop down from the catwalk and get the Minikit inside a cloud of toxic gas (the gas does not affect BB-8). Then roll back to the rotary control switch and launch again to continue.

PULL ON THE HANDLE

The trash compactor has moved, making the chamber smaller. As BB-8, roll to the top of the trash pile and use the small access hatch to move across the chamber to where the rest of the characters are located.

Several small dianogas attack. Defeat them all, and then use Poe's grapple gun on the hook to break up pieces for a Multi-Build. Construct either object to deal with the larger dianoga. Both require BB-8 to power up the charge panel so you can get across the water to the center of the chamber.

Now switch to Admiral Ackbar and use the water access to get him to the chamber's far side. Once there, walk up the pile of garbage and then jump and grab onto the handle to make the walls of the trash compactor move outwards and increase the size of the chamber.

GET C-3PO TO THE PROTOCOL DROID TERMINAL

After fighting off some small dianogas, have Ackbar use the staff switch. Rotate the switch to raise a bridge out of the water so the rest of the group can get to this side of the chamber.

Take control of C-3PO and walk to the right. Use the protocol droid terminal and repeat the code back in order to open the hatch so you can escape from the trash compactor and complete the level.

MINIKIT

After raising the bridge, find a stove on the lower part of the chambers. Switch to a character who can pull on the strength handles to get this Minikit.

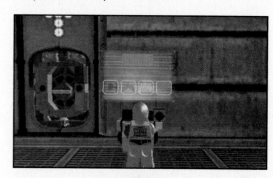

Take control of BB-8 and use the rotary control switch on the chamber's right side. This moves the walls a bit and also drops some bricks for a Multi-build in the middle of the area. You will need to build different objects to help C-3PO reach the catwalk where the protocol droid terminal is located. Assemble the pieces into a jump switch on the right. Then jump on the red button to activate a lift so C-3PO can get to the elevated walkway.

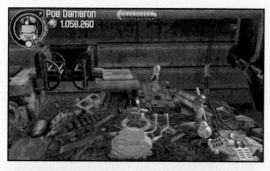

Break up the switch and then reassemble the pieces into a magnetic device in the center. This lowers the small draw bridge so C-3PO can walk across to the left.

RED BRICK
(INFINITE TORPEDOES)

Before using C-3PO to activate the protocol droid terminal, switch to a character who can use the Force to pull a Red Brick down from the catwalk on the right side. The Red Brick is off-screen and you won't see it until you move a Force user to that side of the catwalk.

Destroy the magnetic device and now assemble the pieces into a winch on the left side. This will lower a lift so C-3PO can walk onto it. Then destroy the winch to allow the lift to rise to the catwalk.

Asteroid Escape

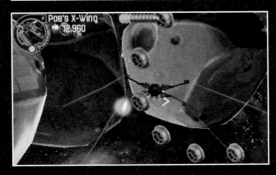

FLY THROUGH THE ASTEROID FIELD

Poe and his group escaped from the Star Destroyer on a landing craft. After changing ships on an asteroid, he is now ready to go on the attack in his own X-wing fighter. At the level's start, dodge the large asteroids and shoot the smaller ones to avoid taking damage.

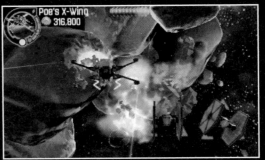

The First Order has sent TIE fighters into the asteroid field to try to stop you. Avoid their fire while shooting them down to eliminate their threats. Keep going until you find a hollow asteroid with a tunnel through it.

CHARACTERS

	Poe Dameron's X-wing

UNLOCKS

	Heavy Trooper (Episode VII)	Complete the level.
	Hot Tub Stormtrooper Alt	Complete All Collectibles challenge.
	O-MR1	Complete Crystal Caves challenge.
	K-3PO	Complete Tunnel Trouble challenge.

MINIKIT

Near the beginning of the level, look for a gold asteroid. Destroy it to get this Minikit.

GOLD BRICK CHALLENGES

Name	Mode	Notes
Level Complete	Any	Complete the level.
True Jedi	Any	Collect 50,000 studs.
All Collectibles	Any	Find all the Minikits.
Crystal Caves	Any	Destroy the 5 crystals in the first part of the cave section.
Tunnel Trouble	Any	Don't take any damage from the oncoming creatures hatching from the cave walls.

COLLECTIBLES

Type	Mode	Notes
Minikit	Any	Destroy the gold asteroid.
Minikit	Any	Destroy the container near the start of the tunnel.
Minikit	Any	Destroy 3 wrecked ships in the crater.

FLY THROUGH THE ASTEROID TUNNEL

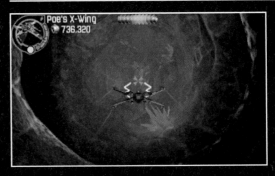

To try to escape from the TIE fighters, Poe flies into the tunnel of a large asteroid. Fly carefully and avoid the walls of the tunnel as well as obstacles inside that can damage your fighter.

CHALLENGE:
CRYSTAL CAVES

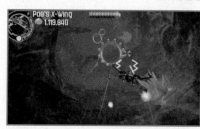

There are five bright crystals inside the tunnel. Shoot and destroy all of them to get a Gold Brick and unlock O-MR1.

MINIKIT

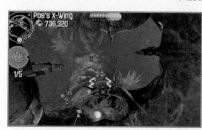

Near the start of the tunnel, just behind the first crystal, you can find a small container in the middle of the screen. Shoot at it to get the second Minikit.

CHALLENGE:
TUNNEL TROUBLE

As you near the tunnel's end, a swarm of mynocks flies around your ship. Stay in the center of the tunnel to avoid having them hit your ship. If they do not damage your ship, you earn a Gold Brick and unlock K-3PO.

DOGFIGHT IN THE CRATER

As you emerge from the tunnel, you now have a dogfight against lots of TIE fighters in a large crater of the asteroid. Your objective is to shoot down 12 TIE fighters. Keep moving around to avoid getting hit while targeting the enemies with your own weapons.

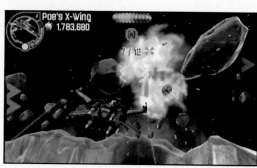

MINIKIT

There are three rust-colored wrecks around the edges of the crater. Shoot all of them to get the third Minikit.

After you've downed 12 TIE fighters, the First Order sends in Special Forces TIE fighters. They are equipped with torpedoes. Destroy them and pick up the torpedoes they leave behind. Now target the silver boulders in the crater and fire torpedoes at them. By destroying them, you open up some small tunnels and release mynocks that will distract the enemy so you can make your escape.

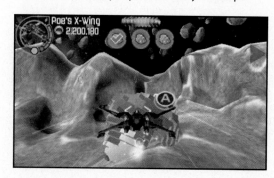

RATHTAR HUNTING

Rathtar Caverns

FIND A WAY OUT OF THE CAVERN

Han Solo and his crew are out hunting rathtar. However, in the cavern, it looks like the tables are turned. Now you just need to get out of the cavern. Wade through the water until you get to the end on the right. Avoid tentacles while you are moving.

CHARACTERS

	Han Solo (Twon Ketee)		Chewbacca (Twon Ketee)
	Varond Jelik (Twon Ketee)		

UNLOCKS

	Adan Mose	Complete All Collectibles challenge.
	Croll Jenkins	Complete Pacifist challenge.
	Zylas	Complete We Need to Get Out of Here! challenge.

GOLD BRICK CHALLENGES

Name	Mode	Notes
Level Complete	Any	Complete the level.
True Jedi	Any	Collect 22,000 studs.
All Collectibles	Free Play	Find all the Minikits.
Pacifist	Any	Leave the rathtar alone when they pounce.
We Need to Get out of Here!	Any	Climb the waterfall in under 110 seconds.

COLLECTIBLES

Type	Mode	Notes
Minikit	Any	Destroy all of the mushrooms.
Minikit	Any	Inside an alcove near top of waterfall.
Minikit	Free Play	Use the Force to get this one at the top of a waterfall.

MINIKIT

There are ten glowing mushrooms in this level. Destroy them all to get the Minikit. The first can be found on the banks of the water. After you exit, move along the bank at the top and to the left to find it. Others are at the base of the waterfall, behind the water midway up the waterfall, and in alcoves where you must climb to them. Be sure to search in areas outside of the main play area so you can get them all.

Follow the trail up the hill to the right until you reach a waterfall. There are several studs at the base of the waterfall. Move forward to pick them up. As you do, some tentacles reach out and try to grab you. Back away from them.

CHALLENGE: PACIFIST

There are two times when tentacles reach out for you along the waterfall. Don't shoot at or attack them. They won't hurt you. By showing restraint, you collect a Gold Brick and unlock Croll Jenkins.

CLIMB THE WATERFALL

After the tentacles retract behind the waterfall, some bricks for a Multi-Build fall out. Build a climbing wall to the right, then switch to Varond Jelik and climb it to the top. Take control of Han Solo and break up the climbing wall. Reassemble the bricks into a pillar that Varond can use to jump across to the waterfall's left side.

CHALLENGE:
WE NEED TO GET OUT OF HERE!

This challenge requires you to get to the top of the waterfall within 110 seconds. To do this, you don't have a lot of time to explore for collectibles. Instead, just make your way to the top as fast as you can. Then you can go back and collect items after completing this challenge or during Free Play. Not only do you get a Gold Brick for this, but you also unlock Zylas.

On the left side, push a large rock along a checkered path so it drops to the ground and breaks. Switch to Chewbacca and assemble the pieces into a flower lift and ride it to the top. Then use his strength to pull on the strength handles and break away the side of the cliff. Use the revealed pink bounce pad to jump to the next level.

Move to the right and break up a large flowery plant into Multi-Build bricks. Assemble them into cupcakes on the left. A couple spiders come to eat them and form handholds so you can reach the top of the waterfall.

MINIKIT

If you assemble the Multi-Build into handholds on the right, you can climb to a small alcove and collect a Minikit. A mushroom is also in this spot.

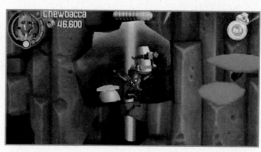

At the top, move toward the pile of rocks on the left. Some tentacles break through the rocks and come at you. Move back and wait for a pile of bricks to drop. Now assemble them into a battering ram. Jump on the pad to make the device start pounding a pile of rocks. Do this a few times to break away the rocks and create an exit. Move through the opening to complete the level.

MINIKIT

During Free Play, once you get to the top of the waterfall, select a Force user and move to the left side near the edge. Use the Force to pull a Minikit down from a ledge and add it to your collection.

Loading Area

CHARACTERS

	Han Solo (Twon Ketee)		Chewbacca (Twon Ketee)
	Varond Jelik (Twon Ketee)		

UNLOCKS

	Oni Jass	Complete True Jedi challenge.
	Croz Danoc	Complete All Collectibles challenge.
	Gaff Kaylek	Complete I Have the High Ground! challenge.
	Ozeer Tenzer	Complete Seasoned Professional challenge.

GOLD BRICK CHALLENGES

Name	Mode	Notes
Level Complete	Any	Complete the level.
True Jedi	Any	Collect 13,000 studs.
All Collectibles	Free Play	Find two Minikits and a Red Brick.
I Have the High Ground!	Any	Defeat 5 Solculvis crew members from high cover.
Seasoned Professional	Any	Capture the rathtar without taking any damage from it.

COLLECTIBLES

Type	Mode	Notes
Minikit	Free Play	Use a rotary control switch to open a weapons crate.
Minikit	Free Play	Dive into a water access.
Red Brick (Super Detonators)	Free Play	Destroy a gold container.

DEFEAT THE SOLCULVIS CREW

As Han Solo and his crew return to the loading area after escaping from the rathtar cavern, they find new trouble. A gang of mercenaries is stealing the rathtar. That just will not do. Move to the right and take cover behind some barricades.

MINIKIT

At the start of the level, during Free Play, you can collect the Minikits. Select BB-8 and use the rotary control switch to open a weapons container. Pick up the revealed Minikit and add it to your collection.

MINIKIT

The second minikit is inside a water access. During Free Play, choose Admiral Ackbar to dive in and get it for you.

Take aim and begin shooting at the enemies below. Watch out for the turret to the right side. When it starts firing at you, take cover.

CHALLENGE:
I HAVE THE HIGH GROUND!

While in the cover section, shooting at the enemies below, defeat five of them to earn a Gold Brick and unlock Gaff Kaylek.

The enemies just keep coming. Maybe you can let the rathtar help you out. Switch to Chewbacca and throw thermal detonators at the silver locks on the rathtar cage. However, that is not enough to release the rathtar.

Take control of Han Solo. Move to the left and take aim at the hook to fire a grapple gun at it. This pulls Han to a higher ledge overlooking the loading area.

Move to the left and use Han's goggles to locate a target on the side of the cage. Now take aim and shoot at the target to release the bands holding the cage together.

RED BRICK
(SUPER DETONATORS)

Once you are on the upper ledge and before you release the rathtar, shoot at a gold container on the opposite side of the loading area with a character with a rapid fire gun such as Captain Phasma or the Guavian Gunner. Destroy it to collect this Red Brick.

DEFEAT THE RATHTAR

Now that the rathtar HAS BEEN released and HAS dealt with the enemies, it is time to defeat the rathtar so you can get it back into a cage. It throws things at you, so move to avoid them. Wait for a pile of bricks to land in the middle of the area. This is a Multi-Build. Quickly build an object to the left.

While the rathtar is momentarily stunned, shoot at it to inflict some damage. Then move out of the way when it recovers. Enemies will appear on the side of the area. Take some time to defeat them, and then get back to work on the rathtar.

The bricks return to the center again. Now build an object in the middle and shoot at the rathtar while it is stunned. Finally, repeat this a third time, building the object on the right side, to defeat the rathtar and complete the level.

CHALLENGE:
SEASONED PROFESSIONAL

If you can defeat the rathtar without taking any damage, you earn a Gold Brick and unlock Ozeer Tenzer. The key to this is once the Multi-Build bricks appear, start building. The faster you defeat the rathar, the less time it has to attack you. Also dodge the rocks it throws at you.

OTTEGAN ASSAULT
Ottegan Pursuit

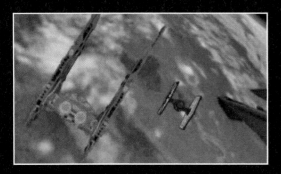

SHOOT DOWN THE RESISTANCE TRANSPORT

Kylo Ren is trying to find the missing map piece to prevent the Resistance from finding Luke Skywalker. He has tracked a Resistance transport to the Ottega system and believes one of the resistance leaders aboard has information he needs. Fly along the exterior of the city and follow the transport. Don't worry about destroying it. Instead, avoid being destroyed yourself.

CHARACTERS

	Kylo Ren's Command Shuttle		Special Forces TIE fighter

UNLOCKS

	Kylo Ren (Masked)	Complete level.
	Captain Phasma	Complete level
	Kaydel Ko Connix	Complete All Collectibles challenge.
	Ottegon Acolyte	Complete Otte-gone challenge.
	R2-Q5	Complete Minor Inconvenience challenge.

RED BRICK
(QUICK BUILD)

There are several Ottegan siege engines along the path. They shoot at you and look like towers with blue on top. Destroy three of these to earn the Red Brick.

CHALLENGE:
MINOR INCONVENIENCE

The Ottegans have placed several space mines to stop intruders. Avoid hitting any of these to earn a Gold Brick and unlock R2-Q5. Some are positioned near the siege engines, so watch out for them as you target the towers.

GOLD BRICK CHALLENGES

Name	Mode	Notes
Level Complete	Any	Complete the level.
True Jedi	Any	Collect 12,000 studs.
All Collectibles	Any	Find all the Minikits.
Otte-gone	Any	Destroy 3 of the Ottegan fighters flying out of the hangars.
Minor Inconvenience	Any	Avoid taking damage from any of the space mines.

COLLECTIBLES

Type	Mode	Notes
Minikit	Any	Destroy container outside of the hangars.
Minikit	Any	Destroy the gold tower.
Red Brick	Any	Destroy 3 Ottegan siege engines.

The chase leads around the hangars where many Ottegan fighters are taking off and fleeing. Shoot them down while continuing your pursuit.

The pursuit leads you into a tunnel-like area. Watch out for Resistance X-wings that attack and small turrets. Continue watching for space mines as well.

As the Resistance transport leaves the tunnels, follow it up to the surface. Other transports are evacuating, but stay on your target and follow it until it begins to land and the level comes to an end.

MINIKIT

Shortly after you begin flying near the hangars, look for a container floating in the center of the screen. Shoot it to collect the Minikit inside.

CHALLENGE:
OTTE-GONE

Shoot down three of the Ottegan fighters as they are fleeing. They can be tough to hit since they are moving from left to right rather than in the same direction as you. Complete this challenge to unlock the Ottegon Acolyte and earn a Gold Brick.

MINIKIT

After going through the tunnels, watch for a gold tower on the left side. Shoot and destroy it to earn this Minikit.

Ottegan Surface

CHARACTERS

	Kylo Ren (Masked)		Captain Phasma

UNLOCKS

	Praster Barrun	Complete True Jedi challenge.
	Ottegan Warrior	Complete All Collectibles challenge.
	Pamich Nerro Goode	Complete Will You Help Me? challenge.
	Trentus Savay	Complete Blind Rage challenge.

GOLD BRICK CHALLENGES

Name	Mode	Notes
Level Complete	Any	Complete the level.
True Jedi	Any	Collect 22,000 studs.
All Collectables	Free Play	Find all the Minikits.
Will you help me?	Any	Defeat an Ottegan by deflecting his bolts back at him as Kylo Ren.
Blind Rage	Any	Lightsaber-cut 3 trees down.

COLLECTIBLES

Type	Mode	Notes
Minikit	Free Play	Go through a cloud of toxic gas.
Minikit	Any	Use the Command ability to destroy a gold statue.
Minikit	Free Play	Use a Resistance terminal.

DEFEAT 20 OTTEGAN WARRIORS

Kylo Ren and Captain Phasma have landed on the surface and must now get to the Resistance transport. However, the Ottegans are not going to make it easy for them. Before you can leave the first area, you must defeat 20 of their warriors.

CHALLENGE:
WILL YOU HELP ME?

For this challenge, you must use Kylo Ren. When he comes under fire from the enemy, use his lightsaber to deflect the bolt back at the enemy to defeat them. This often takes a couple hits. Complete this challenge to earn a Gold Brick and unlock Pamich Nerro Goode.

CHALLENGE:
BLIND RAGE

Kylo Ren likes to use his lightsaber to take out his frustrations. Use it to cut down three trees to earn another Gold Brick and unlock Trentus Savay. One tree is in this area, and the other two are in the final area where the transport is located.

MINIKIT

During Free Play, select a character who is immune to toxic gas, such as BB-8 or Darth Vader, and move through the green cloud on the left side of this first area. A Minikit can be found here.

After all of the Ottegan warriors have been defeated, a security ship appears and begins firing missiles. As Kylo Ren, use the Force to create a barrier around him and stop the missiles. Then target the silver band on the large tree branch and release the missiles. This causes a huge boulder to come crashing down onto the barricaded gate to the right, allowing you to continue your advance to the transport.

DESTROY THE TURRETS

The Ottegans have taken cover behind some barricades and are protected by two missile turrets. You need to destroy both of those turrets in order to get to the transport. As Kylo Ren, use the Force to catch some missiles. Then target the silver crane to the right and throw the missiles at it to break it into pieces for a Multi-Build.

Assemble the pieces into a crane on the right. It then picks up an Ottegan warrior and lifts him in the air. Switch to Captain Phasma and take a shot to defeat this enemy who is no longer behind cover.

After destroying the crane, take control of Kylo Ren and reassemble the pieces into a bomb dispenser on the left side. Wait for a gold bomb to deploy, then use the Force to lift it and hold it over the enemy barricades.

Switch back to Captain Phasma and shoot at the gold bomb until it detonates and takes out the barricades. You can now move closer to the turrets.

A red fuel container is suspended below each turret. Use Captain Phasma's blaster to destroy the gold

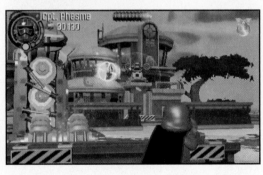

latch to release the container on the right. Switch to Kylo Ren and use the Force to catch some missiles which you can throw back at the silver latch on the left container. Now use the Force to lift each container in turn and use them to destroy the turrets.

OPEN THE LARGE GATE

Now that the turrets are eliminated, you can move to the large gate. However, you must first defeat eight Ottegan warriors. Once they are out of the picture, a First Order landing craft will drop off three stormtroopers. Use Captain Phasma's Command ability to lead them. Use her grappling gun to pull on one of the four hooks on the gate and the stormtroopers will do the same on the other three hooks. Together they can pull the large gate open and clear the way to the transport.

MINIKIT

Before opening the gate and exiting this area, have Captain Phasma lead the stormtroopers to the right so that all four of them can open fire on a gold statue. Destroy the statue to get the Minikit.

MINIKIT

During Free Play, choose a character who can interact with the Resistance terminal to the right of the large gate. After solving the puzzle, a door opens so you can get the Minikit.

You have reached the shuttle. There are six Ottegan warriors guarding the area around the shuttle. Defeat all of them, and then use the Force as Kylo Ren to pull open the transport's door. Six Resistance fighters jump out and begin attacking. Defeat them, and then use the Force to pull off the red panel on the transport. Switch to Captain Phasma and shoot at the gold panel.

The Ottegan leader then activates an energy shield as well as a missile turret on top of the shuttle. Take control of Kylo Ren and use the Force to catch the missiles. Then throw them at the orange generators on either side of the shield to shut it down. The leader is now your prisoner. Through a mental interrogation by Kylo Ren, the leader reveals that the missing map piece is on the desert planet of Jakku.

RESISTANCE BASE HUB

The Resistance Base hub is where the story begins and ends. It also serves as the main hub for the game. While it does not have nearly as many collectibles as the other three hubs, the Resistance Base has several vital features available only at this location.

Medical Bunker

DECARBONIZER DEVICE

The Medical Bunker contains two important consoles. First, you can find the decarbonizer device here. As you explore the four hub planets, you can find characters frozen in carbonite. Once a character is found, return to the Medical Bunker and use the device to remove them from carbonite. You can then select these characters during Free Play and for use at the hub planets.

The second feature here is the custom character creator. One of the cool features of LEGO games is to make your own characters. Not only can you customize their looks, but also their abilities. You can have up to three saved characters at one time. They can be used at the hubs, as well as during Free Play.

CREATING A CUSTOM CHARACTER

Let's take a look at how to make a custom character. First select a character from the three slots you want to customize. Now there are nine different character aspects that can be modified.

Faction

You can choose from three different factions: Light, Neutral, or Dark. Light gives the character Resistance access while Dark gives the character First Order access.

Size

Here you can choose between Minifig and Smallfig. Smallfigs can use small access hatches and also have toxic resistance.

Class

Depending on your Faction and Size, you can choose from two to six different classes. Cycle through them all to see which abilities the classes give your character. Your class can also affect the weapons your character can carry.

Head

There are 118 different heads from which you can choose. These heads also include a hat or hair as well as shape of the head.

Face

There are 84 different faces. However, if you choose a non-human head, you cannot change the face.

Body

Select from 144 different bodies.

Legs

There are 119 different legs you can use to customize your Minifig characters. Smallfig characters' legs are selected as a part of the body.

Ranged

Here you can decide if your character will have a ranged weapon, as well as which type. Some of these weapons have special abilities, such as melting ice or destroying gold or silver objects.

Melee

Do you want your character to have a melee weapon? If you select none, he or she can still fight with their fists. There are a variety of weapons here. If you want to select a lightsaber, you must be sure that your character is of a class with the Force ability.

New Star Wars Adventures

As you play through the story levels and earn Gold Bricks, you unlock access to four different groups of levels which take place before *Star Wars: The Force Awakens*. There are four Level Select terminals for these levels. Once you unlock a terminal, a mini starship appears on the terminal.

Prologue Levels	Gold Bricks to Unlock
Battle of Endor	10
Poe to the Rescue	25
Rathtar Hunting	75
Ottegan Assault	125

WHEN TO PLAY THE NEW STAR WARS ADVENTURES LEVELS

These levels become available as soon as you have the required number of Gold Bricks. If you want to go back and replay some of the story levels in Free Play before playing through all 37 story levels, then do the Prologue levels as soon as you can. These levels allow you to unlock characters that have abilities you can use when trying to acquire all those collectibles during Free Play. For example, in Battle of Endor, you can get some characters who use the Force, such as Luke Skywalker and Darth Vader. Or maybe you need Admiral Ackbar so you can use those water access points? Play through Poe to the Rescue to unlock that Mon Calmari character.

Starkiller Battle Arena

Once you complete the entire story of the game, including the Epilogue, the Starkiller Battle Arena is unlocked. See the Starkiller Battle Arena chapter for more information on playing in this area. The access terminal for the arena is located in the Resistance Base hub just to the right of the Prologue Level Select terminal. You can't miss the mini Starkiller at this terminal.

Collectibles

The Resistance Base Hub has five Minikits and two characters in carbonite. While this is not as many as the other three hub planets, this is a good place to start collecting. Some of the collectibles can be found in the hub. Others require you to complete a side mission in order to earn them.

MINIKITS

Minikit 1

This Minikit is next to the X-wing landing pad. Break up the steps to the landing pad, then reassemble this Multi-Build into a rotary control switch. Switch to BB-8 and use the rotary control switch to launch the droid into the air to get the Minikit.

Minikit 2

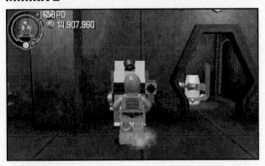

Enter the Command Hangar and select C-3PO or another droid to use the protocol droid terminal to the left. Complete the puzzle to open a door so you can collect the Minikit inside.

Minikit 3

Locate a container with a crack on it behind the Millennium Falcon. Select a character that can break cracked bricks and then destroy the container to get the Minikit.

Minikit 4

You must complete the Resistance Assistance side mission to get this Minikit. Talk to the character just outside of the Command Hangar to get it started. You must train three groups: new recruits, pilots, and commandos. To do this, follow the green studs to each group and defeat three characters. Then return to the start to get your prize.

Minikit 5

This Minikit also requires a side mission: Resistance Hotshot. Move behind a barricade and then begin shooting at hologram targets. Hit ten of them and then return to the start to get the Minikit.

CHARACTERS IN CARBONITE

Gray Squadron Pilot

This character is standing next to the decarbonizer device. Just walk into the Medical Bunker and collect the pilot.

Boba Fett

Boba Fett is located above some large tanks just outside of the Medical Bunker. You need a character with the Force to move the carbonite to the ground so you can collect it.

JAKKU HUB

The Jakku hub is the second hub to which you gain access. Unlike the Resistance Base hub, there are no special features here—only Level Select terminals and collectibles.

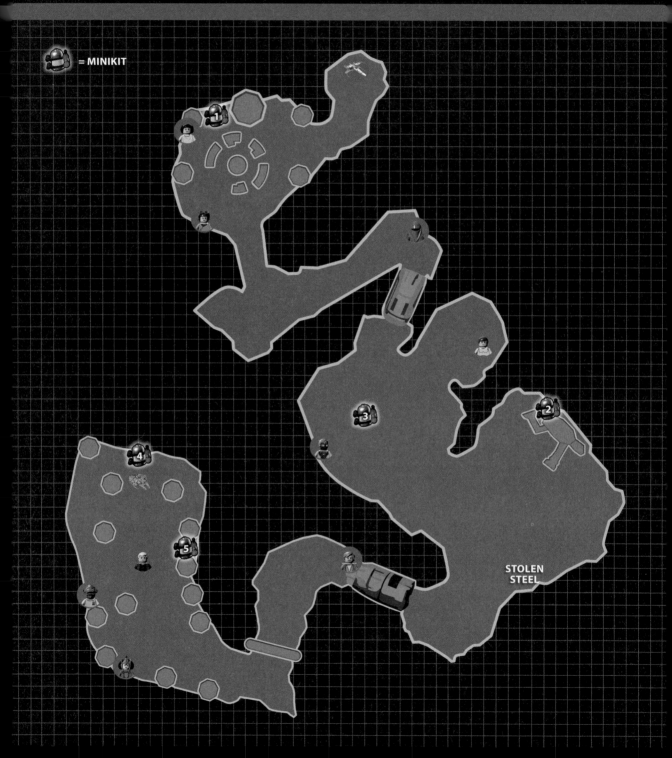

= MINIKIT

STOLEN
STEEL

Collectibles

The Jakku Hub has five Minikits and ten characters in carbonite. There are also six side missions associated with collecting some of those Minikits and characters in carbonite.

FINDING COLLECTIBLES

Unless a collectible is obtained by completing a side mission, they do not appear on the in-game map. Some of these are very hard to find since they do not appear as you move through the hubs. However, if you find, purchase, and activate the Collectible Detector Red Brick, icons will appear on the screen to show you the location of all collectibles.

MINIKITS

Minikit 1

This Minikit is located in the Niima village near the X-wing landing pad. You must complete the Nightwatch side mission. After talking to the character who gives you the mission, follow the trail of green studs into the desert and break a crate. Assemble it into a music device. This lures Nightwatchers out of the sand. Attack and defeat ten to complete this mission. Then return to the start to get the Minikit.

Minikit 2

This Minikit is in a silver container behind the wrecked AT-AT that Rey calls home. Break it open to get the Minikit.

Minikit 3

This Minikit is buried in the sand in the Niima graveyard area. Use the Force to lift it out of the sand.

Minikit 4

Look behind the Millennium Falcon at the Niima Outpost to find a crate with this Minikit inside.

Minikit 5

Complete The Niima Rally side mission to get this Minikit. After talking to the character in the Niima Outpost, go talk to the speeder dealer and pick which speeder you want to race. Walk back to a terminal to start the race. Once the race begins, you must drive through several race gates in under 49 seconds to win the Minikit.

CHARACTERS IN CARBONITE

Admiral Ackbar (Classic)

This character in carbonite is located behind Unkar's hut in the Niima Outpost. Use a character with the Force to bring it to you.

Anakin Skywalker (Episode 1)

To get this character, you need to complete the Speeder Racer side mission. After talking to the character who gives you the mission, go to a hat dispenser and choose a Podracer helmet. Then come back and start the race. Move through all gates within 49 seconds to win the prize.

Chancellor Palpatine

You need a character such as Admiral Ackbar who can dive into water access spots to get this character in carbonite. Once he dives down, the carbonite will come flying out of the water. This is located near the Millennium Falcon in the Niima Outpost.

Han Solo (Stormtrooper)

Locate a silver object in the Jakku graveyard. Throw a thermal detonator or use some other way to break it open and the carbonite will come sliding down the slope.

Luke Skywalker (Episode IV)

This one is also located in the Jakku graveyard. Look for a target on the side of one of the engine tunnels. Shoot it to get the carbonite down.

Princess Leia (Ewok Village)

This character in carbonite is located behind a hut in the Niima Village. Use the Force to get it.

Queen Amidala

You must complete A Secret Service side mission to get this carbonite. This requires you to find three clues. At each clue, you must scan it and then use a character with a special ability to open it. Return to the spy who gave you the mission with the clues. Then use goggles to find the First Order Spy and defeat him to earn your reward.

Royal Guard

Look for a cracked piece in the Jakku graveyard. Then select a character like Grummgar to smash the cracked LEGO and collect this character in the carbonite.

Teebo

Complete the Stolen Steel side mission to get this character in carbonite. First you must melt some ice to free a character who gives you the mission. Then hunt a steelpecker and shoot at this bird at three different locations until it drops the regulator part. Carry it back to the character who needs it to complete the mission.

Tusken Raider

Complete the Scavenger Shakedown side mission to get this carbonite. Follow the trail of green studs and fight off some teedos to get a data card. Then return the data card to the character who gave you the mission.

TAKODANA
HUB

After completing the nine levels on Jakku, you gain access to the Takodana hub. At the beginning, you can only get to a small part of this hub. However, complete all Takodana levels to roam the entire hub.

Collectibles

The Takodana hub has five Minikits and ten characters in carbonite. There are also six side missions associated with collecting some of those Minikits and characters in carbonite.

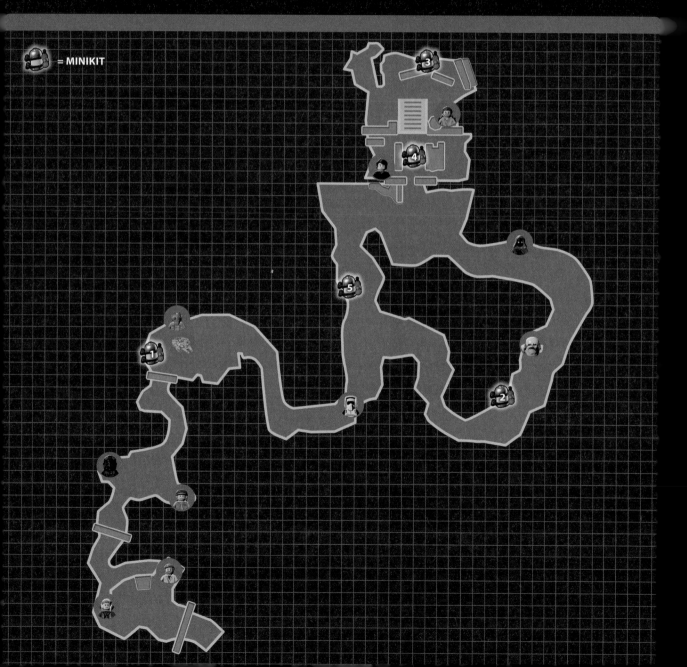

= MINIKIT

MINIKITS

Minikit 1

This Minikit is located in a red and black container next to the Millennium Falcon. Use the Force to break it open and get the Minikit.

Minikit 2

This Minikit is difficult to find without some help. It is out of view as you walk along the forest path. Use the Force to bring it down to where you can collect it.

Minikit 3

Walk all the way to the edge of the waterfront to find this Minikit. You will need to use the Force to bring it to you.

Minikit 4

Complete the Kanata Reconstruction side mission to get this Minikit. You must find three parts to rebuild a statue. One requires diving into a water access. The second requires goggles and the ability to break cracked bricks. The third part requires a lightsaber. Once you have all three parts, return to the start and build the statue to complete the mission and get the Minikit.

Minikit 5

This Minikit is the reward for completing the Resistance Recon side mission. You must gather three parts once again. These require breaking cracked bricks, using the Force, and using an astromech terminal. Once you have all the parts, return and build a mini X-wing. Then race it through the gates within 49 seconds to get the Minikit.

CHARACTERS IN CARBONITE

Anakin Skywalker (Episode III)

You must complete the Takodana Treachery side mission to get this carbonite. Follow the directions to get disguises and then find opposing gangs. You must defeat eight gang members and then return to the start to get your prize.

Arvel Crynyd

This carbonite is the prize for completing The Second Wave side mission. Once again, you need to get three objects. You will need to use goggles, blow up silver objects, and pull on strength handles to get them all. Now take them all to the waterfront and construct a turret. Finally, use the turret to shoot down six TIE fighters.

Greedo

This carbonite is located inside the Millennium Falcon. Use the Force to move a container out of the way so you can reach the collectible.

Jawa

Complete the Express Delivery side mission for this carbonite. You must first use the Force to move a piece of wall, and then destroy a silver safe to get the delivery. After defeating some pirates, return to the smuggler who gave you the mission. Then race through the gates within 49 seconds to earn the reward.

Obi-Wan Kenobi (Episode III)

Break open a cracked brick door to get this character in carbonite.

Qui-Gon Jinn

This carbonite brick is stuck in a wall. Use a lightsaber to cut it out and add it to your collection.

Rebel Commando

You must complete the Rumble in the Jungle side mission to get this collectible. Follow the trail of green studs to a contact. Shoot an apple and bring it to him to get a blueprint. Next, build a trap and defeat some First Order stormtroopers. Finally, return a lunchbox to the Resistance soldiers to complete the mission.

Scout Trooper

This character in carbonite is located in a tree. Use the Force to get it down.

TIE Interceptor Pilot

Look for an orange hook up in a tree. Use a grapple gun to pull on it and get the carbonite inside.

Wampa

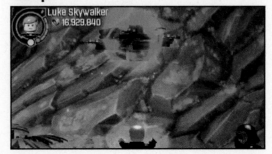

This character in carbonite is on a red and black platform. Use the Force to destroy the platform and the prize will drop down to you.

STARKILLER HUB

The Starkiller hub is the last hub. Unlock all parts of the hub by completing the 9 Starkiller levels.

Collectibles

The Starkiller hub has 5 Minikits and 10 characters in carbonite. There are also 6 side missions associated with collecting some of those Minikits and characters in carbonite.

= MINIKIT

MINIKITS

Minikit 1

The first Minikit is located aboard the Millennium Falcon. Break open a container with a large crack on it to get the goods.

Minikit 2

This Minikit is on top of the wall on the left as you exit the First Order base. Use a grapple gun to pull it down.

Minikit 3

This Minikit is partially buried in the snow. Use the Force to lift it out.

Minikit 4

A minikit is the reward for completing the Ace TIE Pilot side mission. This requires you to repair a TIE fighter and involves strength handles and an astromech terminal. Once the TIE is repaired, you need to take it out for a test flight and fly through all the race gates within 44 seconds.

Minikit 5

Complete the Stormtrooper School side mission to collect this Minikit. You must find three data cards and bring them back to the instructor. You will need to use the Force, activate a First Order terminal, and defeat some stormtroopers to get the cards.

CHARACTERS IN CARBONITE

Count Dooku

This carbonite brick requires you to complete the Parade Practice side mission. This follow-the-leader mission has a leader show you a routine which you must then copy. Complete five of these to come home with the carbonite.

Death Star Trooper

Get ready to do some more flying. You need to complete the Snowspeeder Slalom side mission to get this carbonite brick. Before you can fly it, you must get a snowspeeder out of a snowbank. Start off by using goggles and then breaking a cracked brick. Then use the Force to lift it up and out of the snow. Finally, take it for a spin. Race through the gates within 44 seconds to complete this mission.

Han Solo (Classic)

This character in carbonite is located in an alcove in the Millennium Falcon. Use the Force to lift it out of the alcove so you can add it to your collection.

Luke Skywalker (Stormtrooper)

A protocol droid is supposed to deliver food to various parties around Starkiller base. However, due to the cold, it is unable to move. A carbonite brick is awarded if you complete the Starkiller Chef side mission. Begin by putting on a chef's hat. Then you will need to use goggles, a flamethrower, and even break up a cracked brick to bring food to three groups.

Obi-Wan Kenobi (Episode IV)

This character in carbonite is hard to find. Look for an opening to a pipe covered by red and black bricks. It is located between the Millennium Falcon and the base. Use the Force to pull these bricks away and the carbonite will fall out.

Padmé Amidala

Use a grapple gun to pull this carbonite brick down from a snowy ledge.

Princess Leia (Classic)

This character in carbonite can be found inside a locked container. Blow up the silver lock to open the door. Then switch to a character that is resistant to the cold and get the collectible.

Rebel Scout Trooper

Use the Force to get this carbonite brick down from a ledge inside the First Order base. Using the Collectible Detector Red Brick helps you find this one since it is out of sight as you walk by.

Snowtrooper (Classic)

Feel like a snowball fight? Complete the Snowball Skirmish side mission to get this carbonite brick. This is like a cover shooting section; however, this time you are throwing snowballs at snowtroopers rather than firing a blaster. Hit ten of them without being defeated to win this mission and get the prize.

Yoda

Behind an ice wall, this carbonite brick you will find. Melt through it with a flamethrower, you must.

STARKILLER ARENA

Once you complete the entire story of the game, including the Epilogue, you unlock the Starkiller Battle Arena. The access terminal for the arena is located in the Resistance Base hub just to the right of the Prologue Level Select terminals. While there are no collectibles in this arena, you can still earn five Gold Bricks here.

GOLD BRICK CHALLENGES	
Name	Notes
Bronze Battler	Defeat all waves.
Silver Soldier	Defeat all waves in under 6 minutes.
Gold Guardian	Defeat all waves in under 4 minutes.
It's a Trap	Defeat 25 enemies using traps.
That's One Hell of a Pilot!	Defeat 25 enemies with Poe Dameron.

DEFEAT TEN WAVES OF ENEMIES

This level requires you to defeat ten different waves of attacks by enemies. You are competing against the clock. While you earn one Gold Brick for just completing the level, you earn additional Gold Bricks the faster you defeat the enemies.

The key to getting a better time is going after the enemies instead of letting them come to you. Move around the arena. Most players are tempted to stay near the starting location by the bridge. However, go down the stairs to the right and up the stairs at the top of the level. Hunt the enemies to defeat them more efficiently. Some characters are better than others on this level. For example, Darth Vader and his abilities can come in handy in completing some of the challenges.

CHALLENGE:
IT'S A TRAP

In addition to using ranged and melee attacks to defeat the enemies, there are also several traps you can use. Shoot at the red explosives to defeat any nearby enemies. Also use the terminals by the bridge to retract it; if there are any enemies on the bridge, they will fall and be defeated. There are also other traps. Look for terminals to activate turrets and other defenses. This challenge takes more time to complete, so if you are going for it, don't try for those timed challenges.

CHALLENGE:
THAT'S ONE HELL OF A PILOT!

Poe is the default character for the arena. Just defeat 25 enemies as Poe to get this Gold Brick. Once you have achieved this, try using other characters that might be able to cause more damage in a shorter time.

USING RED BRICKS

You can make the Starkiller Arena easier by using Red Bricks and the special abilities they provide. Here are some you may want to use:

- Regenerate Hearts
- Combat Bar Regen
- Explosive Bolts
- Imperial Inaccuracy
- Mega Melee

COLLECTIBLES CHECKLISTS

This chapter is a quick-reference guide to all of the collectibles in the game—Red Bricks, Gold Bricks, Minikits, Characters in Carbonite, and Vehicles (Characters are covered in their own chapter). You can check off each collectible here as you acquire it and keep track of your progress. If you need more information on acquiring a particular collectible, turn to the corresponding walkthrough or hub chapter.

Red Bricks

Each of the story chapters (which consist of three levels) includes one Red Brick. Some are easy to find, while others are only accessible during Free Play after you unlock additional characters with specific abilities. Once you find a Red Brick, you must then purchase and activate it to use it. This is accomplished from the menu.

RED BRICKS						
Icon	Got It?	Name	Description	Level	How Unlocked?	Price
		Birthday Brick	Replace all explosions with confetti, fireworks, and party noises.	Available at Start	N/A	50,000
		Collectible Detector	Indicates where to find Minikits, Red Bricks, and Gold Bricks.	Available at Start	N/A	200,000
		Combat Bar Regen	Combat bar constantly recharges when emptied, providing infinite specials.	Available at Start	N/A	250,000
		Dark Side	All Jedi Characters can use Sith powers.	Epilogue: Luke's Island	Swim through a water access to a small island.	50,000
		Destroy on Contact	Destroys all LEGO smashables on contact.	Chapter 6: Attack on Takodana—Castle Escape	Use a dark side character with the Force during the cover section on a wall.	50,000
		Droid Sounds	Non-Droid characters make Droid sounds.	Available at Start	N/A	50,000
		Explosive Bolts	Blasters defeat enemies with one hit and knock them back a great distance.	Chapter 9: The Finale—Starkiller Showdown	Use the Force and then go through a small access hatch.	50,000
		Fast Build	Build LEGO objects much faster than usual.	Prologue: Ottegan Assault—Ottegan Pursuit	Destroy 3 Ottegan Siege Engines.	50,000
		Helium Voices	All characters have helium voices.	Available at Start	N/A	50,000
		Imperial Inaccuracy	Enemy blaster accuracy reduced to 0% chance of hit and will always miss the player.	Available at Start	N/A	500,000
		Infinite Torpedoes	Ships are always stocked with the maximum number of torpedoes during flight arena levels.	Prologue: Poe to the Rescue—Trash Compactor	Use the Force near the end of the level.	100,000
		Mega Melee	Melee attacks one-hit KO regular enemies.	Chapter 7: Starkiller Sabotage—Starkiller Crash Site	Defeat the wampa.	100,000
		Perfect Deflect	Block oncoming laser fire with 100% accuracy. Bolts are hit back at who fired them.	Chapter 2: Escape from the Finalizer—Finalizer Hangar 2	Use the Force to move a panel.	100,000
		Quick Access	Instantly complete Astromech, Protocol, First Order, and Resistance panels.	Prologue: The Battle of Endor—Death Star Interior	Use a rotary control switch to get up onto a catwalk.	50,000
		Regenerate Hearts	Health regenerates over time.	Available at Start	N/A	50,000
		Silly Sabers	Lightsaber beams appear as silly LEGO pieces.	Available at Start	N/A	50,000
		Silly Torpedoes	Torpedoes are replaced with silly items.	Available at Start	N/A	50,000
		Stud Magnet	Attracts nearby studs to the player.	Chapter 4: The Eravana—Freighter Battle	Get through a silver door and cold at the end of the level.	50,000
		Stud Multiplier x2	Multiply the value of collected studs by 2!	Chapter 1: Assault on Jakku—Jakku Graveyard	Destroy a gold container.	200,000

RED BRICKS

Icon	Got It?	Name	Description	Level	How Unlocked?	Price
		Stud Multiplier x4	Multiply the value of collected studs by 4!	Chapter 3: Niima Outpost—Niima Outpost	Destroy a cracked LEGO crate and then the gold crate inside.	400,000
		Stud Multiplier x6	Multiply the value of collected studs by 6!	Chapter 5: Maz's Castle—Castle Basement	Use the Force to open a wall in the final room.	600,000
		Stud Multiplier x8	Multiply the value of collected studs by 8!	Chapter 8: Destroy the Starkiller—Rey's Escape	Pick it up near the end of the level.	800,000
		Stud Multiplier x10	Multiply the value of collected studs by 10!	Epilogue: Luke's Island	Destroy a gold object.	1,000,000
		Super Detonators	Thermal Detonators cause a larger explosion radius.	Prologue: Rathtar Hunting—Loading Area	Destroy a gold container.	50,000

SPENDING STUDS

As you begin collecting studs, it is tempting to spend them on new characters or Red Bricks. The best strategy is to save your studs as you play through the story levels. Then purchase the Stud Multiplier Red Bricks as soon as you can and then activate them. The Stud Multiplier x4 Red Brick can be obtained in the third level. Once you have 400,000 studs, you can purchase and activate it. Then as you play through subsequent levels, you earn four times the amount of studs you would normally. The stud multiplier Red Bricks can be activated together. So if you have all four activated, you actually have a stud multiplier of x1,920!

Gold Bricks

Each level has five Gold Bricks, which can be earned for completing challenges.

CHAPTER 1: ASSAULT ON JAKKU—VILLAGE RETREAT

Got It?	Name	Mode	Notes
	Level Complete	Any	Complete the level.
	True Jedi	Any	Collect 18,000 studs.
	All Collectibles	Free Play	Find all the Minikits.
	No DESERTing	Any	Smash 3 containers with villagers hiding in them.
	A Load of Old Bloggins	Any	Return all 3 bloggins to their pen.

CHAPTER 1: ASSAULT ON JAKKU—JAKKU GRAVEYARD

Got It?	Name	Mode	Notes
	Level Complete	Any	Complete the level.
	True Jedi	Any	Collect 35,000 studs.
	All Collectibles	Free Play	Find all the Minikits.
	The Brave Little Droid	Any	Defeat 5 Teedos with BB-8.
	A Proper Scavenger	Any	Destroy every object within the Destroyer as Rey.

CHAPTER 2: ESCAPE FROM THE FINALIZER—FINALIZER HANGAR 2

Got It?	Name	Mode	Notes
	Level Complete	Any	Complete the level.
	True Jedi	Any	Collect 18,000 studs.
	All Collectibles	Free Play	Find all the Minikits.
	TIEd Down	Any	Defeat 15 stormtroopers while in the TIE fighter.
	Keep Your Head On!	Any	Get through cover without getting hit.

CHAPTER 1: ASSAULT ON JAKKU—FIRST ORDER ASSAULT

Got It?	Name	Mode	Notes
	Level Complete	Any	Complete the level.
	True Jedi	Any	Collect 25,000 studs.
	All Collectibles	Free Play	Find all the Minikits.
	Don't Spill a Drop	Any	Complete the Multi-Build puzzle at the end of the level without making any mistakes.
	Cover Commander	Any	Complete the cover section without being defeated.

CHAPTER 2: ESCAPE FROM THE FINALIZER—FINALIZER HANGAR 1

Got It?	Name	Mode	Notes
	Level Complete	Any	Complete the level.
	True Jedi	Any	Collect 15,000 studs.
	All Collectibles	Free Play	Find all the Minikits.
	Dameron Unchained	Any	Return to knock out the First Order crew near the start.
	Dest-droid	Any	Walk the protocol droid to its doom!

CHAPTER 2: ESCAPE FROM THE FINALIZER—STAR DESTROYER EXTERIOR

Got It?	Name	Mode	Notes
	Level Complete	Any	Complete the level.
	True Jedi	Any	Collect 40,000 studs.
	All Collectibles	Any	Find all the Minikits.
	Blow TIE!	Any	Destroy 15 TIE fighters in the arena section.
	Falling with Style	Any	Make it through the flight route toward Jakku without being destroyed.

Gold Bricks continued next page.

CHAPTER 3: NIIMA OUTPOST— NIIMA OUTPOST

Got It?	Name	Mode	Notes
☐	Level Complete	Any	Complete the level.
☐	True Jedi	Any	Collect 30,000 studs.
☐	All Collectibles	Free Play	Find all the Minikits.
☐	Luggabeast Master	Any	Defeat 3 stormtroopers with a captured luggabeast.
☐	Soap Boxing	Any	Smash 4 scrap washing machines.

CHAPTER 3: NIIMA OUTPOST— NIIMA BOMBARDMENT

Got It?	Name	Mode	Notes
☐	Level Complete	Any	Complete the level.
☐	True Jedi	Any	Collect 25,000 studs.
☐	All Collectibles	Free Play	Find all the Minikits.
☐	Group Shot	Any	Defeat 3 stormtroopers with the turret or Bomb Multi-Build.
☐	Flawless Coverage	Any	Complete the Spaceport cover section without being defeated.

CHAPTER 3: NIIMA OUTPOST— JAKKU GRAVEYARD FLIGHT

Got It?	Name	Mode	Notes
☐	Level Complete	Any	Complete the level.
☐	True Jedi	Any	Collect 22,000 studs.
☐	All Collectibles	Any	Find all the Minikits.
☐	Probation	Any	Destroy 5 probe droids.
☐	Golden Sands	Any	Destroy 3 gold LEGO arches.

CHAPTER 4: THE ERAVANA— FREIGHTER BATTLE

Got It?	Name	Mode	Notes
☐	Level Complete	Any	Complete the level.
☐	True Jedi	Any	Collect 30,000 studs.
☐	All Collectibles	Free Play	Find all the Minikits.
☐	Wrath-tar	Any	Avoid the rathtar tentacles.
☐	Once a Stormtrooper, Always a Stormtrooper	Any	Defeat 10 gang members as Finn.

CHAPTER 4: THE ERAVANA— FREIGHTER CHASE

Got It?	Name	Mode	Notes
☐	Level Complete	Any	Complete the level.
☐	True Jedi	Any	Collect 27,000 studs.
☐	All Collectibles	Free Play	Find all the Minikits.
☐	Wookiee Cookie	Free Play	Find Chewbacca's 3 cookie stashes.
☐	No Match for a Good Blaster	Any	Defeat 2 gangers with Han's blaster, without taking any damage.

CHAPTER 4: THE ERAVANA— FREIGHTER SHUTDOWN

Got It?	Name	Mode	Notes
☐	Level Complete	Any	Complete the level.
☐	True Jedi	Any	Collect 16,000 studs.
☐	All Collectibles	Free Play	Find all the Minikits.
☐	The Tentacle Menace	Free Play	Scare off 3 rathtar tentacles.
☐	BB-Ball	Any	Score a basket with BB-8.

CHAPTER 5: MAZ'S CASTLE— CASTLE APPROACH

Got It?	Name	Mode	Notes
☐	Level Complete	Any	Complete the level.
☐	True Jedi	Any	Collect 21,000 studs.
☐	All Collectibles	Free Play	Find all the Minikits.
☐	Classic Misdirection	Any	Point all the signs away from the castle.
☐	Full Stream	Any	Wake Grummgar up in a single attempt.

CHAPTER 5: MAZ'S CASTLE— CASTLE HALL

Got It?	Name	Mode	Notes
☐	Level Complete	Any	Complete the level.
☐	True Jedi	Any	Collect 28,000 studs.
☐	All Collectibles	Free Play	Find all the Minikits.
☐	Just a Helping Hand	Free Play	Help all the patrols of the bar.
☐	Quick Fire Shot	Any	Shoot all 10 bottles in the shooting gallery in less than 15 seconds.

CHAPTER 5: MAZ'S CASTLE— CASTLE BASEMENT

Got It?	Name	Mode	Notes
☐	Level Complete	Any	Complete the level.
☐	True Jedi	Any	Collect 45,000 studs.
☐	All Collectibles	Free Play	Find all the Minikits.
☐	Tidy as You Go	Any	Destroy all of the objects in the first corridor.
☐	Floor is Lava!	Any	Collect the upper gear without touching the ground once you've started.

CHAPTER 6: ATTACK ON TAKODANA— ATTACK ON TAKODANA

Got It?	Name	Mode	Notes
☐	Level Complete	Any	Complete the level.
☐	True Jedi	Any	Collect 20,000 studs.
☐	All Collectibles	Free Play	Find all the Minikits.
☐	Fight Fire with Fire	Free Play	Destroy 5 objects as a Flametrooper with the flamethrower weapon.
☐	I'm Rubber, You're Glue	Free Play	Defeat a stormtrooper by deflecting his bolts back at him.

CHAPTER 6: ATTACK ON TAKODANA— CASTLE ESCAPE

Got It?	Name	Mode	Notes
☐	Level Complete	Any	Complete the level.
☐	True Jedi	Any	Collect 20,000 studs.
☐	All Collectibles	Free Play	Find the Minikit and Red Brick.
☐	Let's Call it a TIE	Any	Don't take any damage from the TIE fighters.
☐	Cook up a Storm	Any	Use each of the Multi-Build models to defeat FN-2199.

CHAPTER 6: ATTACK ON TAKODANA— TAKODANA SKIES

Got It?	Name	Mode	Notes
☐	Level Complete	Any	Complete the level.
☐	True Jedi	Any	Collect 100,000 studs.
☐	All Collectibles	Free Play	Find all the Minikits.
☐	Tower Control	Any	Destroy the 5 towers during the approach to the battlefield.
☐	TIE Die	Any	Save the transporter without it taking damage.

CHAPTER 7: STARKILLER SABOTAGE—STARKILLER CRASH SITE

Got It?	Name	Mode	Notes
	Level Complete	Any	Complete the level.
	True Jedi	Any	Collect 40,000 studs.
	All Collectibles	Free Play	Find the Minikit and Red Brick.
	Power to the People	Any	Complete the Power Bridge puzzle without losing power.
	Wampa Stompa	Free Play	Defeat the wampa.

CHAPTER 7: STARKILLER SABOTAGE—SHIELD ROOM APPROACH

Got It?	Name	Mode	Notes
	Level Complete	Any	Complete the level.
	True Jedi	Any	Collect 40,000 studs.
	All Collectibles	Free Play	Find all the Minikits.
	Smash Hits	Any	Smash 5 First Order radar transmitters.
	Thermal Heating	Any	Take out 3 stormtroopers with a Thermal Detonator.

CHAPTER 7: STARKILLER SABOTAGE—PHASMA

Got It?	Name	Mode	Notes
	Level Complete	Any	Complete the level.
	True Jedi	Any	Collect 20,000 studs.
	All Collectibles	Free Play	Find all the Minikits.
	Evasive Manoeuvres	Any	Successfully avoid 5 of Phasma's missile attacks.
	Mouse Hunt	Any	Exterminate 3 mouse droids.

CHAPTER 8: DESTROY THE STARKILLER—ASSAULT OF STARKILLER

Got It?	Name	Mode	Notes
	Level Complete	Any	Complete the level.
	True Jedi	Any	Collect 20,000 studs.
	All Collectibles	Any	Find all the Minikits.
	Missile Intercept	Any	Shoot 5 missiles out of the air.
	Rapid Oscillator	Any	Hit all the oscillator weak points in 2 minutes.

CHAPTER 8: DESTROY THE STARKILLER—REY'S ESCAPE

Got It?	Name	Mode	Notes
	Level Complete	Any	Complete the level.
	True Jedi	Any	Collect 45,000 studs.
	All Collectibles	Free Play	Find the Minikit and Red Brick.
	Rey Run	Any	Escape within 7 minutes.
	I've Got a Bad Feeling About This	Free Play	What's behind the doors?

CHAPTER 8: DESTROY THE STARKILLER—OSCILLATOR INTERIOR

Got It?	Name	Mode	Notes
	Level Complete	Any	Complete the level.
	True Jedi	Any	Collect 30,000 studs.
	All Collectibles	Free Play	Find all the Minikits.
	No Need for Alarm	Any	Destroy the alarm droid to prevent more stormtroopers from being alerted.
	Post Processing	Any	Smash the 5 posts.

CHAPTER 9: THE FINALE—OSCILLATOR BOMBING RUN

Got It?	Name	Mode	Notes
	Level Complete	Any	Complete the level.
	True Jedi	Any	Collect 36,000 studs.
	All Collectibles	Any	Find all the Minikits.
	Turret Termination	Any	Destroy 5 trench turrets.
	Lap of Honor	Any	Destroy each oscillator panel in one lap.

CHAPTER 9: THE FINALE—STARKILLER FOREST

Got It?	Name	Mode	Notes
	Level Complete	Any	Complete the level.
	True Jedi	Any	Collect 10,000 studs.
	All Collectibles	Free Play	Find all the Minikits.
	Loggerheads	Any	Get Kylo to chop down 3 trees.
	Finn-ess	Any	Defeat Kylo with one life.

CHAPTER 9: THE FINALE—STARKILLER SHOWDOWN

Got It?	Name	Mode	Notes
	Level Complete	Any	Complete the level.
	True Jedi	Any	Collect 7,000 studs.
	All Collectibles	Free Play	Find all the Minikits.
	Snowballed	Any	Take out 3 snowtroopers with one attack.
	Snow BB-8	Any	Build a BB-8 snowman.

EPILOGUE: LUKE'S ISLAND

Got It?	Name	Mode	Notes
	Level Complete	Any	Complete the level.
	True Jedi	Any	Collect 32,000 studs.
	All Collectibles	Free Play	Find both Red Bricks.
	Stud Cove	Free Play	Find the secret area in the level.
	Bush Whacker	Any	Destroy all 3 bush props.

PROLOGUE: THE BATTLE OF ENDOR—ENDOR SHIELD GENERATOR

Got It?	Name	Mode	Notes
	Level Complete	Any	Complete the level.
	True Jedi	Any	Collect 40,000 studs.
	All Collectibles	Free Play	Find all the Minikits.
	Fuel Cells	Any	Take out 3 enemies with fuel cells.
	Chicken Stomp	Any	Stomp on 3 stormtroopers while piloting the AT-ST.

PROLOGUE: THE BATTLE OF ENDOR—DEATH STAR INTERIOR

Got It?	Name	Mode	Notes
	Level Complete	Any	Complete the level.
	True Jedi	Any	Collect 8,000 studs.
	All Collectibles	Free Play	Find the Minikit and the Red Brick.
	Royal Force	Any	Take out 3 Royal Guards with the Force.
	Like Lightning	Any	Defeat the Emperor's Force lightning, as fast as lightning.

Gold Bricks continued next page.

PROLOGUE: THE BATTLE OF ENDOR—ASSAULT OF STARKILLER

Got It?	Name	Mode	Notes
	Level Complete	Any	Complete the level.
	True Jedi	Any	Collect 16,000 studs.
	All Collectibles	Any	Find all the Minikits.
	Quad Lasers	Any	Destroy 4 turbolaser towers.
	Fast Reactor	Any	Destroy the reactor core within 60 seconds.

PROLOGUE: RATHTAR HUNTING—RATHTAR CAVERNS

Got It?	Name	Mode	Notes
	Level Complete	Any	Complete the level.
	True Jedi	Any	Collect 22,000 studs.
	All Collectibles	Free Play	Find all the Minikits.
	Pacifist	Any	Leave the rathtar alone when they pounce.
	We Need to Get out of Here!	Any	Climb the waterfall in under 110 seconds.

PROLOGUE: OTTEGAN ASSAULT—OTTEGAN SURFACE

Got It?	Name	Mode	Notes
	Level Complete	Any	Complete the level.
	True Jedi	Any	Collect 22,000 studs.
	All Collectibles	Free Play	Find all the Minikits.
	Will you help me?	Any	Defeat an Ottegan by deflecting his bolts back at him as Kylo Ren.
	Blind Rage	Any	Lightsaber-cut 3 trees down.

PROLOGUE: POE TO THE RESCUE—TRASH COMPACTOR

Got It?	Name	Mode	Notes
	Level Complete	Any	Complete the level.
	True Jedi	Any	Collect 20,000 studs.
	All Collectibles	Free Play	Find 2 Minikits and the Red Brick.
	Sayonara Dianoga	Any	Build each Multi-Build variant to defeat the dianoga 4 times.
	Fast Reactor	Any	Destroy the reactor core within 60 seconds.

PROLOGUE: RATHTAR HUNTING—LOADING AREA

Got It?	Name	Mode	Notes
	Level Complete	Any	Complete the level.
	True Jedi	Any	Collect 13,000 studs.
	All Collectibles	Free Play	Find two Minikits and a Red Brick.
	I Have the High Ground!	Any	Defeat 5 Solculvis crew members from high cover.
	Seasoned Professional	Any	Capture the rathtar without taking any damage from it.

PROLOGUE: POE TO THE RESCUE—ASTEROID ESCAPE

Got It?	Name	Mode	Notes
	Level Complete	Any	Complete the level.
	True Jedi	Any	Collect 50,000 studs.
	All Collectibles	Any	Find all the Minikits.
	Crystal Caves	Any	Destroy the 5 crystals in the first part of the cave section.
	Tunnel Trouble	Any	Don't take any damage from the oncoming creatures hatching from the cave walls.

PROLOGUE: OTTEGAN ASSAULT—OTTEGAN PURSUIT

Got It?	Name	Mode	Notes
	Level Complete	Any	Complete the level.
	True Jedi	Any	Collect 12,000 studs.
	All Collectibles	Any	Find all the Minikits.
	Otte-gone	Any	Destroy 3 of the Ottegan fighters flying out of the hangars.
	Minor Inconvenience	Any	Avoid taking damage from any of the space mines.

Minikits

There are five Minikits in each chapter as well as five Minikits in each hub planet. Collecting all of the Minikits for a chapter or hub will unlock a vehicle.

CHAPTER 1: ASSAULT ON JAKKU

Got It?	Name	Mode	Notes
	Village Retreat	Any	Return all 3 bloggins to their pen.
	Village Retreat	Free Play	Use the Force to lower this Minikit to the ground.
	First Order Assault	Any	Use goggles and grapple on the X-wing at the start.
	First Order Assault	Free Play	Use a dark side Force user to destroy a panel.
	Jakku Graveyard	Any	Climb up some rails inside the Star Destroyer.

CHAPTER 2: ESCAPE FROM THE FINALIZER

Got It?	Name	Mode	Notes
	Finalizer Hangar 1	Free Play	Use a strong character to pull on orange handles.
	Finalizer Hangar 1	Free Play	Use a small character to go through a small access hatch.
	Finalizer Hangar 2	Any	Destroy all the gold containers with the TIE fighter.
	Star Destroyer Exterior	Any	Shoot a TIE fighter in the interior at the front of the Star Destroyer.
	Star Destroyer Exterior	Any	Destroy 10 turrets.

CHAPTER 3: NIIMA OUTPOST

Got It?	Name	Mode	Notes
	Niima Outpost	Free Play	Use a dark side character with the Force to break a red and black object.
	Niima Bombardment	Free Play	Destroy a silver container.
	Niima Bombardment	Free Play	Move through flames.
	Jakku Graveyard Flight	Any	Destroy 4 gold ships on the ground in the arena section.
	Jakku Graveyard Flight	Any	Destroy a TIE fighter flying around the edge of the arena.

CHAPTER 4: THE ERAVANA

Got It?	Name	Mode	Notes
	Freighter Battle	Free Play	Cut through a door with a lightsaber and then complete a minigame.
	Freighter Chase	Any	Collect this one while being chased by a rathtar.
	Freighter Chase	Free Play	Use a character with the Force to get this Minikit.
	Freighter Shutdown	Free Play	Destroy a gold panel and then use a First Order terminal.
	Freighter Shutdown	Free Play	Use the Force to move a ladder and then to destroy a container.

CHAPTER 5: MAZ'S CASTLE

Got It?	Name	Mode	Notes
	Castle Approach	Free Play	Use a protocol droid.
	Castle Approach	Free Play	Use a small access hatch to get to a balcony.
	Castle Hall	Free Play	Use a lightsaber to cut down a lamp near the entrance.
	Castle Hall	Free Play	Destroy 3 gold lamps.
	Castle Basement	Free Play	Destroy the silver object in the final room.

CHAPTER 6: ATTACK ON TAKODANA

Got It?	Name	Mode	Notes
	Attack on Takodana	Any	Use goggles to find a saber wall and then climb it.
	Attack on Takodana	Free Play	Use the Force to get this Minikit down from the top of a pillar.
	Castle Escape	Free Play	Look in a puddle in the courtyard.
	Takodana Skies	Any	Destroy the jammer tower on the castle.
	Takodana Skies	Any	Destroy the 3 transport ships before they land.

CHAPTER 7: STARKILLER SABOTAGE

Got It?	Name	Mode	Notes
	Starkiller Crash Site	Any	Build a snowman and then jump up it to reach a higher area.
	Shield Room Approach	Free Play	Melt ice and then swim to a higher platform to destroy a snowman.
	Shield Room Approach	Free Play	Use the Force on a panel near the end of the level.
	Phasma	Any	Destroy 3 surveillance cameras.
	Phasma	Free Play	Use the Force to lower this Minikit.

CHAPTER 8: DESTROY THE STARKILLER

Got It?	Name	Mode	Notes
	Assault of Starkiller	Any	Destroy the middle of three falling rocks.
	Assault of Starkiller	Any	Destroy an object near the oscillator.
	Rey's Escape	Free Play	Use the force to move a pipe to get to this Minikit.
	Oscillator Interior	Any	Use a Multi-Build to get this Minikit.
	Oscillator Interior	Free Play	Go through a small access hatch.

CHAPTER 9: THE FINALE

Got It?	Name	Mode	Notes
	Oscillator Bombing Run	Any	Destroy the blue container in the tunnel.
	Oscillator Bombing Run	Any	Destroy the gold pipes in the trench.
	Starkiller Forest	Free Play	Destroy a silver container.
	Starkiller Forest	Free Play	Pull on some strength handles.
	Starkiller Showdown	Free Play	Melt a chunk of ice to get the Minikit inside.

PROLOGUE: THE BATTLE OF ENDOR

Got It?	Name	Mode	Notes
	Endor Shield Generator	Free Play	Use the Force to play some drums up in a tree.
	Endor Shield Generator	Free Play	Use goggles to find a container with the Minikit inside.
	Death Star Interior	Free Play	Use a rotary control switch to get up onto a catwalk.
	Assault of Starkiller	Any	Destroy a container on top of a structure in the trench.
	Assault of Starkiller	Any	Destroy the container towed behind a TIE fighter in the reactor area.

PROLOGUE: POE TO THE RESCUE

Got It?	Name	Mode	Notes
	Trash Compactor	Any	Move through toxic waste.
	Trash Compactor	Free Play	Pull on strength handles.
	Asteroid Escape	Any	Destroy the gold asteroid.
	Asteroid Escape	Any	Destroy the container near the start of the tunnel.
	Asteroid Escape	Any	Destroy 3 wrecked ships in the crater.

PROLOGUE: RATHTAR HUNTING

Got It?	Name	Mode	Notes
	Rathtar Caverns	Any	Destroy all of the mushrooms.
	Rathtar Caverns	Any	Inside an alcove near top of a waterfall.
	Rathtar Caverns	Free Play	Use the force to get this one at the top of a waterfall.
	Loading Area	Free Play	Use a rotary control switch to open a weapons crate.
	Loading Area	Free Play	Dive into a water access.

Minikits continued next page.

	Mode	Notes
Ottegan Pursuit	Any	Destroy container outside of the hangars.
Ottegan Pursuit	Any	Destroy the gold tower.
Ottegan Surface	Free Play	Go through a cloud of toxic gas.
Ottegan Surface	Any	Use the Command ability to destroy a gold statue.
Ottegan Surface	Free Play	Use a Resistance terminal.

OTTEGAN ASSAULT

JAKKU HUB

Got It?	Notes
	Complete the Nightwatch side mission.
	Break open a silver container near Rey's home.
	Use the Force to lift it out of the sand.
	In a crate behind the Millennium Falcon.
	Complete The Niima Rally side mission.

STARKILLER HUB

Got It?	Notes
	Break open a cracked container on the Millennium Falcon.
	Use a grapple gun to pull the Minikit down from a wall.
	Use the Force to lift the Minikit up out of a snowbank.
	Complete the Ace TIE Pilot side mission.
	Complete the Stormtrooper School side mission.

RESISTANCE BASE HUB

Got It?	Notes
	Use Multi-Build to make a rotary control switch near the X-wing pad.
	Use protocol droid terminal inside Command Hangar.
	Break open a cracked container near the Millennium Falcon.
	Complete the Resistance Assistance side mission.
	Complete the Resistance Hotshot side mission.

TAKODANA HUB

Got It?	Notes
	Use the Force to break open a red and black container.
	Use the Force to lower the Minikit to the ground along the forest path.
	Use the Force to bring the Minikit to you from a wall on the waterfront.
	Complete the Kanata Reconstruction side mission.
	Complete the Resistance Recon side mission.

Characters in Carbonite

These 32 characters in carbonite can only be found in the hubs. Once collected, go to the Medical Bunker at the Resistance Base to decarbonize them so you can use the characters.

CHARACTERS IN CARBONITE

Icon	Got It?	Character	Hub	Notes
		Admiral Ackbar (Classic)	Jakku	Use the Force.
		Anakin Skywalker (Episode 1)	Jakku	Complete the Speeder Racer side mission.
		Anakin Skywalker (Episode III)	Takodana	Complete the Takodana Treachery side mission.
		Arvel Crynyd	Takodana	Complete The Second Wave side mission.
		Boba Fett	Resistance Base	Use the Force.
		Chancellor Palpatine	Jakku	Dive into a water access spot.
		Count Dooku	Starkiller	Complete the Parade Practice side mission.
		Death Star Trooper	Starkiller	Complete the Snowspeeder Slalom side mission.
		Gray Squadron Pilot	Resistance Base	Inside Medical Bunker.
		Greedo	Takodana	Use the Force to move a container inside the Millennium Falcon.
		Han Solo (Classic)	Starkiller	Use the Force to lift it out of an alcove on the Millennium Falcon.

CHARACTERS IN CARBONITE

Icon	Got It?	Character	Hub	Notes
		Han Solo (Stormtrooper)	Jakku	Blow up a silver object.
		Jawa	Takodana	Complete the Express Delivery side mission.
		Luke Skywalker (Episode IV)	Jakku	Shoot at a target.
		Luke Skywalker (Stormtrooper)	Starkiller	Complete the Starkiller Chef side mission.
		Obi-Wan Kenobi (Episode III)	Takodana	Break open a cracked brick door.
		Obi-Wan Kenobi (Episode IV)	Starkiller	Use the Force to remove a red and black covering on a pipe.
		Padmé Amidala	Starkiller	Use a grapple gun to pull it down from a snowy ledge.
		Princess Leia (Classic)	Starkiller	Destroy a silver lock, then resist the cold to get it.
		Princess Leia (Ewok Village)	Jakku	Use the Force.
		Queen Amidala	Jakku	Complete A Secret Service side mission.
		Qui-Gon Jinn	Takodana	Cut it out of a wall with a lightsaber.

CHARACTERS IN CARBONITE				
Icon	Got It?	Character	Hub	Notes
		Rebel Commando	Takodana	Complete the Rumble in the Jungle side mission.
		Rebel Scout Trooper	Starkiller	Use the Force to get it down from a ledge.
		Royal Guard	Jakku	Break a cracked object.
		Scout Trooper	Takodana	Use the Force to get it out of a tree.
		Snowtrooper Classic	Starkiller	Complete the Snowball Skirmish side mission.

CHARACTERS IN CARBONITE				
Icon	Got It?	Character	Hub	Notes
		Teebo	Jakku	Complete the Stolen Steel side mission.
		TIE Interceptor Pilot	Takodana	Use a grapple gun to get it out of a tree.
		Tusken Raider	Jakku	Complete the Scavenger Shakedown side mission.
		Wampa	Takodana	Use the Force to destroy a black and red platform in the forest.
		Yoda	Starkiller	Melt through an ice wall.

Vehicles

Many of the vehicles can be used in flying levels. In addition, mini versions of the vehicles you collect can also be summoned for use in the hubs. While several vehicles are available at the start, others must be unlocked by completing story levels or by collecting Minikits.

VEHICLES			
Icon	Got It?	Vehicle	How Obtained?
		Imperial AT-ST	Collect all the Minikits for Prologue: Battle of Endor.
		Rebel Alliance A-Wing	Unlocked at the start.
		Rebel Alliance B-wing	Unlocked at the start.
		Rebel Alliance Snowspeeder	Collect all the Minikits for Starkiller hub.
		Customized Jedi Starfighter	Complete Asteroid Escape level.
		Finalizer	Collect all the Minikits for Chapter 2: Escape from the Finalizer.
		Imperial AT-AT	Collect all the Minikits for Chapter 7: Starkiller Sabotage.
		First Order Transporter	Collect all the Minikits for Chapter 1: Assault on Jakku.
		First Order Snow Speeder	Collect all the Minikits for Chapter 8: Destroy the Starkiller.
		Ghost	Unlocked at the start
		Kylo Ren's Command Shuttle	Complete Ottegan Pursuit level.
		Luke's Landspeeder	Collect all the Minikits for Resistance Base hub.
		Meson Martinet	Unlocked at the start
		Millennium Falcon (Episode VI)	Complete Death Star Escape level.
		Millennium Falcon (Episode VII)	Complete Jakku Graveyard Flight level.
		Ottegan Defense Fighter	Collect all the Minikits for Prologue: Ackbar Capture.
		Prana Ship	Collect all the Minikits for Prologue: Rathtar Hunting.

VEHICLES			
Icon	Got It?	Vehicle	How Obtained?
		Quadjumper	Collect all the Minikits for Jakku hub.
		Han Solo's Freighter (Eravana)	Collect all the Minikits for Chapter 4: The Eravana.
		Rebel Alliance Transport	Unlocked at the start.
		Resistance Transport	Collect all the Minikits for Chapter 6: Attack on Takodana.
		Rey's Speeder	Collect all the Minikits for Chapter 3: Niima Outpost.
		Slave 1	Unlocked at the start.
		Starkiller	Collect all the Minikits for Chapter 9: The Finale.
		Rebel Alliance X-wing	Complete Death Star Escape level.
		Resistance X-wing	Complete Takodana Skies level.
		Poe Dameron's X-wing	Complete Takodana Skies level.
		Takodana Cruiser	Collect all the Minikits for Chapter 5: Maz's Castle.
		Imperial TIE Bomber	Unlocked at the start.
		First Order TIE fighter	Collect all the Minikits for Takodana hub.
		Special Forces TIE fighter	Complete Star Destroyer Exterior level.
		Imperial TIE Intercepter	Collect all the Minikits for Prologue: Trash Compactor.
		Wookiee Gunship	Unlocked at the start.
		Rebel Alliance Y-wing	Unlocked at the start.

TROPHIES

Got It?	Name	Description	Trophy
☐	...It Is Found	Collect all collectibles in the hub.	Silver
☐	...What was the Second Time?	Complete Chapter 4.	Bronze
☐	Less Than 12 Parsecs	Use a Microfighter in each Hub.	Bronze
☐	A Bag Full of Explosives	Complete Chapter 8.	Bronze
☐	A Big Deal in the Resistance	Complete all the Hub Missions.	Bronze
☐	It's True. All of it...	Complete The Battle of Endor.	Bronze
☐	Classic Gamer	Play all the retro arcade games found in the hub levels.	Bronze
☐	Classified? Me too.	Complete Chapter 2.	Bronze
☐	Credit Check	Collect 50,000,000 LEGO studs.	Gold
☐	Cryptosurgeon	Create a custom character.	Bronze
☐	Don't Get Cocky!	Defeat 100 TIE fighters.	Bronze
☐	Don't Let These Dogs Scare You	Complete Chapter 6.	Bronze
☐	Eyes of a Man Who Wants to Run	Complete Chapter 5.	Bronze
☐	Family Reunion	Have Kylo Ren and Han Solo in the same party.	Bronze
☐	Going the Distance	Complete the Bonus Level.	Bronze
☐	Quick on the Draw	In a blaster battle, have Han defeat a character who is preparing an attack.	Bronze
☐	Hope is Not Lost Today...	Collect All Collectibles in the Story Level & Bonus Level.	Silver
☐	I Can Fly Anything	Collect All Minikits in the game.	Silver
☐	I Like That Wookiee...	Complete a Free Play level playing as Maz and Chewbacca.	Bronze
☐	I'll Come Back for You!	Complete Chapter 1.	Bronze
☐	I'm Getting Pretty Good at This!	Get a gold medal in a Blaster Battle.	Bronze
☐	Is There a Garbage Chute?	Complete Chapter 7.	Bronze
☐	It's a Trap!	Complete Ottegan Assault.	Bronze
☐	Just a Scavenger	Collect a Minikit	Bronze

Got It?	Name	Description	Trophy
☐	Just Improvise	Complete 25 Multi-Builds.	Silver
☐	Never Be as Strong as Vader	Defeat Kylo Ren as Darth Vader.	Bronze
☐	Never Tell Me the Odds	Complete Poe to the Rescue.	Bronze
☐	Not the Droid You're Looking For	Use the wrong type of droid on an access panel.	Bronze
☐	Red Leader	Collect all Red Bricks.	Silver
☐	Speechless	Complete the Epilogue.	Bronze
☐	STOP... Kylo Time	Use Force Freeze as Kylo Ren.	Bronze
☐	Stormtrooper Syndrome	Miss your target 10 times in a Blaster Battle.	Bronze
☐	It Belongs to Me!	Complete Chapter 9.	Bronze
☐	Hey! That's Miiiiiiine!	Play as Unkar Plutt on the Millennium Falcon.	Bronze
☐	That's Not Junk	Collect a Minikit Collection.	Silver
☐	That's Not How the Force Works	Enable the Red Brick—Collectible Detector	Bronze
☐	The Force is Strong with This One	Achieve 100% Completion.	Gold
☐	The Force, It's Calling to You	Obtain "True Jedi" in any level.	Bronze
☐	The Garbage Will Do	Complete Chapter 3.	Bronze
☐	The New Jedi Will Rise	Obtain "True Jedi" on all levels.	Silver
☐	There Has Been an Awakening	Complete The Force Awakens.	Gold
☐	They're Shooting at Both Of Us!	Complete a Blaster Battle.	Bronze
☐	Used to Have a Bigger Crew	Complete Rathtar Hunting.	Bronze
☐	We Need More Troops!	Defeat 50 stormtroopers.	Bronze
☐	We'll Figure It Out. We'll Use The Force.	Defeat ten enemies as a Jedi by deflecting fire back at them.	Bronze
☐	Unlearn What You Have Learned	Rebuild a Multi-Build.	Bronze
☐	The Force Awakens	Unlock all Trophies	Platinum

WARS

BE A REBEL.
READ A BOOK.

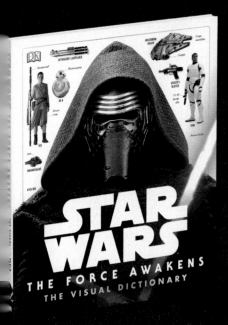

STAR WARS
THE FORCE AWAKENS
THE VISUAL DICTIONARY

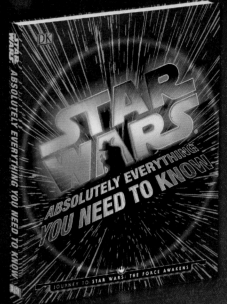

STAR WARS
ABSOLUTELY EVERYTHING YOU NEED TO KNOW

JOURNEY TO STAR WARS: THE FORCE AWAKENS

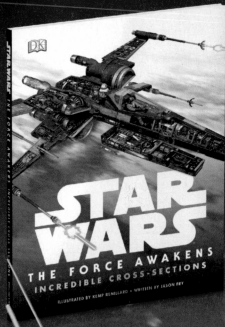

STAR WARS
THE FORCE AWAKENS
INCREDIBLE CROSS-SECTIONS

ILLUSTRATED BY KEMP REMILLARD • WRITTEN BY JASON FRY

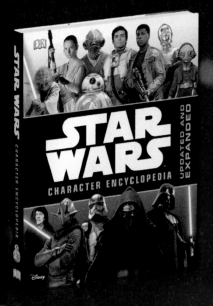

STAR WARS
CHARACTER ENCYCLOPEDIA
UPDATED AND EXPANDED

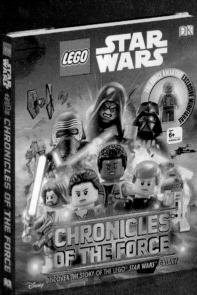

LEGO STAR WARS
CHRONICLES OF THE FORCE
DISCOVER THE STORY OF THE LEGO STAR WARS GALAXY

LEGO

STAR WARS™

LEGO.COM/STARWARS